Perl and LWP

Sean M. Burke

Beijing · Cambridge · Farnham · Köln · Paris · Sebastopol · Taipei · Tokyo

Perl and LWP
by Sean M. Burke

Copyright © 2002 O'Reilly & Associates, Inc. All rights reserved.
Printed in the United States of America.

Published by O'Reilly & Associates, Inc., 1005 Gravenstein Highway North, Sebastopol, CA 95472.

O'Reilly & Associates books may be purchased for educational, business, or sales promotional use. Online editions are also available for most titles (*safari.oreilly.com*). For more information, contact our corporate/institutional sales department: (800) 998-9938 or *corporate@oreilly.com*.

Editor:	Nathan Torkington
Production Editor:	Linley Dolby
Cover Designer:	Emma Colby
Interior Designer:	Melanie Wang

Printing History:

June 2002:	First Edition.

ISBN: 0-596-00178-9   [10/02]
[M]

Table of Contents

Foreword

I started playing around with the Web a long time ago—at least, it feels that way. The first versions of Mosaic had just showed up, Gopher and Wais were still hot technology, and I discovered an HTTP server program called Plexus. What was different was it was implemented in Perl. That made it easy to extend. CGI was not invented yet, so all we had were servlets (although we didn't call them that then). Over time, I moved from hacking on the server side to the client side but stayed with Perl as the programming language of choice. As a result, I got involved in LWP, the Perl web client library.

A lot has happened to the web since then. These days there is almost no end to the information at our fingertips: news, stock quotes, weather, government info, shopping, discussion groups, product info, reviews, games, and other entertainment. And the good news is that LWP can help automate them all.

This book tells you how you can write your own useful web client applications with LWP and its related HTML modules. Sean's done a great job of showing how this powerful library can be used to make tools that automate various tasks on the Web. If you are like me, you probably have many examples of web forms that you find yourself filling out over and over again. Why not write a simple LWP-based tool that does it all for you? Or a tool that does research for you by collecting data from many web pages without you having to spend a single mouse click? After reading this book, you should be well prepared for tasks such as these.

This book's focus is to teach you how to write scripts against services that are set up to serve traditional web browsers. This means services exposed through HTML. Even in a world where people eventually have discovered that the Web can provide real program-to-program interfaces (the current "web services" craze), it is likely that

HTML scraping will continue to be a valuable way to extract information from the Web. I strongly believe that Perl and LWP is one of the best tools to get that job done. Reading *Perl and LWP* is a good way get you started.

It has been fun writing and maintaining the LWP codebase, and Sean's written a fine book about using it. Enjoy!

—Gisle Aas
Primary author and maintainer of LWP

Preface

Perl soared to popularity as a language for creating and managing web content. Perl is equally adept at consuming information on the Web. Most web sites are created for people, but quite often you want to automate tasks that involve accessing a web site in a repetitive way. Such tasks could be as simple as saying "here's a list of URLs; I want to be emailed if any of them stop working," or they could involve more complex processing of any number of pages. This book is about using LWP (the Library for World Wide Web in Perl) and Perl to fetch and process web pages.

For example, if you want to compare the prices of all O'Reilly books on Amazon.com and bn.com, you could look at each page yourself and keep track of the prices. Or you could write an LWP program to fetch the product pages, extract the prices, and generate a report. O'Reilly has a lot of books in print, and after reading this one, you'll be able to write and run the program much more quickly than you could visit every catalog page.

Consider also a situation in which a particular page has links to several dozen files (images, music, and so on) that you want to download. You could download each individually, by monotonously selecting each link in your browser and choosing Save as..., or you could dash off a short LWP program that scans for URLs in that page and downloads each, unattended.

Besides extracting data from web pages, you can also automate submitting data through web forms. Whether this is a matter of uploading 50 image files through your company's intranet interface, or searching the local library's online card catalog every week for any new books with "Navajo" in the title, it's worth the time and piece of mind to automate repetitive processes by writing LWP programs to submit data into forms and scan the resulting data.

Audience for This Book

This book is aimed at someone who already knows Perl and HTML, but I don't assume you're an expert at either. I give quick refreshers on some of the quirkier aspects of HTML (e.g., forms), but in general, I assume you know what each of the HTML tags means. If you know basic regular expressions and are familiar with references and maybe even objects, you have all the Perl skills you need to use this book.

If you're new to Perl, consider reading *Learning Perl* (O'Reilly) and maybe also *The Perl Cookbook* (O'Reilly). If your HTML is shaky, try the *HTML Pocket Reference* or *HTML: The Definitive Guide* (O'Reilly). If you don't feel comfortable using objects in Perl, reading Appendix G in this book should be enough to bring you up to speed.

Structure of This Book

The book is divided into 12 chapters and 7 appendixes, as follows:

Chapter 1, *Introduction to Web Automation*, covers in general terms what LWP does, the alternatives to using LWP, and when you shouldn't use LWP.

Chapter 2, *Web Basics*, explains how the Web works and some easy-to-use yet limited functions for accessing it.

Chapter 3, *The LWP Class Model*, covers the more powerful interface to the Web.

Chapter 4, *URLs*, shows how to parse URLs with the URI class, and how to convert between relative and absolute URLs.

Chapter 5, *Forms*, describes how to submit GET and POST forms.

Chapter 6, *Simple HTML Processing with Regular Expressions*, shows how to extract information from HTML using regular expressions.

Chapter 7, *HTML Processing with Tokens*, provides an alternative approach to extracting data from HTML using the HTML::TokeParser module.

Chapter 8, *Tokenizing Walkthrough*, is a case study of data extraction using tokens.

Chapter 9, *HTML Processing with Trees*, shows how to extract data from HTML using the HTML::TreeBuilder module.

Chapter 10, *Modifying HTML with Trees*, covers the use of HTML::TreeBuilder to modify HTML files.

Chapter 11, *Cookies, Authentication, and Advanced Requests*, deals with the tougher parts of requests.

Chapter 12, *Spiders*, explores the technological issues involved in automating the download of more than one page from a site.

Appendix A, *LWP Modules*, is a complete list of the LWP modules.

Appendix B, *HTTP Status Codes*, is a list of HTTP codes, what they mean, and whether LWP considers them error or success.

Appendix C, *Common MIME Types*, contains the most common MIME types and what they mean.

Appendix D, *Language Tags*, lists the most common language tags and their meanings (e.g., "zh-cn" means Mainland Chinese, while "sv" is Swedish).

Appendix E, *Common Content Encodings*, is a list of the most common character encodings (character sets) and the tags that identify them.

Appendix F, *ASCII Table*, is a table to help you make sense of the most common Unicode characters. It shows each character, its numeric code (in decimal, octal, and hex), and any HTML escapes there may be for it.

Appendix G, *User's View of Object-Oriented Modules*, is an introduction to the use of Perl's object-oriented programming features.

Order of Chapters

The chapters in this book are arranged so that if you read them in order, you will face a minimum of cases where I have to say "you won't understand this part of the code, because we won't cover that topic until two chapters later." However, only some of what each chapter introduces is used in later chapters. For example, Chapter 3 lists all sorts of LWP methods that you are likely to use eventually, but the typical task will use only a few of those, and only a few will show up in later chapters. In cases where you can't infer the meaning of a method from its name, you can always refer back to the earlier chapters or use `perldoc` to see the applicable module's online reference documentation.

Important Standards Documents

The basic protocols and data formats of the Web are specified in a number of Internet RFCs. The most important are:

RFC 2616: HTTP 1.1
   ftp://ftp.isi.edu/in-notes/rfc2616.txt

RFC 2965: HTTP Cookies Specification
   ftp://ftp.isi.edu/in-notes/rfc2965.txt

RFC 2617: HTTP Authentication: Basic and Digest Access Authentication
   ftp://ftp.isi.edu/in-notes/rfc2617.txt

RFC 2396: Uniform Resource Identifiers: Generic Syntax
   ftp://ftp.isi.edu/in-notes/rfc2396.txt

HTML 4.01 specification
   http://www.w3.org/TR/html401/

HTML 4.01 Forms specification
   http://www.w3.org/TR/html401/interact/forms/

Character sets
   http://www.iana.org/assignments/character-sets

Country codes
   http://www.isi.edu/in-notes/iana/assignments/country-codes

Unicode specifications
   http://www.unicode.org

RFC 2279: Encoding Unicode as UTF-8
   ftp://ftp.isi.edu/in-notes/rfc2279.txt

Request For Comments documents
   http://www.rfc-editor.org

IANA protocol assignments
   http://www.iana.org/numbers.htm

Conventions Used in This Book

The following typographic conventions are used in this book:

Italic

> Used for file and directory names, email addresses, and URLs, as well as for new terms where they are defined.

`Constant width`

> Used for code listings and for keywords, variables, function names, command options, parameters, and bits of HTML source where they appear in the text.

`Constant width bold`

> Used to highlight key fragments of larger code examples, or to show the output of a piece of code.

`Constant width italic`

> Used as a general placeholder to indicate terms that should be replaced by actual values in your own programs.

Comments & Questions

Please address comments and questions concerning this book to the publisher:

> O'Reilly & Associates, Inc.
> 1005 Gravenstein Highway North
> Sebastopol, CA 95472
> (800) 998-9938 (in the United States or Canada)
> (707) 829-0515 (international/local)
> (707) 829-0104 (fax)

There is a web page for this book, which lists errata, examples, or any additional information. You can access this page at:

> *http://www.oreilly.com/catalog/perllwp/*

To comment or ask technical questions about this book, send email to:

> *bookquestions@oreilly.com*

For more information about books, conferences, Resource Centers, and the O'Reilly Network, see the O'Reilly web site at:

> *http://www.oreilly.com*

Acknowledgments

It takes a mere village to raise a puny human child, but it took a whole globe-girdling Perl cabal to get this book done! These are the readers who, as a personal favor to me, took the time to read and greatly improve my first sketchy manuscript, each in their own particular, helpful, and careful ways: Gisle Aas, David H. Adler, Tim Allwine, Elaine Ashton, Gene Boggs, Gavin Estey, Scott Francis, Joe Johnston, Kevin Healy, Conrad Heiney, David Huggins-Daines, Samy Kamkar, Joe Kline, Yossef Mendelssohn, Abhijit Menon-Sen, Brad Murray, David Ondrik, Clinton Pierce, Robert Spier, Andrew Stanley, Dennis Taylor, Martin Thurn, and Glenn Wood.

I'm also especially thankful to Elaine Ashton for doing a last-minute review not just of this manuscript's prose, but of all the code blocks. If not for her eagle eye, you'd be scratching your head over variables and subroutines magically renaming themselves all over the place!

I am grateful to Conrad Heiney for suggesting the California Department of Motor Vehicles as an example for Chapter 5. Thanks also to Mark-Jason Dominus for suggesting the ABEBooks web site as an example in that same chapter. Many thanks to Gisle Aas, Michael A. Chase, and Martijn Koster for making LWP such a reliable and indispensable addition to every programmer's toolkit.

And last but not least, thanks to the people at O'Reilly who intrepidly pushed for this book to get done when I really just wanted to stay in bed and play Tetris. The chief author-wrangler is my editor, Nat Torkington, but I'm much obliged also to the many other under-appreciated O'Reilly people who conspired to get this book from my hands to yours: Jon Orwant (of *Perl Journal* fame even before he got to O'Reilly), Neil Walls (who slaved over Appendix F so you can see what a ⊥ looks like!), sage editor Linda Mui, Betsy Waliszewski in marketing, and in the production department, Linley Dolby, the book's production editor and copyeditor and Rob Romano, the book's illustrator.

## CHAPTER 1

Introduction to Web Automation

LWP (short for "Library for World Wide Web in Perl") is a set of Perl modules and object-oriented classes for getting data from the Web and for extracting information from HTML. This chapter provides essential background on the LWP suite. It describes the nature and history of LWP, which platforms it runs on, and how to download and install it. This chapter ends with a quick walkthrough of several LWP programs that illustrate common tasks, such as fetching web pages, extracting information using regular expressions, and submitting forms.

The Web as Data Source

Most web sites are designed for people. User Interface gurus consult for large sums of money to build HTML code that is easy to use and displays correctly on all browsers. User Experience gurus wag their fingers and tell web designers to study their users, so they know the human foibles and desires of the ape descendents who will be viewing the web site.

Fundamentally, though, a web site is home to data and services. A stockbroker has stock prices and the value of your portfolio (data) and forms that let you buy and sell stock (services). Amazon has book ISBNs, titles, authors, reviews, prices, and rankings (data) and forms that let you order those books (services).

It's assumed that the data and services will be accessed by people viewing the rendered HTML. But many a programmer has eyed those data sources and services on the Web and thought "I'd like to use those in a program!" For example, they could page you when your portfolio falls past a certain point or could calculate the "best" book on Perl based on the ratio of its price to its average reader review.

LWP lets you do this kind of *web automation*. With it, you can fetch web pages, submit forms, authenticate, and extract information from HTML. Once you've used it to grab news headlines or check links, you'll never view the Web in the same way again.

As with everything in Perl, there's more than one way to automate accessing the Web. In this book, we'll show you everything from the basic way to access the Web (via the LWP::Simple module), through forms, all the way to the gory details of cookies, authentication, and other types of complex requests.

Screen Scraping

Once you've tackled the fundamentals of how to ask a web server for a particular page, you still have to find the information you want, buried in the HTML response. Most often you won't need more than regular expressions to achieve this. Chapter 6 describes the art of extracting information from HTML using regular expressions, although you'll see the beginnings of it as early as Chapter 2, where we query AltaVista for a word, and use a regexp to match the number in the response that says "We found *[number]* results."

The more discerning LWP connoisseur, however, treats the HTML document as a stream of tokens (Chapter 7, with an extended example in Chapter 8) or as a parse tree (Chapter 9). For example, you'll use a token view and a tree view to consider such tasks as how to catch `<img...>` tags that are missing some of their attributes, how to get the absolute URLs of all the headlines on the BBC News main page, and how to extract content from one web page and insert it into a different template.

In the old days of 80x24 terminals, "screen scraping" referred to the art of programmatically extracting information from the screens of interactive applications. That term has been carried over to mean the act of automatically extracting data from the output of any system that was basically designed for interactive use. That's the term used for getting data out of HTML that was meant to be looked at in a browser, not necessarily extracted for your programs' use.

Brittleness

In some lucky cases, your LWP-related task consists of downloading a file without requiring your program to parse it in any way. But most tasks involve having to extract a piece of data from some part of the returned document, using the screen-scraping tactics as mentioned earlier. An unavoidable problem is that the format of most web content can change at any time. For example in Chapter 8, I discuss the task of extracting data from the program listings at the web site for the radio show *Fresh Air*. The principle I demonstrate for that specific case is true for all extraction tasks: no pattern in the data is permanent and so any data-parsing program will be "brittle."

For example, if you want to match text in section headings, you can write your program to depend on them being inside `<h2>...</h2>` tags, but tomorrow the site's template could be redesigned, and headings could then be in `<h3 class='hdln'>...</h3>` tags, at which point your program won't see anything it considers a section heading.

In practice, any given site's template won't change on a daily basis (nor even yearly, for most sites), but as you read this book and see examples of data extraction, bear in mind that each solution can't be *the* solution, but is just *a* solution, and a temporary and brittle one at that.

As somewhat of a lesson in brittleness, in this book I show you data from various web sites (Amazon.com, the BBC News web site, and many others) and show how to write programs to extract data from them. However, that code is fragile. Some sites get redesigned only every few years; Amazon.com seems to change something every few weeks. So while I've made every effort to provide accurate code for the web sites as they exist at the time of this writing, I hope you will consider the programs in this book valuable as learning tools even after the sites will have changed beyond recognition.

Web Services

Programmers have begun to realize the great value in automating transactions over the Web. There is now a booming industry in *web services*, which is the buzzword for data or services offered over the Web. What differentiates web services from web sites is that web services don't emit HTML for the ultimate reading pleasure of humans, they emit XML for programs.

This removes the need to scrape information out of HTML, neatly solving the problem of ever-changing web sites made brittle by the fickle tastes of the web-browsing public. Some web services standards (SOAP and XML-RPC) even make the remote web service appear to be a set of functions you call from within your program—if you use a SOAP or XML-RPC toolkit, you don't even have to parse XML!

However, there will always be information on the Web that isn't accessible as a web service. For that information, screen scraping is the only choice.

History of LWP

The following history of LWP was written by Gisle Aas, one of the creators of LWP and its current maintainer.

The libwww-perl project was started at the very first WWW conference held in Geneva in 1994. At the conference, Martijn Koster met Roy Fielding who was presenting the work he had done on MOMspider. MOMspider was a Perl program that traversed the Web looking for broken links and built an index of the documents and links discovered. Martijn suggested turning the reusable components of this program into a library. The result was the libwww-perl library for Perl 4 that Roy maintained.

Later the same year, Larry Wall made the first "stable" release of Perl 5 available. It was obvious that the module system and object-oriented features that the new version of Perl provided make Roy's library even better. At one point, both Martijn and myself had made our own separate modifications of libwww-perl. We joined forces, merged our designs, and made several alpha releases. Unfortunately, Martijn ended up in disagreement with his employer about the intellectual property rights of work done outside hours. To safeguard the code's continued availability to the Perl community, he asked me to take over maintenance of it.

The LWP:: module namespace was introduced by Martijn in one of the early alpha releases. This name choice was lively discussed on the libwww mailing list. It was soon pointed out that this name could be confused with what certain implementations of threads called themselves, but no better name alternatives emerged. In the last message on this matter, Martijn concluded, "OK, so we all agree LWP stinks :-)." The name stuck and has established itself.

If you search for "LWP" on Google today, you have to go to 30th position before you find a link about threads.

In May 1996, we made the first non-beta release of libwww-perl for Perl 5. It was called release 5.00 because it was for Perl 5. This made some room for Roy to maintain libwww-perl for Perl 4, called libwww-perl-0.40. Martijn continued to contribute but was unfortunately "rolled over by the Java train."

In 1997–98, I tried to redesign LWP around the concept of an event loop under the name LWPng. This allowed many nice things: multiple requests could be handled in parallel and on the same connection, requests could be pipelined to improve round-trip time, and HTTP/1.1 was actually supported. But the tuits to finish it up never came, so this branch must by now be regarded as dead. I still hope some brave soul shows up and decides to bring it back to life.

1998 was also the year that the HTML:: modules were unbundled from the core LWP distribution and the year after Sean M. Burke showed up and took over maintenance of the HTML-Tree distribution, actually making it handle all the real-world HTML that you will find. I had kind of given up on dealing with all the strange HTML that the web ecology had let develop. Sean had enough dedication to make sense of it.

Today LWP is in strict maintenance mode with a much slower release cycle. The code base seems to be quite solid and capable of doing what most people expect it to.

Installing LWP

LWP and the associated modules are available in various distributions free from the Comprehensive Perl Archive Network (CPAN). The main distributions are listed at the start of Appendix A, although the details of which modules are in which distributions change occasionally.

If you're using ActivePerl for Windows or MacPerl for Mac OS 9, you already have LWP. If you're on Unix and you don't already have LWP installed, you'll need to install it from CPAN using instructions given in the next section.

To test whether you already have LWP installed:

```
% perl -MLWP -le "print(LWP->VERSION)"
```

(The second character in `-le` is a lowercase L, not a digit one.)

If you see:

```
Can't locate LWP in @INC (@INC contains: ...lots of paths...).
BEGIN failed--compilation aborted.
```

or if you see a version number lower than 5.64, you need to install LWP on your system.

There are two ways to install modules: using the CPAN shell or the old-fashioned manual way.

Installing LWP from the CPAN Shell

The CPAN shell is a command-line environment for automatically downloading, building, and installing modules from CPAN.

Configuring

If you have never used the CPAN shell, you will need to configure it before you can use it. It will prompt you for some information before building its configuration file.

Invoke the CPAN shell by entering the following command at a system shell prompt:

```
% perl -MCPAN -eshell
```

If you've never run it before, you'll see this:

```
We have to reconfigure CPAN.pm due to following uninitialized parameters:
```

followed by a number of questions. For each question, the default answer is typically fine, but you may answer otherwise if you know that the default setting is wrong or not optimal. Once you've answered all the questions, a configuration file is created and you can start working with the CPAN shell.

Obtaining help

If you need help at any time, you can read the CPAN shell's manual page by typing `perldoc CPAN` or by starting up the CPAN shell (with `perl -MCPAN -eshell` at a system shell prompt) and entering `h` at the `cpan>` prompt:

```
cpan> h

Display Information
 command  argument       description
 a,b,d,m  WORD or /REGEXP/  about authors, bundles, distributions, modules
 i        WORD or /REGEXP/  about anything of above
 r        NONE           reinstall recommendations
 ls       AUTHOR         about files in the author's directory
```

```
Download, Test, Make, Install...
  get                      download
  make                     make (implies get)
  test      MODULES,       make test (implies make)
  install   DISTS, BUNDLES make install (implies test)
  clean                    make clean
  look                     open subshell in these dists' directories
  readme                   display these dists' README files

Other
  h,?           display this menu    | ! perl-code   eval a perl command
  o conf [opt]  set and query options | q            quit the cpan shell
  reload cpan   load CPAN.pm again    | reload index  load newer indices
  autobundle    Snapshot              | force cmd      unconditionally do cmd
```

Installing LWP

All you have to do is enter:

```
cpan> install Bundle::LWP
```

The CPAN shell will show messages explaining what it's up to. You may need to answer questions to configure the various modules (e.g., libnet asks for mail hosts and so on for testing purposes).

After much activity, you should then have a fresh copy of LWP on your system, with far less work than installing it manually one distribution at a time. At the time of this writing, install Bundle::LWP installs not just the libwww-perl distribution, but also URI and HTML-Parser. It does not install the HTML-Tree distribution that we'll use in Chapters 9 and 10. To do that, enter:

```
cpan> install HTML::Tree
```

These commands do not install the HTML-Format distribution, which was also once part of the LWP distribution. I do not discuss HTML-Format in this book, but if you want to install it so that you have a complete LWP installation, enter this command:

```
cpan> install HTML::Format
```

Remember, LWP may be just about the most popular distribution in CPAN, but that's not all there is! Look around the web-related parts of CPAN (I prefer the interface at *http://search.cpan.org*, but you can also try *http://kobesearch.cpan.org*) as there are dozens of modules, from WWW::Automate to SOAP::Lite, that can simplify your web-related tasks.

Installing LWP Manually

The normal Perl module installation procedure is summed up in the document *perlmodinstall*. You can read this by running perldoc perlmodinstall at a shell prompt or online at *http://theoryx5.uwinnipeg.ca/CPAN/perl/pod/perlmodinstall.html*.

CPAN is a network of a large collection of Perl software and documentation. See the CPAN FAQ at *http://www.cpan.org/misc/cpan-faq.html* for more information about CPAN and modules.

Download distributions

First, download the module distributions. LWP requires several other modules to operate successfully. You'll need to install the distributions given in Table 1-1, in the order in which they are listed.

Table 1-1. Modules used in this book

Distribution	CPAN directory
MIME-Base64	*authors/id/G/GA/GAAS*
libnet	*authors/id/G/GB/GBAAR*
HTML-Tagset	*authors/id/S/SBURKE*
HTML-Parser	*authors/id/G/GA/GAAS*
URI	*authors/id/G/GA/GAAS/URI*
Compress-Zlib	*authors/id/P/PM/PMQS/Compress-Zlib*
Digest-MD5	*authors/id/G/GA/GAAS/Digest-MD5*
libwww-perl	*authors/id/G/GA/GAAS/libwww-perl*
HTML-Tree	*authors/id/S/SB/SBURKE/HTML-Tree*

Fetch these modules from one of the FTP or web sites that form CPAN, listed at *http://www.cpan.org/SITES.html* and *http://mirror.cpan.org*. Sometimes CPAN has several versions of a module in the *authors* directory. Be sure to check the version number and get the latest.

For example to install MIME-Base64, you might first fetch *http://www.cpan.org/authors/id/G/GA/GAAS/* to see which versions are there, then fetch *http://www.cpan.org/authors/id/G/GA/GAAS/MIME-Base64-2.12.tar.gz* and install that.

Unpack and configure

The distributions are gzipped tar archives of source code. Extracting a distribution creates a directory, and in that directory is a *Makefile.PL* Perl program that builds a *Makefile* for you.

```
% tar xzf MIME-Base64-2.12.tar.gz
% cd MIME-Base64-2.12
% perl Makefile.PL
Checking if your kit is complete...
Looks good
Writing Makefile for MIME::Base64
```

Make, test, and install

Compile the code with the make command:

```
% make
cp Base64.pm blib/lib/MIME/Base64.pm
cp QuotedPrint.pm blib/lib/MIME/QuotedPrint.pm
/usr/bin/perl -I/opt/perl5/5.6.1/i386-freebsd -I/opt/perl5/5.6.1
/opt/perl5/5.6.1/ExtUtils/xsubpp  -typemap
/opt/perl5/5.6.1/ExtUtils/typemap Base64.xs > Base64.xsc && mv
  Base64.xsc Base64.c
cc -c  -fno-strict-aliasing -I/usr/local/include -O   -DVERSION=\"2.12\"
  -DXS_VERSION=\"2.12\" -DPIC -fpic -I/opt/perl5/5.6.1/i386-freebsd/CORE
Base64.c
Running Mkbootstrap for MIME::Base64 ()
chmod 644 Base64.bs
rm -f blib/arch/auto/MIME/Base64/Base64.so
LD_RUN_PATH="" cc -o blib/arch/auto/MIME/Base64/Base64.so  -shared
  -L/opt Base64.o
chmod 755 blib/arch/auto/MIME/Base64/Base64.so
cp Base64.bs blib/arch/auto/MIME/Base64/Base64.bs
chmod 644 blib/arch/auto/MIME/Base64/Base64.bs
Manifying blib/man3/MIME::Base64.3
Manifying blib/man3/MIME::QuotedPrint.3
```

Then make sure everything works on your system with make test:

```
% make test
PERL_DL_NONLAZY=1 /usr/bin/perl -Iblib/arch -Iblib/lib
-I/opt/perl5/5.6.1/i386-freebsd -I/opt/perl5/5.6.1 -e 'use Test::Harness
  qw(&runtests $verbose); $verbose=0; runtests @ARGV;' t/*.t
t/base64..........ok
t/quoted-print....ok
t/unicode.........skipped test on this platform
All tests successful, 1 test skipped.
Files=3, Tests=306,  1 wallclock secs ( 0.52 cusr +  0.06 csys =  0.58 CPU)
```

If it passes the tests, install it with make install (as the superuser):

```
# make install
Installing /opt/perl5/site_perl/5.6.1/i386-freebsd/auto/MIME/Base64/Base64.so
Installing /opt/perl5/site_perl/5.6.1/i386-freebsd/auto/MIME/Base64/Base64.bs
Files found in blib/arch: installing files in blib/lib into architecture
  dependent library tree
Installing /opt/perl5/site_perl/5.6.1/i386-freebsd/MIME/Base64.pm
Installing /opt/perl5/site_perl/5.6.1/i386-freebsd/MIME/QuotedPrint.pm
Installing /usr/local/man/man3/MIME::Base64.3
Installing /usr/local/man/man3/MIME::QuotedPrint.3
Writing /opt/perl5/site_perl/5.6.1/i386-freebsd/auto/MIME/Base64/.packlist
Appending installation info to /opt/perl5/5.6.1/i386-freebsd/perllocal.pod
```

Words of Caution

In theory, the underlying mechanisms of the Web make no difference between a browser getting data and displaying it to you, and your LWP-based program getting data and doing something else with it. However, in practice, almost all the data on the Web was put there with the assumption (sometimes implicit, sometimes explicit) that it would be looked at directly in a browser. When you write an LWP program that downloads that data, you are working against that assumption. The trick is to do this in as considerate a way as possible.

Network and Server Load

When you access a web server, you are using scarce resources. You are using your bandwidth and the web server's bandwidth. Moreover, processing your request places a load on the remote server, particularly if the page you're requesting has to be dynamically generated, and especially if that dynamic generation involves database access. If you're writing a program that requests several pages from a given server but you don't need the pages immediately, you should write delays into your program (such as sleep 60, to sleep for one minute), so that the load that you're placing on the network and on the web server is spread unobtrusively over a longer period of time.

If possible, you might even want to consider having your program run in the middle of the night (*modulo* the relevant time zones), when network usage is low and the web server is not likely to be busy handling a lot of requests. Do this only if you *know* there is no risk of your program behaving unpredictably. In Chapter 12, we discuss programs with definite risk of that happening; do not let such programs run unattended until you have added appropriate safeguards and carefully checked that they behave as you expect them to.

Copyright

While the complexities of national and international copyright law can't be covered in a page or two (or even a library or two), the short story is that just because you can get some data off the Web doesn't mean you can do whatever you want with it. The things you do with data on the Web form a continuum, as far as their relation to copyright law. At the one end is direct use, where you sit at your browser, downloading and reading pages as the site owners clearly intended. At the other end is illegal use, where you run a program that hammers a remote server as it copies and saves copyrighted data that was not meant for free public consumption, then saves it all to your public web server, which you then encourage people to visit so that you can make money off of the ad banners you've put there. Between these extremes, there are many gray areas involving considerations of "fair use," a tricky concept. The safest guide in trying to stay on the right side of copyright law is to ask, by using the data this way, could I possibly be depriving the original web site of some money that it would/could otherwise get?

For example, suppose that you set up a program that copies data every hour from the Yahoo! Weather site, for the 50 most populous towns in your state. You then copy the data directly to your public web site and encourage everyone to visit it. Even though "no one owns the weather," even if any particular bit of weather data is in the public domain (which it may be, depending on its source), Yahoo! Weather put time and effort into making a collection of that data, presented in a certain way. And as such, the *collection* of data is copyrighted.

Moreover, by posting the data publicly, you are almost definitely taking viewers away from Yahoo! Weather, which means less ad revenue for them. Even if Yahoo! Weather didn't have any ads and so wasn't obviously making any money off of viewers, your having the data online elsewhere means that if Yahoo! Weather wanted to start having ads tomorrow, they'd be unable to make as much money at it, because there would be people in the habit of looking at your web site's weather data instead of at theirs.

Acceptable Use

Besides the protection provided by copyright law, many web sites have "terms of use" or "acceptable use" policies, where the web site owners basically say "as a user, you may do this and this, but not that or that, and if you don't abide by these terms, then we don't want you using this web site." For example, a search engine's terms of use might stipulate that you should not make "automated queries" to their system, nor should you show the search data on another site.

Before you start pulling data off of a web site, you should put good effort into looking around for its terms of service document, and take the time to read it and reasonably interpret what it says. When in doubt, ask the web site's administrators whether what you have in mind would bother them.

LWP in Action

Enough of why you should be careful when you automate the Web. Let's look at the types of things you'll be learning in this book. Chapter 2 introduces web automation and LWP, presenting straightforward functions to let you fetch web pages. Example 1-1 shows how to fetch the O'Reilly home page and count the number of times Perl is mentioned.

Example 1-1. Count "Perl" in the O'Reilly catalog

```
#!/usr/bin/perl -w
use strict;
use LWP::Simple;

my $catalog = get("http://www.oreilly.com/catalog");
my $count = 0;
$count++ while $catalog =~ m{Perl}gi;
print "$count\n";
```

The LWP::Simple module's get( ) function returns the document at a given URL or undef if an error occurred. A regular expression match in a loop counts the number of occurrences.

The Object-Oriented Interface

Chapter 3 goes beyond LWP::Simple to show larger LWP's powerful object-oriented interface. Most useful of all the features it covers are how to set headers in requests and check the headers of responses. Example 1-2 prints the identifying string that every server returns.

Example 1-2. Identify a server

```
#!/usr/bin/perl -w
use strict;
use LWP;

my $browser = LWP::UserAgent->new( );
my $response = $browser->get("http://www.oreilly.com/");
print $response->header("Server"), "\n";
```

The two variables, $browser and $response, are references to objects. LWP::UserAgent object $browser makes requests of a server and creates HTTP::Response objects such as $response to represent the server's reply. In Example 1-2, we call the header( ) method on the response to check one of the HTTP header values.

Forms

Chapter 5 shows how to analyze and submit forms with LWP, including both GET and POST submissions. Example 1-3 makes queries of the California license plate database to see whether a personalized plate is available.

Example 1-3. Query California license plate database

```
#!/usr/bin/perl -w
# pl8.pl -  query California license plate database
```

Example 1-3. Query California license plate database (continued)

```
use strict;
use LWP::UserAgent;
my $plate = $ARGV[0] || die "Plate to search for?\n";
$plate = uc $plate;
$plate =~ tr/O/0/;  # we use zero for letter-oh
die "$plate is invalid.\n"
 unless $plate =~ m/^[A-Z0-9]{2,7}$/
    and $plate !~ m/^\d+$/;  # no all-digit plates

my $browser = LWP::UserAgent->new;
my $response = $browser->post(
  'http://plates.ca.gov/search/search.php3',
  [
    'plate'  => $plate,
    'search' => 'Check Plate Availability'
  ],
);
die "Error: ", $response->status_line
 unless $response->is_success;

if($response->content =~ m/is unavailable/) {
  print "$plate is already taken.\n";
} elsif($response->content =~ m/and available/) {
  print "$plate is AVAILABLE!\n";
} else {
  print "$plate... Can't make sense of response?!\n";
}
exit;
```

Here's how you might use it:

```
% p18.pl knee
KNEE is already taken.
% p18.pl ankle
ANKLE is AVAILABLE!
```

We use the post( ) method on an LWP::UserAgent object to POST form parameters to a page.

Parsing HTML

The regular expression techniques in Examples 1-1 and 1-3 are discussed in detail in Chapter 6. Chapter 7 shows a different approach, where the HTML::TokeParser module turns a string of HTML into a stream of chunks ("start-tag," "text," "close-tag," and so on). Chapter 8 is a detailed step-by-step walkthrough showing how to solve a problem using HTML::TokeParser. Example 1-4 uses HTML::TokeParser to extract the src parts of all img tags in the O'Reilly home page.

Example 1-4. Extract image locations

```perl
#!/usr/bin/perl -w

use strict;
use LWP::Simple;
use HTML::TokeParser;

my $html   = get("http://www.oreilly.com/");
my $stream = HTML::TokeParser->new(\$html);
my %image  = ();

while (my $token = $stream->get_token) {
    if ($token->[0] eq 'S' && $token->[1] eq 'img') {
        # store src value in %image
        $image{ $token->[2]{'src'} }++;
    }
}

foreach my $pic (sort keys %image) {
    print "$pic\n";
}
```

The get_token() method on our HTML::TokeParser object returns an array reference, representing a token. If the first array element is S, it's a token representing the start of a tag. The second array element is the type of tag, and the third array element is a hash mapping attribute to value. The %image hash holds the images we find.

Chapters 9 and 10 show how to use tree data structures to represent HTML. The HTML::TreeBuilder module constructs such trees and provides operations for searching and manipulating them. Example 1-5 extracts image locations using a tree.

Example 1-5. Extracting image locations with a tree

```perl
#!/usr/bin/perl -w

use strict;
use LWP::Simple;
use HTML::TreeBuilder;

my $html = get("http://www.oreilly.com/");
my $root = HTML::TreeBuilder->new_from_content($html);
my %images;
foreach my $node ($root->find_by_tag_name('img')) {
    $images{ $node->attr('src') }++;
}

foreach my $pic (sort keys %images) {
    print "$pic\n";
}
```

We create a new tree from the HTML in the O'Reilly home page. The tree has methods to help us search, such as find_by_tag_name( ), which returns a list of nodes corresponding to those tags. We use that to find the img tags, then use the attr( ) method to get their src attributes.

Authentication

Chapter 11 talks about advanced request features such as cookies (used to identify a user between web page accesses) and authentication. Example 1-6 shows how easy it is to request a protected page with LWP.

Example 1-6. Authenticating

```
#!/usr/bin/perl -w

use strict;
use LWP;

my $browser = LWP::UserAgent->new( );
$browser->credentials("www.example.com:80", "music", "fred" => "l33t1");
my $response = $browser->get("http://www.example.com/mp3s");
# ...
```

The credentials( ) method on an LWP::UserAgent adds the authentication information (the host, realm, and username/password pair are the parameters). The realm identifies which username and password are expected if there are multiple protected areas on a single host. When we request a document using that LWP::UserAgent object, the authentication information is used if necessary.

## CHAPTER 2

Web Basics

Three things made the Web possible: HTML for encoding documents, HTTP for transferring them, and URLs for identifying them. To fetch and extract information from web pages, you must know all three—you construct a URL for the page you wish to fetch, make an HTTP request for it and decode the HTTP response, then parse the HTML to extract information. This chapter covers the construction of URLs and the concepts behind HTTP. HTML parsing is tricky and gets its own chapters later, as does the module that lets you manipulate URLs.

You'll also learn how to automate the most basic web tasks with the LWP::Simple module. As its name suggests, this module has a very simple interface. You'll learn the limitations of that interface and see how to use other LWP modules to fetch web pages without the limitations of LWP::Simple.

URLs

A Uniform Resource Locator (URL) is the address of something on the Web. For example:

> *http://www.oreilly.com/news/bikeweek_day1.html*

URLs have a structure, given in RFC 2396. That RFC runs to 40 pages, largely because of the wide variety of things for which you can construct URLs. Because we are interested only in HTTP and FTP URLs, the components of a URL, with the delimiters that separate them, are:

> `scheme://username@server:port/path?query`

In the case of our example URL, the scheme is *http*, the server is *www.oreilly.com*, and the path is */news/bikeweek_day1.html*.

This is an FTP URL:

> *ftp://ftp.is.co.za/rfc/rfc1808.txt*

The scheme is *ftp*, the host is *ftp.is.co.za*, and the path is */rfc/rfc1808.txt*. The scheme and the hostname are not case sensitive, but the rest is. That is, *ftp://ftp.is.co.za/rfc/rfc1808.txt* and *fTp://ftp.Is.cO.ZA/rfc/rfc1808.txt* are the same, but *ftp://ftp.is.co.za/rfc/rfc1808.txt* and *ftp://ftp.is.co.za/rfc/RFC1808.txt* are not, unless that server happens to forgive case differences in requests.

We're ignoring the URLs that don't designate things that a web client can retrieve. For example, *telnet://melvyl.ucop.edu/* designates a host with which you can start a Telnet session, and *mailto:mojo@jojo.int* designates an email address to which you can send.

The only characters allowed in the path portions of a URL are the US-ASCII characters A through Z, a through z, and 0–9 (but excluding extended ASCII characters such as ü and Unicode characters such as Ω or ⊆), and these permitted punctuation characters:

```
-    _    .    !    ~    *    '    ,
:    @    &    +    $    (    )    /
```

For a query component, the same rule holds, except that the only punctuation characters allowed are these:

```
-    _    .    !    ~    *    '    (    )
```

Any other characters must be *URL encoded*, i.e., expressed as a percent sign followed by the two hexadecimal digits for that character. So if you wanted to use a space in a URL, it would have to be expressed as %20, because space is character 32 in ASCII, and the number 32 expressed in hexadecimal is 20.

Incidentally, sometimes you might also see some of these characters in a URL:

```
{    }    |    \    ^    [    ]    `
```

But the document that defines URLs, RFC 2396, refers to the use of these as unreliable and "unwise." When in doubt, encode it!

The query portion of a URL assigns values to parameters:

```
name=Hiram%20Veeblefeetzer+age=35+country=Madagascar
```

There are three parameters in that query string: name, with the value "Hiram Veeblefeetzer" (the space has been encoded); age, with the value 35; and country, with the value "Madagascar".

The URI::Escape module provides the uri_escape() function to help you build URLs:

```
use URI::Escape;
encoded_string = uri_escape(raw_string);
```

For example, to build the name, age, and country query string:

```
$n = uri_escape("Hiram Veeblefeetzer");
$a = uri_escape(35);
```

```
$c = uri_escape("Madagascar");
$query = "name=$n+age=$a+country=$c";
print $query;
name=Hiram%20Veeblefeetzer+age=35+country=Madagascar
```

An HTTP Transaction

The Hypertext Transfer Protocol (HTTP) is used to fetch most documents on the Web. It is formally specified in RFC 2616, but this section explains everything you need to know to use LWP.

HTTP is a server/client protocol: the server has the file, and the client wants it. In regular web surfing, the client is a web browser such as Mozilla or Internet Explorer. The URL for a document identifies the server, which the browser contacts and requests the document from. The server returns either in error ("file not found") or success (in which case the document is attached).

Example 2-1 contains a sample request from a client.

Example 2-1. An HTTP request

```
GET /daily/2001/01/05/1.html HTTP/1.1
Host: www.suck.com
User-Agent: Super Duper Browser 14.6
```
blank line

A successful response is given in Example 2-2.

Example 2-2. A successful HTTP response

```
HTTP/1.1 200 OK
Content-type: text/html
Content-length: 24204
```
blank line
and then 24,204 bytes of HTML code

A response indicating failure is given in Example 2-3.

Example 2-3. An unsuccessful HTTP response

```
HTTP/1.1 404 Not Found
Content-type: text/html
Content-length: 135
```

```
<html><head><title>Not Found</title></head><body>
Sorry, the object you requested was not found.
</body><html>
```
and then the server closes the connection

Request

An HTTP request has three parts: the request line, the headers, and the body of the request (normally used to pass form parameters).

The request line says what the client wants to do (the *method*), what it wants to do it to (the *path*), and what protocol it's speaking. Although the HTTP standard defines several methods, the most common are GET and POST. The path is part of the URL being requested (in Example 2-1 the path is */daily/2001/01/05/1.html*). The protocol version is generally HTTP/1.1.

Each header line consists of a key and a value (for example, User-Agent: SuperDuperBrowser/14.6). In versions of HTTP previous to 1.1, header lines were optional. In HTTP 1.1, the Host: header must be present, to name the server to which the browser is talking. This is the "server" part of the URL being requested (e.g., *www.suck.com*). The headers are terminated with a blank line, which must be present regardless of whether there are any headers.

The optional message body can contain arbitrary data. If a body is sent, the request's Content-Type and Content-Length headers help the server decode the data. GET queries don't have any attached data, so this area is blank (that is, nothing is sent by the browser). For our purposes, only POST queries use this third part of the HTTP request.

The following are the most useful headers sent in an HTTP request.

Host: *www.youthere.int*
> This mandatory header line tells the server the hostname from the URL being requested. It may sound odd to be telling a server its own name, but this header line was added in HTTP 1.1 to deal with cases where a single HTTP server answers requests for several different hostnames.

User-Agent: *Thing/1.23 details...*
> This optional header line identifies the make and model of this browser (virtual or otherwise). For an interactive browser, it's usually something like Mozilla/4.76 [en] (Win98; U) or Mozilla/4.0 (compatible; MSIE 5.12; Mac_PowerPC). By default, LWP sends a User-Agent header of libwww-perl/5.64 (or whatever your exact LWP version is).

Referer: *http://www.thingamabob.int/stuff.html*
> This optional header line tells the remote server the URL of the page that contained a link to the page being requested.

Accept-Language: *en-US, en, es, de*
> This optional header line tells the remote server the natural languages in which the user would prefer to see content, using language tags. For example, the above list means the user would prefer content in U.S. English, or (in order of decreasing preference) any kind of English, Spanish, or German. (Appendix D

lists the most common language tags.) Many browsers do not send this header, and those that do usually send the default header appropriate to the version of the browser that the user installed. For example, if the browser is Netscape with a Spanish-language interface, it would probably send Accept-Language: es, unless the user has dutifully gone through the browser's preferences menus to specify other languages.

Response

The server's response also has three parts: the status line, some headers, and an optional body.

The status line states which protocol the server is speaking, then gives a numeric status code and a short message. For example, "HTTP/1.1 404 Not Found." The numeric status codes are grouped—200–299 are success, 400–499 are permanent failures, and so on. A full list of HTTP status codes is given in Appendix B.

The header lines let the server send additional information about the response. For example, if authentication is required, the server uses headers to indicate the type of authentication. The most common header—almost always present for both successful and unsuccessful requests—is Content-Type, which helps the browser interpret the body. Headers are terminated with a blank line, which must be present even if no headers are sent.

Many responses contain a Content-Length line that specifies the length, in bytes, of the body. However, this line is rarely present on dynamically generated pages, and because you never know which pages are dynamically generated, you can't rely on that header line being there.

(Other, rarer header lines are used for specifying that the content has moved to a given URL, or that the server wants the browser to send HTTP cookies, and so on; however, these things are generally handled for you automatically by LWP.)

The body of the response follows the blank line and can be any arbitrary data. In the case of a typical web request, this is the HTML document to be displayed. If an error occurs, the message body doesn't contain the document that was requested but usually consists of a server-generated error message (generally in HTML, but sometimes not) explaining the error.

LWP::Simple

GET is the simplest and most common type of HTTP request. Form parameters may be supplied in the URL, but there is never a body to the request. The LWP::Simple module has several functions for quickly fetching a document with a GET request. Some functions return the document, others save or print the document.

Basic Document Fetch

The LWP::Simple module's get( ) function takes a URL and returns the body of the document:

```
$document = get("http://www.suck.com/daily/2001/01/05/1.html");
```

If the document can't be fetched, get( ) returns undef. Incidentally, if LWP requests that URL and the server replies that it has moved to some other URL, LWP requests that other URL and returns that.

With LWP::Simple's get( ) function, there's no way to set headers to be sent with the GET request or get more information about the response, such as the status code. These are important things, because some web servers have copies of documents in different languages and use the HTTP language header to determine which document to return. Likewise, the HTTP response code can let us distinguish between permanent failures (e.g., "404 Not Found") and temporary failures ("505 Service [Temporarily] Unavailable").

Even the most common type of nontrivial web robot (a link checker), benefits from access to response codes. A 403 ("Forbidden," usually because of file permissions) could be automatically corrected, whereas a 404 ("Not Found") error implies an out-of-date link that requires fixing. But if you want access to these codes or other parts of the response besides just the main content, your task is no longer a simple one, and so you shouldn't use LWP::Simple for it. The "simple" in LWP::Simple refers not just to the style of its interface, but also to the kind of tasks for which it's meant.

Fetch and Store

One way to get the status code is to use LWP::Simple's getstore( ) function, which writes the document to a file and returns the status code from the response:

```
$status = getstore("http://www.suck.com/daily/2001/01/05/1.html",
                   "/tmp/web.html");
```

There are two problems with this. The first is that the document is now stored in a file instead of in a variable where you can process it (extract information, convert to another format, etc.). This is readily solved by reading the file using Perl's built-in open( ) and <FH> operators; see below for an example.

The other problem is that a status code by itself isn't very useful: how do you know whether it was successful? That is, does the file contain a document? LWP::Simple offers the is_success( ) and is_error( ) functions to answer that question:

```
$successful = is_success(status);
$failed     = is_error(status);
```

If the status code *status* indicates a successful request (is in the 200–299 range), is_success( ) returns true. If *status* is an error (400–599), is_error( ) returns true.

For example, this bit of code saves the BookTV (CSPAN2) listings schedule and emits a message if Gore Vidal is mentioned:

```perl
use strict;
use warnings;
use LWP::Simple;
my $url  = 'http://www.booktv.org/schedule/';
my $file = 'booktv.html';
my $status = getstore($url, $file);
die "Error $status on $url" unless is_success($status);
open(IN, "<$file") || die "Can't open $file: $!";
while (<IN>) {
  if (m/Gore\s+Vidal/) {
    print "Look!  Gore Vidal!  $url\n";
    last;
  }
}
close(IN);
```

Fetch and Print

LWP::Simple also exports the getprint( ) function:

```perl
$status = getprint(url);
```

The document is printed to the currently selected output filehandle (usually STD-OUT). In other respects, it behaves like getstore( ). This can be very handy in one-liners such as:

```
% perl -MLWP::Simple -e "getprint('http://cpan.org/RECENT')||die" | grep Apache
```

That retrieves *http://cpan.org/RECENT*, which lists the past week's uploads in CPAN (it's a plain text file, not HTML), then sends it to STDOUT, where grep passes through the lines that contain "Apache."

Previewing with HEAD

LWP::Simple also exports the head( ) function, which asks the server, "If I were to request this item with GET, what headers would it have?" This is useful when you are checking links. Although, not all servers support HEAD requests properly, if head( ) says the document is retrievable, then it almost definitely is. (However, if head( ) says it's not, that might just be because the server doesn't support HEAD requests.)

The return value of head( ) depends on whether you call it in scalar context or list context. In scalar context, it is simply:

```perl
$is_success = head(url);
```

If the server answers the HEAD request with a successful status code, this returns a true value. Otherwise, it returns a false value. You can use this like so:

```perl
die "I don't think I'll be able to get $url" unless head($url);
```

Regrettably, however, some old servers, and most CGIs running on newer servers, do not understand HEAD requests. In that case, they should reply with a "405 Method Not Allowed" message, but some actually respond as if you had performed a GET request. With the minimal interface that head( ) provides, you can't really deal with either of those cases, because you can't get the status code on unsuccessful requests, nor can you get the content (which, in theory, there should never be any).

In list context, head( ) returns a list of five values, if the request is successful:

```
(content_type, document_length, modified_time, expires, server)
    = head(url);
```

The *content_type* value is the MIME type string of the form *type/subtype*; the most common MIME types are listed in Appendix C. The *document_length* value is whatever is in the Content-Length header, which, if present, should be the number of bytes in the document that you would have gotten if you'd performed a GET request. The *modified_time* value is the contents of the Last-Modified header converted to a number like you would get from Perl's time( ) function. For normal files (GIFs, HTML files, etc.), the Last-Modified value is just the modification time of that file, but dynamically generated content will not typically have a Last-Modified header.

The last two values are rarely useful; the *expires* value is a time (expressed as a number like you would get from Perl's time( ) function) from the seldom used Expires header, indicating when the data should no longer be considered valid. The *server* value is the contents of the Server header line that the server can send, to tell you what kind of software it's running. A typical value is Apache/1.3.22 (Unix).

An unsuccessful request, in list context, returns an empty list. So when you're copying the return list into a bunch of scalars, they will each get assigned undef. Note also that you don't need to save all the values—you can save just the first few, as in Example 2-4.

Example 2-4. Link checking with HEAD

```
use strict;
use LWP::Simple;
foreach my $url (
  'http://us.a1.yimg.com/us.yimg.com/i/ww/m5v9.gif',
  'http://hooboy.no-such-host.int/',
  'http://www.yahoo.com',
  'http://www.ora.com/ask_tim/graphics/asktim_header_main.gif',
  'http://www.guardian.co.uk/',
  'http://www.pixunlimited.co.uk/siteheaders/Guardian.gif',
) {
  print "\n$url\n";

  my ($type, $length, $mod) = head($url);
  # so we don't even save the expires or server values!
```

Example 2-4. Link checking with HEAD (continued)

```
  unless (defined $type) {
    print "Couldn't get $url\n";
    next;
  }
  print "That $type document is ", $length || "???", " bytes long.\n";
  if ($mod) {
    my $ago = time( ) - $mod;
    print "It was modified $ago seconds ago; that's about ",
      int(.5 + $ago / (24 * 60 * 60)), " days ago, at ",
      scalar(localtime($mod)), "!\n";
  } else {
    print "I don't know when it was last modified.\n";
  }
}
```

Currently, that program prints the following, when run:

```
http://us.a1.yimg.com/us.yimg.com/i/ww/m5v9.gif
That image/gif document is 5611 bytes long.
It was modified 251207569 seconds ago; that's about 2907 days ago, at Thu Apr 14 18:
00:00 1994!

http://hooboy.no-such-host.int/
Couldn't get http://hooboy.no-such-host.int/

http://www.yahoo.com
That text/html document is ??? bytes long.
I don't know when it was last modified.

http://www.ora.com/ask_tim/graphics/asktim_header_main.gif
That image/gif document is 8588 bytes long.
It was modified 62185120 seconds ago; that's about 720 days ago, at Mon Apr 10 12:14:
13 2000!

http://www.guardian.co.uk/
That text/html document is ??? bytes long.
I don't know when it was last modified.

http://www.pixunlimited.co.uk/siteheaders/Guardian.gif
That image/gif document is 4659 bytes long.
It was modified 24518302 seconds ago; that's about 284 days ago, at Wed Jun 20 11:14:
33 2001!
```

Incidentally, if you are using the very popular CGI.pm module, be aware that it
exports a function called head( ) too. To avoid a clash, you can just tell LWP::Simple
to export every function it normally would except for head( ):

```
use LWP::Simple qw(!head);
use CGI qw(:standard);
```

If not for that qw(!head), LWP::Simple would export head( ), then CGI would export
head( ) (as it's in that module's :standard group), which would clash, producing a
mildly cryptic warning such as "Prototype mismatch: sub main::head ($) vs none."

Because any program using the CGI library is almost definitely a CGI script, any such warning (or, in fact, any message to STDERR) is usually enough to abort that CGI with a "500 Internal Server Error" message.

Fetching Documents Without LWP::Simple

LWP::Simple is convenient but not all powerful. In particular, we can't make POST requests or set request headers or query response headers. To do these things, we need to go beyond LWP::Simple.

The general all-purpose way to do HTTP GET queries is by using the do_GET( ) subroutine shown in Example 2-5.

Example 2-5. The do_GET subroutine

```
use LWP;
my $browser;
sub do_GET {
  # Parameters: the URL,
  #  and then, optionally, any header lines: (key,value, key,value)
  $browser = LWP::UserAgent->new( ) unless $browser;
  my $resp = $browser->get(@_);
  return ($resp->content, $resp->status_line, $resp->is_success, $resp)
    if wantarray;
  return unless $resp->is_success;
  return $resp->content;
}
```

A full explanation of the internals of do_GET( ) is given in Chapter 3. Until then, we'll be using it without fully understanding how it works.

You can call the do_GET( ) function in either scalar or list context:

```
doc = do_GET(URL [header, value, ...]);
(doc, status, successful, response) = do_GET(URL [header, value, ...]);
```

In scalar context, it returns the document or undef if there is an error. In list context, it returns the document (if any), the status line from the HTTP response, a Boolean value indicating whether the status code indicates a successful response, and an object we can interrogate to find out more about the response.

Recall that assigning to undef discards that value. For example, this is how you fetch a document into a string and learn whether it is successful:

```
($doc, undef, $successful, undef) = do_GET('http://www.suck.com/');
```

The optional header and value arguments to do_GET( ) let you add headers to the request. For example, to attempt to fetch the German language version of the European Union home page:

```
$body = do_GET("http://europa.eu.int/",
  "Accept-language" => "de",
);
```

The do_GET( ) function that we'll use in this chapter provides the same basic convenience as LWP::Simple's get( ) but without the limitations.

Example: AltaVista

Every so often, two people, somewhere, somehow, will come to argue over a point of English spelling—one of them will hold up a dictionary recommending one spelling, and the other will hold up a dictionary recommending something else. In olden times, such conflicts were tidily settled with a fight to the death, but in these days of overspecialization, it is common for one of the spelling combatants to say "Let's ask a linguist. He'll know I'm right and you're wrong!" And so I am contacted, and my supposedly expert opinion is requested. And if I happen to be answering mail that month, my response is often something like:

> Dear Mr. Hing:
>
> I have read with intense interest your letter detailing your struggle with the question of whether your favorite savory spice should be spelled in English as "asafoetida" or whether you should heed your secretary's admonishment that all the kids today are spelling it "asafetida."
>
> I could note various factors potentially involved here; notably, the fact that in many cases, British/Commonwealth spelling retains many "ae"/"oe" digraphs whereas U.S./ Canadian spelling strongly prefers an "e" ("foetus"/"fetus," etc.). But I will instead be (merely) democratic about this and note that if you use AltaVista (*http://altavista.com*, a well-known search engine) to run a search on "asafetida," it will say that across all the pages that AltaVista has indexed, there are "about 4,170" matched; whereas for "asafoetida" there are many more, "about 8,720."
>
> So you, with the "oe," are apparently in the majority.

To automate the task of producing such reports, I've written a small program called *alta_count*, which queries AltaVista for each term given and reports the count of documents matched:

```
% alta_count asafetida asafoetida
asafetida: 4,170 matches
asafoetida: 8,720 matches
```

At time of this writing, going to *http://altavista.com*, putting a word or phrase in the search box, and hitting the Submit button yields a result page with a URL that looks like this:

```
http://www.altavista.com/sites/search/web?q=%22asafetida%22&kl=XX
```

Now, you could construct these URLs for any phrase with something like:

```
$url = 'http://www.altavista.com/sites/search/web?q=%22'
     . $phrase
     . '%22&kl=XX'  ;
```

But that doesn't take into account the need to encode characters such as spaces in URLs. If I want to run a search on the frequency of "boy toy" (as compared to the alternate spelling "boytoy"), the space in that phrase needs to be encoded as %20, and if I want to run a search on the frequency of "résumé," each "é" needs to be encoded as %E9.

The correct way to generate the query strings is to use the URI::Escape module:

```
use URI::Escape;    # That gives us the uri_escape function
$url = 'http://www.altavista.com/sites/search/web?q=%22'
       . uri_escape($phrase)
       . '%22&kl=XX'  ;
```

Now we just have to request that URL and skim the returned content for AltaVista's standard phrase "We found [number] results." (That's assuming the response comes with an okay status code, as we should get unless AltaVista is somehow down or inaccessible.)

Example 2-6 is the complete *alta_count* program.

Example 2-6. The alta_count program

```
#!/usr/bin/perl -w
use strict;
use URI::Escape;
foreach my $word (@ARGV) {
  next unless length $word; # sanity-checking
  my $url = 'http://www.altavista.com/sites/search/web?q=%22'
    . uri_escape($word) . '%22&kl=XX';
  my ($content, $status, $is_success) = do_GET($url);
  if (!$is_success) {
    print "Sorry, failed: $status\n";
  } elsif ($content =~ m/>We found ([0-9,]+) results?/) { # like "1,952"
    print "$word: $1 matches\n";
  } else {
    print "$word: Page not processable, at $url\n";
  }
  sleep 2; # Be nice to AltaVista's servers!!!
}


# And then my favorite do_GET routine:
use LWP; # loads lots of necessary classes.
my $browser;
sub do_GET {
  $browser = LWP::UserAgent->new unless $browser;
  my $resp = $browser->get(@_);
  return ($resp->content, $resp->status_line, $resp->is_success, $resp)
    if wantarray;
  return unless $resp->is_success;
  return $resp->content;
}
```

With that, I can run:

```
% alta_count boytoy 'boy toy'
boytoy: 6,290 matches
boy toy: 26,100 matches
```

knowing that when it searches for the frequency of "boy toy," it is duly URL-encoding the space character.

This approach to HTTP GET query parameters, where we insert one or two values into an otherwise precooked URL, works fine for most cases. For a more general approach (where we produce the part after the ? completely from scratch in the URL), see Chapter 5.

HTTP POST

Some forms use GET to submit their parameters to the server, but many use POST. The difference is POST requests pass the parameters in the body of the request, whereas GET requests encode the parameters into the URL being requested.

Babelfish (*http://babelfish.altavista.com*) is a service that lets you translate text from one human language into another. If you're accessing Babelfish from a browser, you see an HTML form where you paste in the text you want translated, specify the language you want it translated from and to, and hit Translate. After a few seconds, a new page appears, with your translation.

Behind the scenes, the browser takes the key/value pairs in the form:

```
urltext = I like pie
lp = en_fr
enc = utf8
```

and rolls them into a HTTP request:

```
POST /translate.dyn HTTP/1.1
Host: babelfish.altavista.com
User-Agent: SuperDuperBrowser/14.6
Content-Type: application/x-www-form-urlencoded
Content-Length: 40

urltext=I%20like%20pie&lp=en_fr&enc=utf8
```

Just as we used a do_GET( ) function to automate a GET query, Example 2-7 uses a do_POST( ) function to automate POST queries.

Example 2-7. The do_POST subroutine

```
use LWP;
my $browser;
sub do_POST {
  # Parameters:
  #  the URL,
  #  an arrayref or hashref for the key/value pairs,
  #  and then, optionally, any header lines: (key,value, key,value)
  $browser = LWP::UserAgent->new( ) unless $browser;
  my $resp = $browser->post(@_);
  return ($resp->content, $resp->status_line, $resp->is_success, $resp)
    if wantarray;
```

Example 2-7. The do_POST subroutine (continued)

```
  return unless $resp->is_success;
  return $resp->content;
}
```

Use do_POST( ) like this:

```
    doc = do_POST(URL, [form_ref, [headers_ref]]);
    (doc, status, success, resp) = do_GET(URL, [form_ref, [headers_ref]]);
```

The return values in scalar and list context are as for do_GET( ). The *form_ref* parameter is a reference to a hash containing the form parameters. The *headers_ref* parameter is a reference to a hash containing headers you want sent in the request.

Example: Babelfish

Submitting a POST query to Babelfish is as simple as:

```
    my ($content, $message, $is_success) = do_POST(
      'http://babelfish.altavista.com/translate.dyn',
      [ 'urltext' => "I like pie", 'lp' => "en_fr", 'enc' => 'utf8' ],
    );
```

If the request succeeded ($is_success will tell us this), $content will be an HTML page that contains the translation text. At time of this writing, the translation is inside the only textarea element on the page, so it can be extracted with just this regexp:

```
    $content =~ m{<textarea.*?>(.*?)</textarea>}is;
```

The translated text is now in $1, if the match succeeded.

Knowing this, it's easy to wrap this whole procedure up in a function that takes the text to translate and a specification of what language from and to, and returns the translation. Example 2-8 is such a function.

Example 2-8. Using Babelfish to translate

```
sub translate {
  my ($text, $language_path) = @_;

  my ($content, $message, $is_success) = do_POST(
    'http://babelfish.altavista.com/translate.dyn',
    [ 'urltext' => $text, 'lp' => $language_path, 'enc' => 'utf8' ],
  );
  die "Error in translation $language_path: $message\n"
   unless $is_success;

  if ($content =~ m{<textarea.*?>(.*?)</textarea>}is) {
    my $translation;
    $translation = $1;
    # Trim whitespace:
    $translation =~ s/\s+/ /g;
```

Example 2-8. Using Babelfish to translate (continued)

```
      $translation =~ s/^ //s;
      $translation =~ s/ $//s;
      return $translation;
  } else {
      die "Can't find translation in response to $language_path";
  }
}
```

The translate( ) subroutine constructs the request and extracts the translation from the response, cleaning up any whitespace that may surround it. If the request couldn't be completed, the subroutine throws an exception by calling die( ).

The translate( ) subroutine could be used to automate on-demand translation of important content from one language to another. But machine translation is still a fairly new technology, and the real value of it is to be found in translating from English into another language and then back into English, just for fun. (Incidentally, there's a CPAN module that takes care of all these details for you, called Lingua::Translate, but here we're interested in how to carry out the task, rather than whether someone's already figured it out and posted it to CPAN.)

The *alienate* program given in Example 2-9 does just this (the definitions of translate( ) and do_POST( ) have been omitted from the listing for brevity).

Example 2-9. The alienate program

```
#!/usr/bin/perl -w
# alienate - translate text
use strict;
my $lang;
if (@ARGV and $ARGV[0] =~ m/^-(\w\w)$/s) {
   # If the language is specified as a switch like "-fr"
   $lang = lc $1;
   shift @ARGV;
} else {
   # Otherwise just pick a language at random:
   my @languages = qw(it fr de es ja pt);
   # I.e.: Italian, French, German, Spanish, Japanese, Portugese.
   $lang = $languages[rand @languages];
}

die "What to translate?\n" unless @ARGV;
my $in = join(' ', @ARGV);

print " => via $lang => ",
   translate(
      translate($in, 'en_' . $lang),
      $lang . '_en'
   ), "\n";
exit;

# definitions of do_POST() and translate() go here
```

Call the alienate program like this:

```
% alienate [-lang] phrase
```

Specify a language with -lang, for example -fr to translate via French. If you don't specify a language, one will be randomly chosen for you. The phrase to translate is taken from the command line following any switches.

Here are some runs of *alienate*:

```
% alienate -de "Pearls before swine!"
=> via de => Beads before pigs!

% alienate "Bond, James Bond"
=> via fr => Link, Link Of James

% alienate "Shaken, not stirred"
=> via pt => Agitated, not agitated

% alienate -it "Shaken, not stirred"
=> via it => Mental patient, not stirred

% alienate -it "Guess what! I'm a computer!"
=> via it => Conjecture that what! They are a calculating!

% alienate 'It was more fun than a barrel of monkeys'
=> via de => It was more fun than a barrel drop hammer

% alienate -ja 'It was more fun than a barrel of monkeys'
=> via ja => That the barrel of monkey at times was many pleasures
```

## CHAPTER 3

The LWP Class Model

For full access to every part of an HTTP transaction—request headers and body, response status line, headers and body—you have to go beyond LWP::Simple, to the object-oriented modules that form the heart of the LWP suite. This chapter introduces the classes that LWP uses to represent browser objects (which you use for making requests) and response objects (which are the result of making a request). You'll learn the basic mechanics of customizing requests and inspecting responses, which we'll use in later chapters for cookies, language selection, spidering, and more.

The Basic Classes

In LWP's object model, you perform GET, HEAD, and POST requests via a browser object (a.k.a. a user agent object) of class LWP::UserAgent, and the result is an HTTP response of the aptly named class HTTP::Response. These are the two main classes, with other incidental classes providing features such as cookie management and user agents that act as spiders. Still more classes deal with non-HTTP aspects of the Web, such as HTML. In this chapter, we'll deal with the classes needed to perform web requests.

The classes can be loaded individually:

```
use LWP::UserAgent;
use HTTP::Response;
```

But it's easiest to simply use the LWP convenience class, which loads LWP::User-Agent and HTTP::Response for you:

```
use LWP;                # same as previous two lines
```

If you're familiar with object-oriented programming in Perl, the LWP classes will hold few real surprises for you. All you need is to learn the names of the basic classes and accessors. If you're not familiar with object-oriented programming in any language, you have some catching up to do. Appendix G will give you a bit of conceptual background on the object-oriented approach to things. To learn more (including information on how to write your own classes), check out *Programming Perl* (O'Reilly).

Programming with LWP Classes

The first step in writing a program that uses the LWP classes is to create and initialize the browser object, which can be used throughout the rest of the program. You need a browser object to perform HTTP requests, and although you could use several browser objects per program, I've never run into a reason to use more than one.

The browser object can use a proxy (a server that fetches web pages for you, such as a firewall, or a web cache such as Squid). It's good form to check the environment for proxy settings by calling env_proxy():

```
use LWP::UserAgent;
my $browser = LWP::UserAgent->new( );
$browser->env_proxy( ); # if we're behind a firewall
```

That's all the initialization that most user agents will ever need. Once you've done that, you usually won't do anything with it for the rest of the program, aside from calling its get( ), head( ), or post( ) methods, to get what's at a URL, or to perform HTTP HEAD or POST requests on it. For example:

```
$url = 'http://www.guardian.co.uk/';
my $response = $browser->get($url);
```

Then you call methods on the response to check the status, extract the content, and so on. For example, this code checks to make sure we successfully fetched an HTML document that isn't worryingly short, then prints a message depending on whether the words "Madonna" or "Arkansas" appear in the content:

```
die "Hmm, error \"", $response->status_line( ),
   "\" when getting $url"  unless $response->is_success( );
my $content_type = $response->content_type( );
die "Hm, unexpected content type $content_type from $url"
   unless $content_type eq 'text/html';
my $content = $response->content( );
die "Odd, the content from $url is awfully short!"
   if length($content) < 3000;
if($content =~ m/Madonna|Arkansas/i) {
   print "<!-- The news today is IMPORTANT -->\n",
        $content;
} else {
   print "$url has no news of ANY CONCEIVABLE IMPORTANCE!\n";
}
```

As you see, the response object contains all the data from the web server's response (or an error message about how that server wasn't reachable!), and we use method calls to get at the data. There are accessors for the different parts of the response (e.g., the status line) and convenience functions to tell us whether the response was successful (is_success( )).

And that's a working and complete LWP program!

Inside the do_GET and do_POST Functions

You now know enough to follow the do_GET( ) and do_POST( ) functions introduced in Chapter 2. Let's look at do_GET( ) first.

Start by loading the module, then declare the $browser variable that will hold the user agent. It's declared outside the scope of the do_GET( ) subroutine, so it's essentially a static variable, retaining its value between calls to the subroutine. For example, if you turn on support for HTTP cookies, this browser could persist between calls to do_GET( ), and cookies set by the server in one call would be sent back in a subsequent call.

```
use LWP;
my $browser;
sub do_GET {
```

Next, create the user agent if it doesn't already exist:

```
$browser = LWP::UserAgent->new( ) unless $browser;
```

Enable proxying, if you're behind a firewall:

```
$browser->env_proxy();
```

Then perform a GET request based on the subroutine's parameters:

```
my $response = $browser->request(@_);
```

In list context, you return information provided by the response object: the content, status line, a Boolean indicating whether the status meant success, and the response object itself:

```
return($response->content, $response->status_line, $response->is_success, $response)
    if wantarray;
```

If there was a problem and you called in scalar context, we return undef:

```
return unless $response->is_success;
```

Otherwise we return the content:

```
    return $response->content;
}
```

The do_POST( ) subroutine is just like do_GET( ), only it uses the post( ) method instead of get( ).

The rest of this chapter is a detailed reference to the two classes we've covered so far: LWP::UserAgent and HTTP::Response.

User Agents

The first and simplest use of LWP's two basic classes is LWP::UserAgent, which manages HTTP connections and performs requests for you. The new( ) constructor makes a user agent object:

```
$browser = LWP::UserAgent->new(%options);
```

The *options* and their default values are summarized in Table 3-1. The options are attributes whose values can be fetched or altered by the method calls described in the next section.

Table 3-1. Constructor options and default values for LWP::UserAgent

Key	Default
agent	"libwww-perl/#.###"
conn_cache	undef
cookie_jar	undef
from	undef
max_size	undef
parse_head	1
protocols_allowed	undef
protocols_forbidden	undef
requests_redirectable	['GET', 'HEAD']
timeout	180

If you have a user agent object and want a copy of it (for example, you want to run the same requests over two connections, one persistent with KeepAlive and one without) use the clone( ) method:

```
$copy = $browser->clone( );
```

This object represents a browser and has attributes you can get and set by calling methods on the object. Attributes modify future connections (e.g., proxying, timeouts, and whether the HTTP connection can be persistent) or the requests sent over the connection (e.g., authentication and cookies, or HTTP headers).

Connection Parameters

The timeout( ) attribute represents how long LWP will wait for a server to respond to a request:

```
$oldval = $browser->timeout([newval]);
```

That is, if you want to set the value, you'd do it like so:

```
$browser->timeout(newval);
```

And if you wanted to read the value, you'd do it like this:

```
$value = $browser->timeout( );
```

And you could even set the value and get back the old value at the same time:

```
$previously = $browser->timeout(newval);
```

The default value of the timeout attribute is 180 seconds. If you're spidering, you might want to change this to a lower number to prevent your spider from wasting a lot of time on unreachable sites:

```
$oldval = $browser->timeout( );
$browser->timeout(10);
print "Changed timeout from $oldval to 10\n";
Changed timeout from 180 to 10
```

The max_size( ) method limits the number of bytes of an HTTP response that the user agent will read:

```
$size = $browser->max_size([bytes])
```

The default value of the max_size( ) attribute is undef, signifying no limit. If the maximum size is exceeded, the response will have a Client-Aborted header. Here's how to test for that:

```
$response = $browser->request($req);
if ($response->header("Client-Aborted")) {
  warn "Response exceeded maximum size."
}
```

To have your browser object support HTTP Keep-Alive, call the conn_cache( ) method to a *connection cache object*, of class LWP::ConnCache. This is done like so:

```
use LWP::ConnCache;
$cache = $browser->conn_cache(LWP::ConnCache->new( ));
```

The newly created connection cache object will cache only one connection at a time. To have it cache more, you access its total_capacity attribute. Here's how to increase that cache to 10 connections:

```
$browser->conn_cache->total_capacity(10);
```

To cache all connections (no limits):

```
$browser->conn_cache->total_capacity(undef);
```

Request Parameters

The agent( ) attribute gets and sets the string that LWP sends for the User-Agent header:

```
$oldval = $browser->agent([agent_string]);
```

Some web sites use this string to identify the browser. To pretend to be Netscape to get past web servers that check to see whether you're using a "supported browser," do this:

```
print "My user agent name is ", $browser->agent( ), ".\n";
$browser->agent("Mozilla/4.76 [en] (Windows NT 5.0; U)");
print "And now I'm calling myself ", $browser->agent( ), "!\n";
My user agent name is libwww-perl/5.60.
And now I'm calling myself Mozilla/4.76 [en] (Windows NT 5.0; U)!
```

The from( ) attribute controls the From header, which contains the email address of the user making the request:

```
$old_address = $browser->from([email_address]);
```

The default value is undef, which indicates no From header should be sent.

The user agent object can manage the sending and receiving of cookies for you. Control this with the cookie_jar( ) method:

```
$old_cj_obj = $browser->cookie_jar([cj_obj])
```

This reads or sets the HTTP::Cookies object that's used for holding all this browser's cookies. By default, there is no cookie jar, in which case the user agent ignores cookies.

To create a temporary cookie jar, which will keep cookies only for the duration of the user agent object:

```
$browser->cookie_jar(HTTP::Cookies->new);
```

To use a file as a persistent store for cookies:

```
my $some_file = '/home/mojojojo/cookies.lwp';
$browser->cookie_jar(HTTP::Cookies->new(
  'file' => $some_file, 'autosave' => 1
));
```

Cookies are discussed in more detail in Chapter 11.

Protocols

LWP allows you to control the protocols with which a user agent can fetch documents. You can choose to allow only a certain set of protocols, or allow all but a few. You can also test a protocol to see whether it's supported by LWP and by this particular browser object.

The protocols_allowed( ) and protocols_forbidden( ) methods explicitly permit or forbid certain protocols (e.g., FTP or HTTP) from being used by this user agent:

```
$aref_maybe = $browser->protocols_allowed([\@protocols]);
$aref_maybe = $browser->protocols_forbidden([\@protocols]);
```

Call the methods with no arguments to get an array reference containing the allowed or forbidden protocols, or undef if the attribute isn't set. By default, neither is set, which means that this browser supports all the protocols that your installation of LWP supports.

For example, if you're processing a list of URLs and don't want to parse them to weed out the FTP URLs, you could write this:

```
$browser->protocols_forbidden(["ftp"]);
```

Then you can blindly execute requests, and any ftp URLs will fail automatically. That is, if you request an ftp URL, the browser object returns an error response without performing any actual request.

Instead of forbidden protocols, you can specify which to allow by using the protocols_allowed method. For example, to set this browser object to support only http and gopher URLs, you could write this:

```
$browser->protocols_allowed(["http", "gopher"]);
```

To check if LWP and this particular browser support a particular URL protocol, use the is_protocol_supported( ) method. It returns true if LWP supports the protocol, isn't in protocols_forbidden, and it has been allowed in a protocols_allowed list set. You call it like this:

```
$boolean = $browser->is_protocol_supported(scheme);
```

For example:

```
unless ($browser->is_protocol_supported("https")) {
  warn "Cannot process https:// URLs.\n";
}
```

Redirection

A server can reply to a request with a response that redirects the user agent to a new location. A user agent can automatically follow redirections for you. By default, LWP::UserAgent objects follow GET and HEAD method redirections.

The requests_redirectable( ) attribute controls the list of methods for which the user agent will automatically follow redirections:

```
$aref = $browser->requests_redirectable([\@methods]);
```

To disable the automatic following of redirections, pass in a reference to an empty array:

```
$browser->requests_redirectable([]);
```

To add POST to the list of redirectable methods:

```
push @{$browser->requests_redirectable}, 'POST';
```

You can test a request to see whether the method in that request is one for which the user agent will follow redirections:

```
$boolean = $browser->redirect_ok(request);
```

The redirect_ok( ) method returns true if redirections are permitted for the method in the request.

Authentication

The user agent can manage authentication information for a series of requests to the same site. The credentials( ) method sets a username and password for a particular realm on a site:

```
$browser->credentials(host_port, realm, uname, pass);
```

A *realm* is a string that's used to identify the locked-off area on the given server and port. In interactive browsers, the realm is the string that's displayed as part of the pop-up window that appears. For example, if the pop-up window says "Enter username for Unicode-MailList-Archives at www.unicode.org," then the realm string is Unicode-MailList-Archives, and the *host_port* value is www.unicode.org:80. (The browser doesn't typically show the :80 part for HTTP, nor the :443 part for HTTPS, as those are the default port numbers.)

The username, password, and realm can be sent for every request whose hostname and port match the one given in *host_port*, and that require authorization. For example:

```
$browser->credentials("intranet.example.int:80", "Finances",
                      "fred", "3l1t3");
```

From that point on, any requests this browser makes to port 80 that require authentication with a realm name of "Finances," will be tried with a username "fred" and a password "3l1t3."

For more information on authentication, see Chapter 11.

Proxies

One potentially important function of the user agent object is managing proxies. The env_proxy( ) method configures the proxy settings:

```
$browser->env_proxy( );
```

This method inspects proxy settings from environment variables such as http_proxy, gopher_proxy, and no_proxy. If you don't use a proxy, those environment variables aren't set, and the call to env_proxy( ) has no effect.

To set proxying from within your program, use the proxy( ) and no_proxy( ) methods. The proxy( ) method sets or retrieves the proxy for a particular scheme:

```
$browser->proxy(scheme, proxy);
$browser->proxy(\@schemes, proxy);
$proxy = $browser->proxy(scheme);
```

The first two forms set the proxy for one or more schemes. The third form returns the proxy for a particular scheme. For example:

```
$p = $browser->proxy("ftp");
$browser->proxy("ftp", "http://firewall:8001/");
print "Changed proxy from $p to our firewall.\n";
```

The no_proxy( ) method lets you disable proxying for particular domains:

```
$browser->no_proxy([ domain, ... ]);
```

Pass a list of domains to no_proxy( ) to add them to the list of domains that are not proxied (e.g., those within your corporate firewall). For example:

```
$browser->no_proxy("c64.example.int", "localhost", "server");
```

Call no_proxy( ) with no arguments to clear the list of unproxied domains:

```
$browser->no_proxy( );  # no exceptions to proxying
```

Request Methods

There are three basic request methods:

```
$resp = $browser->get(url);
$resp = $browser->head(url);
$resp = $browser->post(url, \@form_data);
```

If you're specifying extra header lines to be sent with the request, do it like this:

```
$resp = $browser->get(url, Header1 => Value1, Header2 => Value2, ...);
$resp = $browser->head(url, Header1 => Value1, Header2 => Value2, ...);
$resp = $browser->post(url, \@form_data,
                       Header1 => Value1, Header2 => Value2, ...);
```

For example:

```
$resp = $browser->get("http://www.nato.int",
  'Accept-Language' => 'en-US',
  'Accept-Charset' => 'iso-8859-1,*,utf-8',
  'Accept-Encoding' => 'gzip',
  'Accept' =>
  "image/gif, image/x-xbitmap, image/jpeg, image/pjpeg, image/png, */*",
);
```

Saving response content to a file

With normal requests, the body of the response is stored in the response object's $response->content( ) attribute by default. That's fine when the response body is a moderately small piece of data such as a 20-kilobyte HTML file. But a 6-megabyte MP3 file should probably be saved to disk without saving it in memory first.

The request methods support this by providing sort of fake header lines that don't turn into real headers in the request but act as options for LWP's handling of the request. Each option/header starts with a ":" character, a character that no real HTTP header name could contain. The simplest option is ':content_file' => filename.

```
$resp = $browser->get(url, ':content_file' => filename, ...);
$resp = $browser->head(url, ':content_file' => filename, ...);
$resp = $browser->post(url, \@form_data,
  ':content_file' => filename, ...);
```

With this option, the content of the response is saved to the given filename, overwriting whatever might be in that file already. (In theory, no response to a HEAD request should ever have content, so it seems odd to specify where content should be saved. However, in practice, some strange servers and many CGIs on otherwise normal servers do respond to HEAD requests as if they were GET requests.)

A typical example:

```
my $out = 'weather_satellite.jpg';
my $resp = $browser->get('http://weathersys.int/',
  ':content_file' => $out,
);
die "Couldn't get the weather picture: ", $response->status_line
  unless $response->is_success;
```

This feature is also useful for cases in which you were planning on saving the content to that file anyway. Also see the mirror( ) method described below, which does something similar to $browser->get($url, ':content_file' => filename, ...).

Sending response content to a callback

If you instead provide an option/header pair consisting of ':content_cb' and a subroutine reference, LWP won't save the content in memory or to a file but will instead call the subroutine every so often, as new data comes in over the connection to the remote server. This is the syntax for specifying such a callback routine:

```
$resp = $browser->get(url, ':content_cb' => \&mysub, ...);
$resp = $browser->head(url, ':content_cb' => \&mysub, ...);
$resp = $browser->post(url, \@form_data,
  ':content_cb' => \&mysub, ...);
```

Whatever subroutine you define will get chunks of the newly received data passed in as the first parameter, and the second parameter will be the new HTTP::Response object that will eventually get returned from the current get/head/post call. So you should probably start every callback routine like this:

```
sub callbackname {
  my($data, $response) = @_;
  ...
```

Here, for example, is a routine that hex-dumps whatever data is received as a response to this request:

```
my $resp = $browser->get('http://www.perl.com'
  ':content_cb' => \&hexy,
);
sub hexy {
  my($data, $resp) = @_;
  print length($data), " bytes:\n";
  print '  ', unpack('H*', substr($data,0,16,'')), "\n"
```

```
      while length $data;
    return;
  }
```

In fact, you can pass an anonymous routine as the callback. The above could just as well be expressed like this:

```
my $resp = $browser->get('http://www.perl.com/'
  ':content_cb' => sub {
    my($data, $resp) = @_;
    print length($data), " bytes:\n";
    print '   ', unpack('H*', substr($data,0,16,'')), "\n"
     while length $data;
    return;
  }
);
```

The size of the $data string is unpredictable. If it matters to you how big each is, you can specify another option, :read_size_hint => *byte_count*, which LWP will take as a hint for how many bytes you want the typical $data string to be:

```
$resp = $browser->get(url,
  ':content_cb' => \&mysub,
  ':read_size_hint' => byte_count,
  ...,
);
$resp = $browser->head(url,
  ':content_cb' => \&mysub,
  ':read_size_hint' => byte_count,
  ...,
);
$resp = $browser->post(url, \@form_data,
  ':content_cb' => \&mysub,
  ':read_size_hint' => byte_count,
  ...,
);
```

We can modify our hex-dumper routine to be called like this:

```
my $resp = $browser->get('http://www.perl.com'
  ':content_cb' => \&hexy,
  ':read_size_hint' => 1024,
);
```

However, there is no guarantee that's how big the $data string will actually be. It is merely a hint, which LWP may disregard.

Mirroring a URL to a file

The mirror( ) method GETs a URL and stores the result to a file:

```
$response = $browser->mirror(url_to_get, filename)
```

But it has the added feature that it uses an HTTP If-Modified-Since header line on the request it performs, to avoid transferring the remote file unless it has changed since the local file (*filename*) was last changed. The mirror( ) method returns a new

HTTP::Response object but without a content attribute (any interesting content will have been written to the local file). You should at least check $response->is_error( ):

```
$response = $browser->mirror("http://www.cpan.org/",
                             "cpan_home.html");
if( $response->is_error( ) ){
  die "Couldn't access the CPAN home page: " .
    $response->status_line;
}
```

Advanced Methods

The HTML specification permits meta tags in the head of a document, some of which are alternatives to HTTP headers. By default, if the Response object is an HTML object, its head section is parsed, and some of the content of the head tags is copied into the HTTP::Response object's headers. For example, consider an HTML document that starts like this:

```
<html>
<head><title>Kiki's Pie Page</title>
 <base href="http://cakecity.int/">
 <meta name="Notes" content="I like pie!">
 <meta http-equiv="Description" content="PIE RECIPES FROM KIKI">
</head>
```

If you request that document and call print $response->headers_as_string on it, you'll see this:

```
Date: Fri, 05 Apr 2002 11:19:51 GMT
Accept-Ranges: bytes
Server: Apache/1.3.23
Content-Base: http://cakecity.int/
Content-Length: 204
Content-Type: text/html
Last-Modified: Fri, 05 Apr 2002 11:19:38 GMT
Client-Date: Fri, 05 Apr 2002 11:19:51 GMT
Description: PIE RECIPES FROM KIKI
Title: Kiki's Pie Page
X-Meta-Notes: I like pie!
```

You can access those headers individually with $response->header('Content-Base'), $response->header('Description'), $response->header('Title'), and $response->header('X-Meta-Notes'), respectively, as we shall see in the next section.

The documentation for the HTML::HeadParser module, which LWP uses to implement this feature, explains the exact details.

HTTP::Response Objects

You have to manually create most objects your programs work with by calling an explicit constructor, with the syntax *ClassName*->new( ). HTTP::Response objects are a notable exception. You never need to call HTTP::Response->new( ) to make them;

instead, you just get them back as the result of a request made with one of the request methods (get( ), post( ), and head( )).

That is, when writing web clients, you never need to create a response yourself. Instead, a user agent creates it for you, to encapsulate the results of a request it made. You do, however, interrogate a response object's attributes. For example, the code( ) method returns the HTTP status code:

```
print "HTTP status: ", $response->code( ), "\n";
HTTP status: 404
```

HTTP::Response objects also have convenience methods. For example, is_success( ) returns a true value if the response had a successful HTTP status code, or false if it didn't (e.g., 404, 403, 500, etc.). Always check your responses, like so:

```
die "Couldn't get the document"
  unless $response->is_success( );
```

You might prefer something a bit more verbose, like this:

```
# Given $response and $url ...
die "Error getting $url\n", $response->status_line
  unless $response->is_success( );
```

Status Line

The status_line( ) method returns the entire HTTP status line:

```
$sl = $response->status_line( );
```

This includes both the numeric code and the explanation. For example:

```
$resp = $browser->get("http://www.cpan.org/nonesuch");
print $response->status_line( );
404 Not Found
```

To get only the status code, use the code( ) method:

```
$code = $response->code( );
```

To access only the explanatory message, use the message( ) method:

```
$msg = $response->message( );
```

For example:

```
$resp = $browser->get("http://www.cpan.org/nonesuch");
print $response->code(), " (that means ", $response->message(), " )\n";
404 (that means Not Found)
```

Four methods test for types of status codes in the response: is_error( ), is_success( ), is_redirect( ), and is_info( ). They return true if the status code corresponds to an error, a successful fetch, a redirection, or informational (e.g., "102 Processing").

```
$boolean = $response->is_error( );
$boolean = $response->is_success( );
$boolean = $response->is_redirect( );
$boolean = $response->is_info( );
```

Exactly what codes count as what sort of status, is explained in greater detail in Appendix B.

Content

Most responses contain content after their headers. This content is accessible with the content( ) method:

```
$the_file_data = $response->content( );
```

In some cases, it's easier (and more efficient) to get a scalar reference to the content, instead of the value of the content itself. For that, use the content_ref( ) method:

```
$data_ref = $response->content_ref( );
```

For example in Chapter 7, we use a class called HTML::TokeParser that parses HTML starting with a reference to a big block of HTML source. We could use that module to parse the HTML in an HTTP::Response object by using do{ my $x = $response->content( ); \$x}, but we could avoid the unnecessary copying by just using $response->content_ref( ).

Headers

To fetch the value of an HTTP header in the response, use the header( ) method:

```
$value = $response->header(header_name);
```

For example, if you know there will be useful data in a header called Description, access it as $response->header('Description'). The header( ) method returns undef if there is no such header in this response.

HTTP::Response provides some methods for accessing the most commonly used header fields:

```
$type = $response->content_type( );
```

The Content-Type header contains the MIME type of the body. This is "text/html" for HTML files, "image/jpeg" for JPEG files, and so on. Appendix C contains a list of common MIME types.

```
$length = $response->content_length( );
```

The Content-Length header contains the size of the body (in bytes) sent from the browser but is not always present. If you need the real length of the response, use length($response->content).

```
$lm = $response->last_modified( );
```

The Last-Modified header contains a timestamp indicating when the content was last modified, but it is sometimes not present.

```
$encoding = response->content_encoding( );
```

The Content-Encoding header contains the name of the character set this document is declared as using. The most common value is iso-8859-1 meaning Latin-1. An increasingly common runner-up is utf-8, meaning Unicode expressed in the UTF-8 encoding. Less-common encodings are listed in Appendix E. But be warned: this header is occasionally inaccurate, in cases where content is clearly in one encoding, but the document fails to declare it as such. For example, a document might be in Chinese in the big5 encoding but might erroneously report itself as being in iso-8859-1.

This brings us to a regrettably even less-used header:

```
$language = $response->content_language();
```

Rarely present, the Content-Language header contains the language tag(s) for the document's content. Appendix D lists common language tags.

If you want to get all the headers as one string, call $response->headers_as_string. This is useful for debugging, as in:

```
print "Weird response!!\n",
  $response->headers_as_string, "\n\n"
unless $response->content_type();
```

Expiration Times

Most servers send a Date header as well as an Expires or Last-Modified header with their responses. Four methods on HTTP::Response objects use these headers to calculate the age of the document and various caching statistics.

The current_age() method returns the number of seconds since the server sent the document:

```
$age = $response->current_age();
```

For example:

```
$age   = $response->current_age();
$days  = int($age/86400);      $age -= $days * 86400;
$hours = int($age/3600);       $age -= $hours * 3600;
$mins  = int($age/60);         $age -= $minutes * 60;
$secs  = $age;
print "The document is $days days, $hours hours, $mins minutes, and $secs
seconds old.\n";
The document is 0 days, 0 hours, 5 minutes, and 33
seconds old.
```

The freshness_lifetime() method returns the number of seconds until the document expires:

```
$lifetime = $response->freshness_lifetime();
```

For example:

```
$time  = $response->freshness_lifetime();
$days  = int($time/86400);      $time -= $days * 86400;
$hours = int($time/3600);       $time -= $hours * 3600;
```

```
$mins  = int($time/60);          $time -= $mins * 60;
$secs  = int($time);
print "The document expires in $days days, $hours hours, $mins minutes, and
$secs seconds.\n";
```
The document expires in 0 days, 23 hours, 6 minutes, and 15 seconds.

The is_fresh( ) method returns true if the document has not expired yet:

```
$boolean = $response->is_fresh( );
```

If the document is not fresh, your program should reissue the request to the server. This is an issue only if your program runs for a long time and you keep responses for later interrogation.

The fresh_until( ) entry returns the time when the document expires:

```
$expires = $response->fresh_until( );
```

For example:

```
$expires = $response->fresh_until( );
print "This document is good until ", scalar(localtime($expires)), "\n";
```
This document is good until Tue Feb 26 07:36:08 2004

Base for Relative URLs

An HTML document can have relative URLs in it. For example:

```
<img src="my_face.gif">
```

This generally refers to the *my_face.gif* that's located in the same directory as the HTML page. Turning these relative URLs into absolute URLs that can be requested via LWP is covered in the next chapter. To do that, you must know the URL of the current page.

The base( ) method returns the URL of the document in the response.

```
$url = $response->base( );
```

This base URL is normally the URL you requested but can sometimes differ: if there was a redirection (which LWP normally follows through on), the URL of the final response isn't the same as the requested URL. Moreover, the Base, Content-Base, and Content-Location headers in a response specify the address against which you resolve relative URLs. And finally, if the response content is an HTML document and has a <base href="..."> tag in its head, that definitively sets the base URL.

Debugging

When an error occurs (as indicated by the is_error( ) method), error_as_HTML( ) returns an error page in HTML:

```
$error_page = $response->error_as_HTML( );
print "The server said:\n<blockquote>$error_page</blockquote>\n";
```

Because a user agent can follow redirections and automatically answer authentication challenges, the request you gave to the user agent object might not be the request represented by your object. That is, you could have said to get one URL, but that could have directed to another, which could have redirected to another, producing not one response but a chain of responses. For the sake of simplicity, you get back only the one $response object, which is the last in the chain. But if you need to, you can work your way back, using the previous( ) method:

```
$previous_response = $response->previous( );
```

The previous( ) method returns undef when there is no previous method (i.e., on the response to the request you gave the user agent, at the head of the chain). Moreover, each response stores the HTTP::Request object that LWP used for making the request, and you can access it with the $response->request( ). HTTP::Request objects support most of the same methods as HTTP::Response objects, notably $request->as_string, which is useful in debugging.

From each response, you can get the corresponding request and recreate the HTTP dialog. For example:

```
$last = $response;
while ($response) {
  print $response->code( ), " after ";
    # Or you could print even dump the whole
    #   thing, with $response->as_string( )

  $last = $response;
  $response = $response->previous( );
}
print "the original request, which was:\n",
  $last->request->as_string;

200 after 401 after 301 after the original request, which was:
GET http://some.crazy.redirector.int/thing.html
User-Agent: libwww-perl/5.5394
```

LWP Classes: Behind the Scenes

To get data off the Web with LWP, you really only need to know about LWP::User-Agent objects and HTTP::Response objects (although a rudimentary knowledge of the URI class and the LWP::Cookies class can help too). But behind the scenes, there are dozens and dozens of classes that you generally don't need to know about, but that are still busily doing their work. Most of them are documented in the LWP manual pages, and you may see them mentioned in the documentation for the modules about which you *do* need to know. For completeness, they are listed in Appendix A.

CHAPTER 4

URLs

Now that you've seen how LWP models HTTP requests and responses, let's study the facilities it provides for working with URLs. A URL tells you how to get to something: "use HTTP with this host and request this," "connect via FTP to this host and retrieve this file," or "send email to this address."

The great variety inherent in URLs is both a blessing and a curse. On one hand, you can stretch the URL syntax to address almost any type of network resource. However, this very flexibility means attempts to parse arbitrary URLs with regular expressions rapidly run into a quagmire of special cases.

The LWP suite of modules provides the URI class to manage URLs. This chapter describes how to create objects that represent URLs, extract information from those objects, and convert between absolute and relative URLs. This last task is particularly useful for link checkers and spiders, which take partial URLs from HTML links and turn those into absolute URLs to request.

Parsing URLs

Rather than attempt to pull apart URLs with regular expressions, which is difficult to do in a way that works with all the many types of URLs, you should use the URI class. When you create an object representing a URL, it has attributes for each part of a URL (scheme, username, hostname, port, etc.). Make method calls to get and set these attributes.

Example 4-1 creates a URI object representing a complex URL, then calls methods to discover the various components of the URL.

Example 4-1. Decomposing a URL

```
use URI;
my $url = URI->new('http://user:pass@example.int:4345/hello.php?user=12');
print "Scheme: ", $url->scheme(), "\n";
print "Userinfo: ", $url->userinfo(), "\n";
```

Example 4-1. Decomposing a URL (continued)

```
print "Hostname: ", $url->host( ), "\n";
print "Port: ", $url->port( ), "\n";
print "Path: ", $url->path( ), "\n";
print "Query: ", $url->query( ), "\n";
```

Example 4-1 prints:

```
Scheme: http
Userinfo: user:pass
Hostname: example.int
Port: 4345
Path: /hello.php
Query: user=12
```

Besides reading the parts of a URL, methods such as host( ) can also alter the parts of a URL, using the familiar convention that $object->method reads an attribute's value and $object->method(*newvalue*) alters an attribute:

```
use URI;
my $uri = URI->new("http://www.perl.com/I/like/pie.html");
$uri->host('testing.perl.com');
print $uri,"\n";
http://testing.perl.com/I/like/pie.html
```

Now let's look at the methods in more depth.

Constructors

An object of the URI class represents a URL. (Actually, a URI object can also represent a kind of URL-like string called a URN, but you're unlikely to run into one of those any time soon.) To create a URI object from a string containing a URL, use the new( ) constructor:

```
$url = URI->new(url [, scheme ]);
```

If *url* is a relative URL (a fragment such as staff/alicia.html), *scheme* determines the scheme you plan for this URL to have (http, ftp, etc.). But in most cases, you call URI->new only when you know you won't have a relative URL; for relative URLs or URLs that just *might* be relative, use the URI->new_abs method, discussed below.

The URI module strips out quotes, angle brackets, and whitespace from the new URL. So these statements all create identical URI objects:

```
$url = URI->new('<http://www.oreilly.com/>');
$url = URI->new('"http://www.oreilly.com/"');
$url = URI->new('          http://www.oreilly.com/');
$url = URI->new('http://www.oreilly.com/    ');
```

The URI class automatically escapes any characters that the URL standard (RFC 2396) says can't appear in a URL. So these two are equivalent:

```
$url = URI->new('http://www.oreilly.com/bad page');
$url = URI->new('http://www.oreilly.com/bad%20page');
```

If you already have a URI object, the clone( ) method will produce another URI object with identical attributes:

```
$copy = $url->clone( );
```

Example 4-2 clones a URI object and changes an attribute.

Example 4-2. Cloning a URI

```
use URI;
my $url = URI->new('http://www.oreilly.com/catalog/');
$dup = $url->clone( );
$url->path('/weblogs');
print "Changed path: ", $url->path( ), "\n";
print "Original path: ", $dup->path( ), "\n";
```

When run, Example 4-2 prints:

```
Changed path: /weblogs
Original path: /catalog/
```

Output

Treat a URI object as a string and you'll get the URL:

```
$url = URI->new('http://www.example.int');
$url->path('/search.cgi');
print "The URL is now: $url\n";
The URL is now: http://www.example.int/search.cgi
```

You might find it useful to *normalize* the URL before printing it:

```
$url->canonical( );
```

Exactly what this does depends on the specific type of URL, but it typically converts the hostname to lowercase, removes the port if it's the default port (for example, *http://www.eXample.int:80* becomes *http://www.example.int*), makes escape sequences uppercase (e.g., %2e becomes %2E), and unescapes characters that don't need to be escaped (e.g., %41 becomes A). In Chapter 12, we'll walk through a program that harvests data but avoids harvesting the same URL more than once. It keeps track of the URLs it's visited in a hash called %seen_url_before; if there's an entry for a given URL, it's been harvested. The trick is to call canonical on all URLs before entering them into that hash and before checking whether one exists in that hash. If not for calling canonical, you might have visited *http://www.example.int:80* in the past, and might be planning to visit *http://www.EXample.int*, and you would see no duplication there. But when you call canonical on both, they both become *http://www.example.int*, so you can tell you'd be harvesting the same URL twice. If you think such duplication problems might arise in your programs, when in doubt, call canonical right when you construct the URL, like so:

```
$url = URI->new('http://www.example.int')->canonical;
```

Comparison

To compare two URLs, use the eq( ) method:

```
if ($url_one->eq(url_two)) { ... }
```

For example:

```
use URI;
my $url_one = URI->new('http://www.example.int');
my $url_two = URI->new('http://www.example.int/search.cgi');
$url_one->path('/search.cgi');
if ($url_one->eq($url_two)) {
  print "The two URLs are equal.\n";
}
The two URLs are equal.
```

Two URLs are equal if they are represented by the same string when normalized. The eq( ) method is faster than the eq string operator:

```
if ($url_one eq $url_two) { ... } # inefficient!
```

To see if two values refer not just to the same URL, but to the same URI object, use the == operator:

```
if ($url_one == $url_two) { ... }
```

For example:

```
use URI;
my $url = URI->new('http://www.example.int');
$that_one = $url;
if ($that_one == $url) {
  print "Same object.\n";
}
Same object.
```

Components of a URL

A generic URL looks like Figure 4-1.

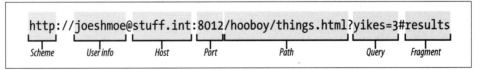

Figure 4-1. Components of a URL

The URI class provides methods to access each component. Some components are available only on some schemes (for example, mailto: URLs do not support the *userinfo*, *server*, or *port* components).

In addition to the obvious scheme( ), userinfo( ), server( ), port( ), path( ), query( ), and fragment( ) methods, there are some useful but less-intuitive ones.

```
$url->path_query([newval]);
```
The path and query components as a single string, e.g., /hello.php?user=21.

```
$url->path_segments([segment, ...]);
```
In scalar context, it is the same as path( ), but in list context, it returns a list of path segments (directories and maybe a filename). For example:

```
$url = URI->new('http://www.example.int/eye/sea/ewe.cgi');
@bits = $url->path_segments( );
for ($i=0; $i < @bits; $i++) {
  print "$i {$bits[$i]}\n";
}
print "\n\n";
0 {}
1 {eye}
2 {sea}
3 {ewe.cgi}
```

```
$url->host_port([newval])
```
The hostname and port as one value, e.g., www.example.int:8080.

```
$url->default_port( );
```
The default port for this scheme (e.g., 80 for http and 21 for ftp).

For a URL that simply lacks one of those parts, the method for that part generally returns undef:

```
use URI;
my $uri = URI->new("http://stuff.int/things.html");
my $query = $uri->query;
print defined($query) ? "Query: <$query>\n" : "No query\n";
No query
```

However, some kinds of URLs can't have certain components. For example, a mailto: URL doesn't have a *host* component, so code that calls host( ) on a mailto: URL will die. For example:

```
use URI;
my $uri = URI->new('mailto:hey-you@mail.int');
print $uri->host;
Can't locate object method "host" via package "URI::mailto"
```

This has real-world implications. Consider extracting all the URLs in a document and going through them like this:

```
foreach my $url (@urls) {
  $url = URI->new($url);
  my $hostname = $url->host;
  next unless $Hosts_to_ignore{$hostname};
  ...otherwise ...
}
```

This will die on a mailto: URL, which doesn't have a host( ) method. You can avoid this by using can( ) to see if you can call a given method:

```
foreach my $url (@urls) {
  $url = URI->new($url);
  next unless $uri->can('host');
  my $hostname = $url->host;
  ...
```

or a bit less directly:

```
foreach my $url (@urls) {
  $url = URI->new($url);
  unless('http' eq $uri->scheme) {
    print "Odd, $url is not an http url!  Skipping.\n";
    next;
  }
  my $hostname = $url->host;
  ...and so forth...
```

Because all URIs offer a scheme method, and all http: URIs provide a host( ) method, this is assuredly safe.[*] For the curious, what URI schemes allow for what is explained in the documentation for the URI class, as well as the documentation for some specific subclasses like URI::ldap.

Queries

The URI class has two methods for dealing with query data above and beyond the query( ) and path_query( ) methods we've already discussed.

In the very early days of the web, queries were simply text strings. Spaces were encoded as plus (+) characters:

```
http://www.example.int/search?i+like+pie
```

The query_keywords( ) method works with these types of queries, accepting and returning a list of keywords:

```
@words = $url->query_keywords([keywords, ...]);
```

For example:

```
use URI;
my $url = URI->new('http://www.example.int/search?i+like+pie');
@words = $url->query_keywords( );
print $words[-1], "\n";
pie
```

More modern queries accept a list of named values. A name and its value are separated by an equals sign (=), and such pairs are separated from each other with ampersands (&):

```
http://www.example.int/search?food=pie&action=like
```

---

[*] Of the methods illustrated above, scheme, path, and fragment are the only ones that are *always* provided. It would be surprising to find a fragment on a mailto: URL—and who knows what it would mean—but it's syntactically possible. In practical terms, this means even if you have a mailto: URL, you can call $url->fragment without it being an error.

The query_form( ) method lets you treat each such query as a list of keys and values:

```
@params = $url->query_form([key,value,...]);
```

For example:

```
use URI;
my $url = URI->new('http://www.example.int/search?food=pie&action=like');
@params = $url->query_form( );
for ($i=0; $i < @params; $i++) {
  print "$i {$params[$i]}\n";
}
0 {food}
1 {pie}
2 {action}
3 {like}
```

Relative URLs

URL paths are either absolute or relative. An absolute URL starts with a scheme, then has whatever data this scheme requires. For an HTTP URL, this means a hostname and a path:

```
http://phee.phye.phoe.fm/thingamajig/stuff.html
```

Any URL that doesn't start with a scheme is relative. To interpret a relative URL, you need a base URL that is absolute (just as you don't know the GPS coordinates of "800 miles west of here" unless you know the GPS coordinates of "here").

A relative URL leaves some information implicit, which you look to its base URL for. For example, if your base URL is *http://phee.phye.phoe.fm/thingamajig/stuff.html*, and you see a relative URL of */also.html*, then the implicit information is "with the same scheme (http)" and "on the same host (*phee.phye.phoe.fm*)," and the explicit information is "with the path */also.html*." So this is equivalent to an absolute URL of:

```
http://phee.phye.phoe.fm/also.html
```

Some kinds of relative URLs require information from the path of the base URL in a way that closely mirrors relative filespecs in Unix filesystems, where ".." means "up one level", "." means "in this level", and anything else means "in this directory". So a relative URL of just *zing.xml* interpreted relative to *http://phee.phye.phoe.fm/thingamajig/stuff.html* yields this absolute URL:

```
http://phee.phye.phoe.fm/thingamajig/zing.xml
```

That is, we use all but the last bit of the absolute URL's path, then append the new component.

Similarly, a relative URL of *../hi_there.jpg* interpreted against the absolute URL *http://phee.phye.phoe.fm/thingamajig/stuff.html* gives us this URL:

```
http://phee.phye.phoe.fm/hi_there.jpg
```

In figuring this out, start with *http://phee.phye.phoe.fm/thingamajig/* and the "`..`" tells us to go up one level, giving us *http://phee.phye.phoe.fm/*. Append *hi_there.jpg* giving us the URL you see above.

There's a third kind of relative URL, which consists entirely of a fragment, such as *#endnotes*. This is commonly met with in HTML documents, in code like so:

```
<a href="#endnotes">See the endnotes for the full citation</a>
```

Interpreting a fragment-only relative URL involves taking the base URL, stripping off any fragment that's already there, and adding the new one. So if the base URL is this:

```
http://phee.phye.phoe.fm/thingamajig/stuff.html
```

and the relative URL is *#endnotes*, then the new absolute URL is this:

```
http://phee.phye.phoe.fm/thingamajig/stuff.html#endnotes
```

We've looked at relative URLs from the perspective of starting with a relative URL and an absolute base, and getting the equivalent absolute URL. But you can also look at it the other way: starting with an absolute URL and asking "what is the relative URL that gets me there, relative to an absolute base URL?". This is best explained by putting the URLs one on top of the other:

```
Base: http://phee.phye.phoe.fm/thingamajig/stuff.xml
Goal: http://phee.phye.phoe.fm/thingamajig/zing.html
```

To get from the base to the goal, the shortest relative URL is simply *zing.xml*. However, if the goal is a directory higher:

```
Base: http://phee.phye.phoe.fm/thingamajig/stuff.xml
Goal: http://phee.phye.phoe.fm/hi_there.jpg
```

then a relative path is *../hi_there.jpg*. And in this case, simply starting from the document root and having a relative path of */hi_there.jpg* would also get you there.

The logic behind parsing relative URLs and converting between them and absolute URLs is not simple and is very easy to get wrong. The fact that the URI class provides functions for doing it all for us is one of its greatest benefits. You are likely to have two kinds of dealings with relative URLs: wanting to turn an absolute URL into a relative URL and wanting to turn a relative URL into an absolute URL.

Converting Absolute URLs to Relative

A relative URL path assumes you're in a directory and the path elements are relative to that directory. For example, if you're in */staff/*, these are the same:

```
roster/search.cgi
/staff/roster/search.cgi
```

If you're in */students/*, this is the path to */staff/roster/search.cgi*:

```
../staff/roster/search.cgi
```

The URI class includes a method rel( ), which creates a relative URL out of an absolute goal URI object. The newly created relative URL is how you could get to that original URL, starting from the absolute base URL.

```
$relative = $absolute_goal->rel(absolute_base);
```

The *absolute_base* is the URL path in which you're assumed to be; it can be a string, or a real URI object. But $absolute_goal must be a URI object. The rel( ) method returns a URI object.

For example:

```
use URI;
my $base = URI->new('http://phee.phye.phoe.fm/thingamajig/zing.xml');
my $goal = URI->new('http://phee.phye.phoe.fm/hi_there.jpg');
print $goal->rel($base), "\n";
../hi_there.jpg
```

If you start with normal strings, simplify this to URI->new($abs_goal)->rel($base), as shown here:

```
use URI;
my $base = 'http://phee.phye.phoe.fm/thingamajig/zing.xml';
my $goal = 'http://phee.phye.phoe.fm/hi_there.jpg';
print URI->new($goal)->rel($base), "\n";
../hi_there.jpg
```

Incidentally, the trailing slash in a base URL can be very important. Consider:

```
use URI;
my $base = 'http://phee.phye.phoe.fm/englishmen/blood';
my $goal = 'http://phee.phye.phoe.fm/englishmen/tony.jpg';
print URI->new($goal)->rel($base), "\n";
tony.jpg
```

But add a slash to the base URL and see the change:

```
use URI;
my $base = 'http://phee.phye.phoe.fm/englishmen/blood/';
my $goal = 'http://phee.phye.phoe.fm/englishmen/tony.jpg';
print URI->new($goal)->rel($base), "\n";
../tony.jpg
```

That's because in the first case, "blood" is not considered a directory, whereas in the second case, it is. You may be accustomed to treating /blood and /blood/ as the same, when blood is a directory. Web servers maintain your illusion by invisibly redirecting requests for /blood to /blood/, but you can't ever tell when this is actually going to happen just by looking at a URL.

Converting Relative URLs to Absolute

By far the most common task involving URLs is converting relative URLs to absolute ones. The new_abs( ) method does all the hard work:

```
$abs_url = URI->new_abs(relative, base);
```

If *rel_url* is actually an absolute URL, *base_url* is ignored. This lets you pass all URLs from a document through new_abs( ), rather than trying to work out which are relative and which are absolute. So if you process the HTML at *http://www.oreilly.com/catalog/* and you find a link to *pperl3/toc.html*, you can get the full URL like this:

```
$abs_url = URI->new_abs('pperl3/toc.html', 'http://www.oreilly.com/catalog/');
```

Another example:

```
use URI;
my $base_url = "http://w3.thing.int/stuff/diary.html";
my $rel_url  = "../minesweeper_hints/";
my $abs_url  = URI->new_abs($rel_url, $base_url);
print $abs_url, "\n";
http://w3.thing.int/minesweeper_hints/
```

You can even pass the output of new_abs to the canonical method that we discussed earlier, to get the normalized absolute representation of a URL. So if you're parsing possibly relative, oddly escaped URLs in a document (each in $href, such as you'd get from an <a href="..."> tag), the expression to remember is this:

```
$new_abs = URI->new_abs($href, $abs_base)->canonical;
```

You'll see this expression come up often in the rest of the book.

CHAPTER 5

Forms

Much of the interesting data of the Web is accessible only through HTML forms. This chapter shows you how to write programs to submit form data and get the resulting page. In covering this unavoidably complex topic, we consider packing form data into GET and POST requests, how each type of HTML form element produces form data, and how to automate the process of submitting form data and processing the responses.

The basic model for the Web is that the typical item is a "document" with a known URL, and when you want to access it (whether it's the *Rhoda* episode guide, or the front page of today's *Boston Globe*), you just get it, no questions asked. Even when there are cookies or HTTP authentication involved, these are basically just addenda to the process of requesting the known URL from the appropriate server. But some web resources require parameters beyond just their URL, parameters that are generally fed in by the user through HTML forms, and that the browser then sends either as dynamic parts of a URL (in the case of a GET request) or as content of a POST request.

A program on the receiving end of form data may simply use it as a query for searching other data, such as scanning all the RFCs and listing the ones by specific authors. Or a program may store the data, as with taking the user's data and saving it as a new post to a message base. Or a program may do grander things with the user-provided data, such as debiting the credit card number provided, logging the products being ordered, and putting them on the roster of items to be sent out. The details of writing those kinds of programs are covered in uncountable books on CGI, mod_perl, ASP, and the like. You are probably familiar with writing server-side programs in at least one of these frameworks, probably through having written CGIs in Perl, maybe with the huge and hugely popular Perl library, CGI.pm.

But what we are interested in here is the process of data getting from HTML forms into those server-side programs. Once you understand that process, you can write LWP programs that simulate that process, by providing the same kind of data as a real live user would provide keying data into a real live browser.

Elements of an HTML Form

A good example of a straightforward form is the U.S. Census Bureau's Gazetteer (geographical index) system. The search form, at *http://www.census.gov/cgi-bin/gazetteer*, consists of:

```
<form method=get action=/cgi-bin/gazetteer>
<hr noshade>
<h3>
<font size=+2>S</font>earch for a <font size=+2>P</font>lace in the
<font size=+2>US</font>
</h3>
<p>
Name: <input name="city" size=15>
State (optional): <input name="state" size=3><br>
or a 5-digit zip code: <input name="zip" size=8>
<p>
<input type="submit" value="Search">
</form>
```

We've highlighted the interesting bits. The method attribute of the `<form>` tag says whether to use GET or POST to submit the form data. The action attribute gives the URL to receive the form data. The components of a form are text fields, drop-down lists, checkboxes, and so on, each identified by a name. Here the `<input>` tags define text fields with the names city and state, and a submit button called zip. The browser submits the state of the form components (what's been typed into the text boxes, which checkboxes are checked, which submit button you pressed) as a set of *name=value* pairs. If you typed "Dulce" into the city field, part of the browser's request for */cgi-bin/gazetteer* would be city=Dulce.

Which part of the request contains the submitted *name=value* pairs depends on whether it's a GET or POST request. GET requests encode the pairs in the URL being requested, each pair separated by an ampersand (&) character, while POST requests encode them in the body of the request, one pair per line. In both cases the names and values are URL encoded.

LWP and GET Requests

The way you submit form data with LWP depends on whether the form's action is GET or POST. If it's a GET form, you construct a URL with encoded form data (possibly using the `$url->query_form( )` method) and call `$browser->get( )`. If it's a POST form, you call to call `$browser->post( )` and pass a reference to an array of form parameters. We cover POST later in this chapter.

GETting Fixed URLs

If you know everything about the GET form ahead of time, and you know everything about what you'd be typing (as if you're always searching on the name

"Dulce"), you know the URL! Because the same data from the same GET form always makes for the same URL, you can just hardcode that:

```
$resp = $browser->get(
  'http://www.census.gov/cgi-bin/gazetteer?city=Dulce&state=&zip='
);
```

And if there is a great big URL in which only one thing ever changes, you could just drop in the value, after URL-encoding it:

```
use URI::Escape ('uri_escape');
$resp = $browser->get(
  'http://www.census.gov/cgi-bin/gazetteer?city=' .
  uri_escape($city) .
  '&state=&zip='
);
```

Note that you should not simply interpolate a raw unencoded value, like this:

```
$resp = $browser->get(
  'http://www.census.gov/cgi-bin/gazetteer?city=' .
  $city .      # wrong!
  '&state=&zip='
);
```

The problem with doing it that way is that you have no real assurance that $city's value doesn't need URL encoding. You may "know" that no unencoded town name ever needs escaping, but it's better to escape it anyway.

If you're piecing together the parts of URLs and you find yourself calling uri_escape more than once per URL, then you should use the next method, query_form, which is simpler for URLs with lots of variable data.

GETting a query_form( ) URL

The tidiest way to submit GET form data is to make a new URI object, then add in the form pairs using the query_form method, before performing a $browser-> get($url) request:

```
$url->query_form(name => value, name => value, ...);
```

For example:

```
use URI;
my $url = URI->new( 'http://www.census.gov/cgi-bin/gazetteer' );
my($city,$state,$zip) = ("Some City","Some State","Some Zip");
$url->query_form(
  # All form pairs:
  'city'  => $city,
  'state' => $state,
  'zip'   => $zip,
);

print $url, "\n"; # so we can see it
```

Prints:

```
http://www.census.gov/cgi-bin/gazetteer?city=Some+City&state=Some+State&zip=Some+Zip
```

From this, it's easy to write a small program (shown in Example 5-1) to perform a request on this URL and use some simple regexps to extract the data from the HTML.

Example 5-1. gazetteer.pl

```perl
#!/usr/bin/perl -w
# gazetteer.pl - query the US Cenus Gazetteer database

use strict;
use URI;
use LWP::UserAgent;

die "Usage: $0 \"That Town\"\n" unless @ARGV == 1;
my $name = $ARGV[0];
my $url = URI->new('http://www.census.gov/cgi-bin/gazetteer');
$url->query_form( 'city' => $name, 'state' => '', 'zip' => '' );
print $url, "\n";

my $response = LWP::UserAgent->new->get( $url );
die "Error: ", $response->status_line unless $response->is_success;
extract_and_sort($response->content);

sub extract_and_sort {  # A simple data extractor routine
  die "No <ul>...</ul> in content" unless $_[0] =~ m{<ul>(.*?)</ul>}s;
  my @pop_and_town;
  foreach my $entry (split /<li>/, $1) {
    next unless $entry =~ m{^<strong>(.*?)</strong>(.*?)<br>}s;
    my $town = "$1 $2";
    next unless $entry =~ m{^Population \((.*?\): (\d+)<br>}m;
    push @pop_and_town, sprintf "%10s %s\n", $1, $town;
  }
  print reverse sort @pop_and_town;
}
```

Then run it from a prompt:

```
% perl gazetteer.pl Dulce
http://www.census.gov/cgi-bin/gazetteer?city=Dulce&state=&zip=
      2438 Dulce, NM  (cdp)
       794 Agua Dulce, TX  (city)
       136 Guayabo Dulce Barrio, PR  (county subdivision)

% perl gazetteer.pl IEG
http://www.census.gov/cgi-bin/gazetteer?city=IEG&state=&zip=
   2498016 San Diego County, CA  (county)
   1886748 San Diego Division, CA  (county subdivision)
   1110549 San Diego, CA  (city)
     67229 Boca Ciega Division, FL  (county subdivision)
      6977 Rancho San Diego, CA  (cdp)
```

```
6874 San Diego Country Estates, CA  (cdp)
5018 San Diego Division, TX  (county subdivision)
4983 San Diego, TX  (city)
1110 Diego Herna]Ndez Barrio, PR  (county subdivision)
 912 Riegelsville, PA  (county subdivision)
 912 Riegelsville, PA  (borough)
 298 New Riegel, OH  (village)
```

Automating Form Analysis

Rather than searching through HTML hoping that you've found all the form components, you can automate the task. Example 5-2 contains a program, *formpairs.pl*, that extracts the names and values from GET or POST requests.

Example 5-2. formpairs.pl

```perl
#!/usr/local/bin/perl -w
# formpairs.pl - extract names and values from HTTP requests

use strict;
my $data;
if(! $ENV{'REQUEST_METHOD'}) { # not run as a CGI
  die "Usage: $0 \"url\"\n" unless $ARGV[0];
  $data = $ARGV[0];
  $data = $1 if $data =~ s/^\w+\:.*?\?(.+)//;
  print "Data from that URL:\n(\n";
} elsif($ENV{'REQUEST_METHOD'} eq 'POST') {
  read(STDIN, $data, $ENV{'CONTENT_LENGTH'});
  print "Content-type: text/plain\n\nPOST data:\n(\n";
} else {
  $data = $ENV{'QUERY_STRING'};
  print "Content-type: text/plain\n\nGET data:\n(\n";
}
for (split '&', $data, -1) {   # Assumes proper URLencoded input
  tr/+/ /;   s/"/\\"/g;   s/=/\" => \"/;   s/%20/ /g;
  s/%/\\x/g;  # so %0d => \x0d
  print "  \"$_\",\n";
}
print ")\n";
```

That program, when run as a command-line utility, takes a URL as its one argument, decodes the encoded GET query, and prints it in more Perlish terms:

```
% perl formpairs.pl "http://www.census.gov/cgi-bin/gazetteer?city=IEG
&state=&zip="
Data from that URL:
(
  "city" => "IEG",
  "state" => "",
  "zip" => "",
)
```

Using a more complex URL (wrapped here for readability) illustrates the benefit of it:

```
% perl -w formpairs.pl http://www.altavista.com/sites/search/web?q=
pie+AND+rhubarb+AND+strawberry%0D%0AAND+NOT+crumb&kl=en&r=&dt=tmperiod
&d2=0&d0=&d1=&sc=on&nbq=30&pg=aq&search=Search
Data from that URL:
(
  "q" => "pie AND rhubarb AND strawberry\x0D\x0AAND NOT crumb",
  "kl" => "en",
  "r" => "",
  "dt" => "tmperiod",
  "d2" => "0",
  "d0" => "",
  "d1" => "",
  "sc" => "on",
  "nbq" => "30",
  "pg" => "aq",
  "search" => "Search",
)
```

The same program also functions as a CGI, so if you want to see what data a given form ends up submitting, you can simply change the form element's action attribute to a URL where you've set up that program as a CGI. As a CGI, it accepts both GET and POST methods.

For example:

```
<form method="post" action="http://myhost.int/cgi-bin/formpairs.pl">
Kind of pie: <input name="what pie" size=15>
<input type="submit" value="Mmm pie">
</form>
```

When you fill the one blank out with "tasty pie!" and press the "Mmm pie" button, the CGI will print:

```
POST data:
(
  "what pie" => "tasty pie\x21",
)
```

A more ad hoc solution that doesn't involve bothering with a CGI is to take the local copy of the form, set the form tag's method attribute to get, set its action attribute to dummy.txt, and create a file *dummy.txt* consisting of the text "Look at my URL!" or the like. Then, when you submit the form, you will see only the "Look at my URL!" page, but the browser's "Location"/"Address"/"URL" window will show a URL like this:

```
file:///C%7C/form_work/dummy.txt?what+pie=tasty+pie%21
```

You can then copy that URL into a shell window as the argument to *formpairs.pl*:

```
% perl formpairs.pl "file:///C%7C/form_work/dummy.txt?what+pie=tasty+pie%21"
Data from that URL:
(
  "what pie" => "tasty pie\x21",
)
```

Idiosyncrasies of HTML Forms

This section explains how the various form fields (hidden data, text boxes, etc.) are turned into data that is sent to the server. For information on the cosmetic features, such as the attributes that control how big the form object appears on the screen, see *Web Design in a Nutshell* (O'Reilly), *HTML & XHTML: The Definitive Guide* (O'Reilly), or the W3C's explanation of HTML 4.01 forms at *http://www.w3.org/TR/html401/interact/forms*.

Hidden Elements

An input element with `type=hidden` creates a form pair consisting of the value of its name attribute and the value of its `value` attribute. For example, this element:

```
<input type=hidden name="pie" value="meringue">
```

This doesn't display anything to the user, but when submitted, creates a form pair `pie=meringue`.

Text Elements

An input element with `type=text` (or with no type attribute at all) creates a one-line form box in which the user can type whatever she wants to send on this form. If there's a `value` attribute, its value is what's filled in when the form is first rendered, or when the user hits a Reset form button.

For example, this element:

```
<input type=text name="pie_filling" value="cherry">
```

creates a form box with "cherry" filled in. If the user submits the form as is, this will make a form pair `pie_filling=cherry`. If the user changes this to crème brûlée, this will make a form pair `pie_filling=crème brûlée`, or, after it gets URL encoded, `pie_filling=cr%E8me+br%FBl%E9e`.

Password Elements

An input element with `type=password` works exactly as if it had `type=text`, except the characters on screen in that box are made unreadable to anyone who might be looking over the user's shoulder. This is typically done by showing every character of the current value as *. For example:

```
<input type=password name="pie_filling" value="cherry">
```

This will have the initial value `cherry`, except it will appear as ******. If the user enters crème brûlée, that will be the current value, but it will display as ************. The form pairs submitted are just as if it were `type=text`, that is, `pie_filling=cherry` or `pie_filling=crème brûlée`.

Checkboxes

An input element with `type=checkbox` creates an on/off form button. The user cannot change the value of the element beyond just turning it on or off. For example:

```
<input type=checkbox name="à la mode" value="Pretty please!">
```

If the user checks this box and submits the form, it will send the form pair consisting of the element's `name` and `value` attribute's values. In this case, the pair is `à la mode=Pretty please!`, or, after it gets URL encoded, `%E0+la+mode=Pretty+please%21`. Note that if there is no value attribute, you get the pair *name*=on, as if there were a `value="on"` in this element. Incidentally, the user doesn't typically see whatever is specified for the `value` attribute.

Note that this differs from `type=text` input elements in this way: in `type=text` input elements, the `value` attribute sets the default value of the form, but in `type=checkbox` elements, the `value` attribute controls what value is sent if the checkbox is turned on when the form is submitted. By default, a checkbox is off upon rendering a new form (or when the user hits Reset); to make a checkbox element on by default, add the `checked` attribute:

```
<input type=checkbox name="à la mode" ivalue="Pretty please!" checked>
```

Radio Buttons

Input elements with `type=radio` behave like checkboxes, except that turning one radio button element on will turn off any other radio button elements with the same name value in that form. As the name "radio button" suggests, this is meant to be like the station preset buttons on many models of old car radios, where pressing in one button would make any selected one pop out.

Moreover, there is typically no way to turn off a radio button except by selecting another in the same group. An example group of radio buttons:

```
<input type=radio name="à la mode" value="nope" checked>
 nope <br>
<input type=radio name="à la mode" value="w/lemon" >
 with lemon sorbet <br>
<input type=radio name="à la mode" value="w/vanilla" >
 with vanilla ice cream<br>
<input type=radio name="à la mode" value="w/chocolate" >
 with chocolate ice cream <br>
```

By default, the `nope` element is on. If the user submits this form unchanged, this will send the form pair `à la mode=nope`. Selecting the second option ("with lemon sorbet") also deselects the first one (or whatever other "à la mode" element is selected), and if the user submits this, it well send the form pair `à la mode=w/lemon`.

Note that the checked attribute can be used to turn a `type=radio` element on by default, just as with `type=checkbox` elements. Different browsers behave differently when a radio button group has no checked element in it, or more than one. If you need to emulate the behavior of a particular browser in that case, experiment with the *formpairs.pl* program explained earlier, to see what form pair(s) are sent.

Submit Buttons

An input element with type=submit produces a button that, when pressed, submits the form data. There are two types of submit buttons: with or without a name attribute.

```
<input type=submit value="Go!">
```

The name-less element forms a button on screen that says "Go!". When pressed, that button submits the form data.

```
<input type=submit value="Go!" name="verb">
```

This displays the same as the name-less element, but when pressed, it also creates a form pair in the form it submits, consisting of verb=Go! (or after URL encoding, verb=Go%21). Note that the value attribute is doing double duty here, supplying both the value to be submitted as well as what should be displayed on the face of the button.

The purpose of this sort of button is to distinguish which of several submit buttons is pressed. Consider a form that contains these three submit buttons:

```
<input type=submit name="what_to_do" value="Continue Shopping">
<input type=submit name="what_to_do" value="Check Out">
<input type=submit name="what_to_do" value="Erase Order">
```

All of these will submit the form, but only if the first one is pressed will there be a what_to_do=Continue Shopping pair in the form data; only if the second one is pressed will there be a what_to_do=Check Out pair in the form data; and only if the third one is pressed will there be a what_to_do=Erase Order pair in the form data.

Note, incidentally, that in some cases, it is possible to submit a form without pressing a submit button! This is not specified in the HTML standard, but many browsers have the feature that if a form contains only one type=text field, if the user hits Enter while the cursor is in that field, the form is submitted. For example, consider this form:

```
<form type=get action="searcher.cgi">
  <input type=hidden name="session" value="3.14159">
  <input type=text name="key" value="">
  <input type=submit name="verb" value="Search!">
</form>
```

If the user types "meringue" in the input box, then hits the "Search!" button with the mouse pointer, there will be *three* form pairs submitted: session=3.14159, key=meringue, and verb=Search!. But if the user merely types "meringue" in the input box and hits the Enter key, there will be only *two* form pairs submitted: session=3.14159 and key=meringue. No form pair for the submit button is sent then, because it wasn't actually pressed.

Image Buttons

An input element with type=image is somewhat like a type=submit element, except instead of producing a button that the user presses in order to submit the form, it produces an inline image that the user clicks on to submit the form.

Also, whereas a type=submit button generates one form pair when pressed, *name=value*, from the element's name and value attributes, a type=image element generates two form pairs when pressed: *name.x=across* and *name.y=down*, reflecting the point in the image where the user's pointer was when he clicked on it. An example of typical type=image element syntax will illustrate this:

```
<input type=image name="woohah" src="do_it.gif">
```

And suppose that *do_it.gif* is an image 100 pixels wide by 40 high, and looks like the image in Figure 5-1.

Figure 5-1. A sample submit button

If the user clicks the pointer over the absolute top-leftmost pixel of that image as drawn by the above <input type=image ...> element inside a larger form element, it will submit the form along with two form pairs: woohah.x=0 and woohah.y=0. If the user instead clicks the pointer over the four-corners design in the middle of the "O" in "DO IT!", this happens to be 38 pixels from the left edge of the image, and 19 pixels from the top edge of the image, the form is submitted with the two form pairs woohah.x=38 and woohah.y=19.

While this imagemap-like feature of input type=image elements would obviously be quite useful for, say, click-to-zoom maps, most uses of input type=image elements are actually merely cosmetic, and the inlined image is just a fancy-looking version of the submit button. As such, the programs that process most such forms will just ignore the values of the name.x and name.y form pairs.

Consider this simple form:

```
<form type=post action="searcher.cgi">
  <input type=hidden name="session" value="3.14159">
  <input type=text name="key" value="">
  <input type=image name="in-english" src="usa_flag.png">
  <input type=image name="in-spanish" src="mex_flag.png">
</form>
```

This will render an input box followed by a U.S. flag image, then a Mexican flag image. There are three possible ways this can be submitted. First, if the user selects the input box to plant the cursor there, types "chocolate", and presses Enter, this will submit the form (via a POST method) to the form *searcher.cgi* with just two form pairs: session=3.14159 and key=chocolate.

Secondly, if the user types "chocolate", then puts the pointer over the U.S. flag and clicks it, it will submit the form with four form pairs: session=3.14159, key=chocolate, in-english.x=12, and in-english.y=34, where 12 and 34 are the across and down coordinates of the point in the U.S. flag where the user clicked.

Or thirdly, if the user types "chocolate", then puts the pointer over the Mexican flag and clicks it, it will submit the form with four form pairs: session=3.14159, key=chocolate, in-spanish.x=12, and in-spanish.y=34, where 12 and 34 are the across and down coordinates of the point in the Mexican flag where the user clicked.

Incidentally, the HTML specifications do not say how browsers should behave when there is no name=*whatever* attribute present in an input type=image element, but common practice is to create form pairs with keys named x and y (i.e., x=38 and y=19).

Reset Buttons

A type=reset input element produces no form pair and does not submit the form. It merely creates a button that the user can press to reset the form's contents to their default values, back to the way they were when the form was first rendered. The value attribute is used only to put text on the button's face. For example:

```
<input type=reset value="Nevermind">
```

This creates a reset button with the text "Nevermind" on it. It has no other effect.

File Selection Elements

A type=file input element provides some set of controls with which the user can select a local file. Usually this appears as a "Browse..." button that brings up an "Open File..." window and a text box that lists the name of whatever file is selected. When a file is selected, it sets the value of the form pair as the content of the file. File parameters, however, work in quite a different way from regular forms, and we deal with them in the "File Uploads" section later in this chapter.

Textarea Elements

A textarea element is like an <input type=text ...> element, except the user can enter many lines of text instead of just one. Moreover, the syntax is different. Whereas an <input type=text ...> element consists of just one tag, with the default content in the value attribute, like so:

```
<input type=text name="pairname" value="default content">
```

a textarea element consists of a start-tag, default content, and an end-tag:

```
<textarea name="pairname">Default content, first line.
Another line.
The last line.</textarea>
```

Select Elements and Option Elements

One final construct for expressing form controls is a select element containing some number of option elements. This is usually rendered as a drop-down/pop-up menu or occasionally as a scrollable list. In either case, the behavior is the same: the user selects an option from the list. The syntax is:

```
<select name="à la mode">
  <option value="nope">Nope</option>
  <option value="w/lemon">with lemon sorbet</option>
  <option value="w/vanilla">with vanilla ice cream</option>
  <option value="w/chocolate">with chocolate ice cream</option>
</select>
```

That is, one select element with a name=*string* attribute contains some option elements, each of which has a value=*string* attribute. The select element generates one form pair, using the select element's *name*=string attribute and the value=*string* attribute from the chosen option element. So in the example above, if the user chooses the option that showed on the screen as "with lemon sorbet", this sends the form pair à la mode=w/lemon, or, once it's URL encoded, %E0+la+mode=w%2Flemon.

Any option elements that have no value=*string* attribute get their values from the content of the element. So these option elements:

```
<option>This &amp; That</option>
<option>And the other
```

mean the same thing as:

```
<option value="This &amp; That">This &amp; That</option>
<option value="And the other">And the other</option>
```

When the form is first rendered, the first element is typically selected by default, and selecting any other deselects it. By providing a selected attribute in an option element, you can force it to be the selected one when the form first renders, just as the checked attribute does for checkbox input elements. Also, the </option> end-tag is optional.

Putting all that together, this code:

```
<select name="pie_filling">
  <option>Apple crunch
  <option selected>Pumpkin
  <option value="Mince-meat">Mince
  <option>Blueberry
  <option>Quince
</select>
```

means the same thing as this code:

```
<select name="pie_filling">
  <option value="Apple crunch">Apple crunch</option>
  <option value="Pumpkin">Pumpkin</option>
  <option value="Mince-meat">Mince</option>
```

```
<option value="Blueberry" selected>Blueberry</option>
<option value="Quince">Quince</option>
</select>
```

with the single exception that when the first one is rendered on the screen, it starts out with "Pumpkin" selected by default, whereas in the second one, "Blueberry" is selected by default.

There are two other kinds of differences in the code: the latter has `</option>` tags, but the former does not, and the former leaves out some `value="..."` attributes where the latter always has them. However, neither of these two kinds of differences are significant; the browser sees both blocks of code as meaning the same thing.

If the select element has a `multiple` attribute, as here:

```
<select name="à la mode" multiple>
  <option value="nope">Nope</option>
  <option value="w/lemon">with lemon sorbet</option>
  <option value="w/vanilla">with vanilla ice cream</option>
  <option value="w/chocolate">with chocolate ice cream</option>
</select>
```

the user is allowed to select more than one option at a time. (And incidentally, this typically forces the options to appear as a scrollable list instead of as a drop-down/pop-up menu.) This `multiple` feature is rarely used in practice.

POST Example: License Plates

Second only to the issues surrounding tattooing and tattoo removal, the hardest decision one ever has to make is, upon moving to California and buying a convertible, what personalized license plate should one get? In the past, this was a slow and embarrassing process, requiring one to go to the Motor Vehicles office, shuffle up to the clerk, and meekly request "HOTBABE," only to receive the crushing news that someone else has, somehow, already thought of that and taken it as her own personalized license plate. While there are 66,220,518,000 possible combinations,[*] it is apparently a devoted pursuit of the state's 30-odd million residents to think of personalized license plates. As with Internet domain names, if you can think of it, someone probably already has it.

But now the California Department of Motor Vehicles has understood our plight, and has put up the web site *plates.ca.gov* so that we can sit at home and use the Web to see which of our license plate ideas is available. It has a simple HTML form interface, shown in Figure 5-2.

However, it's so draining to have to plant the mouse in the search box, type "PL8DV8" or whatever other license plate you want, mouse over to the submit but-

---

[*] This is based on the formula: $c += 35 ** \$\_ - 10 ** \$\_$ for 2 .. 7; print c;. (The 35 is because letter O is treated as digit zero. The 10 is because all-digit plates are not allowed.)

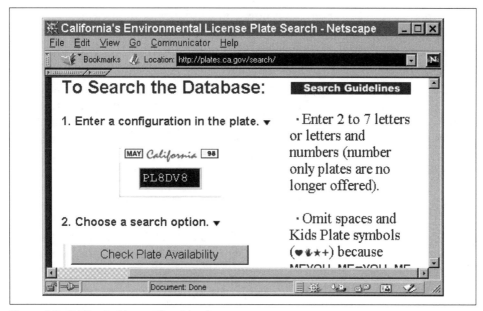

Figure 5-2. California License Plate Search

ton and press it, see the next screen report either "Plate configuration PL8DV8 is unavailable" or "this plate is tentatively acceptable and available," then mouse over to the Back button, press it, and so on for every possibility that occurs to us. Just as a true power user would never use the web interface to *whois* but would instead insist on the command-line tool, we too would be happiest with a command-line interface to this license plate search form.

The Form

Viewing the source of the search form at *http://plates.ca.gov/search/* shows that, omitting some table-formatting codes, it really just consists of:

```
<form method=POST action="search.php3">
<input type=text size=7 name=plate maxlength=7>
<br>
2. Choose a search option.
<br>
<input type=submit value="Check Plate Availability" name="search">
<br>Use this method to see if your exact configuration is available.
<br>
<input type=submit value="See Existing Similar Plates" name="search">
...
Enter 2 to 7 letters or letters and numbers (number only plates are no
longer offered)
...
</form>
```

From what we learned earlier about how different kinds of form elements produce different kinds of pairs, we can deduce that filling "PL8DV8" in the type=text box, then pressing the "Check Plate Availability" button will cause two form pairs to be submitted: plate=PL8DV8 and search=Check Plate Availability.

In each case, the first part of the form pair comes from the element's name attribute. With the first pair, we follow the rule for text input elements, and get the value from whatever the user has typed into that box (or whatever is there by default). With either submit button, we follow the rule for type=submit elements and make a form pair from the value attribute (if there is such an attribute and if this is the button that the user is pressing in order to submit the form).

Use formpairs.pl

We can save a local copy of the form's HTML source and edit the form element's action attribute to point to some server where we've set up as a CGI the *formpairs.pl* program from earlier in this chapter. The form element will then read:

```
<form method=POST action="http://someserver.int/cgi-bin/formpairs.pl">
```

If we then open the local copy of the form in our browser, fill in "PL8DV8" in the search box, and hit the first Submit button, *formpairs.pl* will report:

```
POST data:
(
  "plate" => "PL8DV8",
  "search" => "Check Plate Availability",
)
```

Our idea of what form pairs get sent was correct! (The second button would predictably send a "search" value of "See Existing Similar Plates", but that function is outside the scope of our interest.)

Translating This into LWP

Simply put that list of form pairs into a call to $browser->post(url, *pairs_arrayref*). Specifically, the call will look like this:

```
my $response = $browser->post(
  'http://plates.ca.gov/search/search.php3',
  [
    'plate'  => $plate,
    'search' => 'Check Plate Availability'
  ],
);
```

Knowing this, it's simple to write code that takes an argument from the command line and puts it into $plate, performs the above POST request, then checks the response. Example 5-3 is the complete program.

Example 5-3. pl8.pl

```perl
#!/usr/bin/perl -w
# pl8.pl -  query California license plate database

use strict;
use LWP::UserAgent;
my $plate = $ARGV[0] || die "Plate to search for?\n";
$plate = uc $plate;
$plate =~ tr/O/0/;  # we use zero for letter-oh
die "$plate is invalid.\n"
 unless $plate =~ m/^[A-Z0-9]{2,7}$/
    and $plate !~ m/^\d+$/;  # no all-digit plates

my $browser = LWP::UserAgent->new;
my $response = $browser->post(
  'http://plates.ca.gov/search/search.php3',
  [
    'plate'  => $plate,
    'search' => 'Check Plate Availability'
  ],
);
die "Error: ", $response->status_line
 unless $response->is_success;

if($response->content =~ m/is unavailable/) {
  print "$plate is already taken.\n";
} elsif($response->content =~ m/and available/) {
  print "$plate is AVAILABLE!\n";
} else {
  print "$plate... Can't make sense of response?!\n";
}
exit;
```

Saved into *pl8.pl*, it runs happily from the command line:

```
% perl pl8.pl
Plate to search for?
% perl pl8.pl 314159
314159 is invalid.
% perl pl8.pl pl8dv8
PL8DV8 is AVAILABLE!
% perl pl8.pl elbarto
ELBARTO is already taken.
% perl pl8.pl ilikepie
ILIKEPIE is invalid.
% perl pl8.pl pieman
PIEMAN is already taken.
% perl pl8.pl pielady
PIELADY is already taken.
% perl pl8.pl pieboy
PIEBOY is AVAILABLE!
% perl pl8.pl piegirl
PIEGIRL is AVAILABLE!
```

```
% perl p18.pl shazbot
SHAZBOT is already taken.
% perl p18.pl lwpbot
LWPBOT is AVAILABLE!
```

POST Example: ABEBooks.com

ABEBooks.com is a web site that allows users to search the database of the books for sale at hundreds of used bookstores mostly in the U.S. and Canada. An eagle-eyed user can find anything from a $2 used copy of *Swahili for Travellers*, to an €11,000 complete set of the 1777 edition of Diderot's *Encyclopédie*. The trick, as with any kind of bargain hunting, is to always keep looking, because one never knows when something new and interesting will arrive. The manual way of doing this is to fastidiously keep a list of titles, authors, and subjects for which you're keeping an eye out, and to routinely visit the ABEBooks site, key in each of your searches into the HTML search form, and look for anything new. However, this is precisely the kind of drudgery that computers were meant to do for us; so we'll now consider how to automate that task.

As with the license plate form in the previous section, the first step in automating form submission is to understand the form in question. ABEBooks's "Advanced Search" system consists of one form, which is shown in Figure 5-3.

The process of searching with this form is just a matter of filling in the applicable fields and hitting "Start Search"; the web site then returns a web page listing the results. For example, entering "Codex Seraphinianus" in the "Title" field returns the web page shown in Figure 5-4.

The Form

In the previous section, the form's source was simple enough that we could tell at a glance what form pairs it would produce, and our use of *formpairs.pl* merely confirmed that we understood it. However, this ABEBooks form is obviously much more complex, so let's start with using *formpairs.pl* and look to the details of the form source only as necessary. Save a local copy of the form and change its form action attribute from this:

```
<FORM ACTION="BookSearch" METHOD=post>
```

to this:

```
<FORM ACTION="http://someserver.int/cgi-bin/formpairs.pl" METHOD=post>
```

or to whatever URL you've put a copy of *formpairs.pl* at. If you then open that newly altered HTML file in a browser, fill in "Codex Seraphinianus" in the "Title" blank,

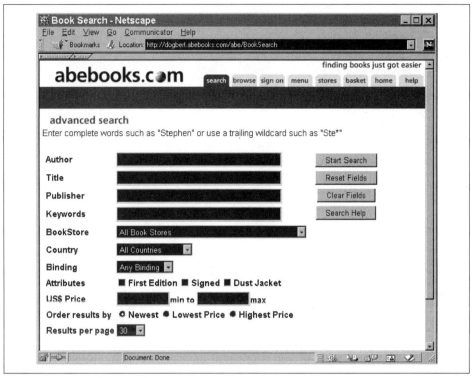

Figure 5-3. ABEBooks query form

set "Order results by" to "Newest," set "Results per page" to "100," and hit "Start Search," our *formpairs.pl* program shows the form pairs that the browser sends:

```
POST data:
(
  "ph" => "2",
  "an" => "",
  "tn" => "Codex Seraphinianus",
  "pn" => "",
  "sn" => "",
  "gpnm" => "ALL",
  "cty" => "",
  "bi" => "",
  "prl" => "",
  "prh" => "",
  "sortby" => "0",
  "ds" => "30",
  "bu" => "Start Search",
)
```

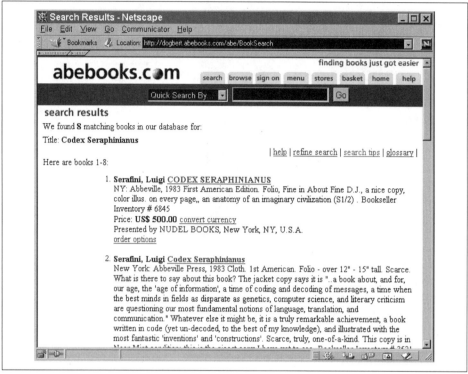

Figure 5-4. ABEBooks results page

Translating This into LWP

These form pairs can be pasted into a simple program for saving the result of that search, using a call to $browser->post(url, *pairs_arrayref*) such as you'll recognize from the previous section. Example 5-4 demonstrates.

Example 5-4. seraph.pl

```
#!/usr/bin/perl -w
# seraph.pl - search for Codex Seraphinianus on abebooks

use strict;
my $out_file = "result_seraph.html";  # where to save it

use LWP;
my $browser = LWP::UserAgent->new;
my $response = $browser->post(
  'http://dogbert.abebooks.com/abe/BookSearch',
   # That's the URL that the real form submits to.
  [
    "ph" => "2",
    "an" => "",
    "tn" => "Codex Seraphinianus",
    "pn" => "",
```

Example 5-4. seraph.pl (continued)

```
    "sn" => "",
    "gpnm" => "All Book Stores",
    "cty" => "All Countries",
    "bi" => "Any Binding",
    "prl" => "",
    "prh" => "",
    "sortby" => "0",
    "ds" => "100",
    "bu" => "Start Search",
  ]
);

die "Error: ", $response->status_line, "\n"
 unless $response->is_success;

open(OUT, ">$out_file") || die "Can't write-open $out_file: $!";
binmode(OUT);
print OUT $response->content;
close(OUT);
print "Bytes saved: ", -s $out_file, " in $out_file\n";
```

When run, this program successfully saves to *result_seraph.html* all the HTML that results from running a 100-newest-items search on the title "Codex Seraphinianus".

Adding Features

A little more experimentation with the form would show that a search on an author's name, instead of the title name, shows up in the an=*author_name* form pair, instead of the tn=*title_name* form pair. That is what we see if we go sifting through the HTML source to the search form:

```
...
<TR><TH ALIGN=LEFT>Author</TH>
<TD><INPUT TYPE=text NAME=an VALUE="" SIZE=35 MAXLENGTH=254></TD></TR>
<TR><TH ALIGN=LEFT>Title</TH>
<TD><INPUT TYPE=text NAME=tn VALUE="" SIZE=35 MAXLENGTH=254></TD></TR>
...
```

We could alter our program to set the form pairs with something like this:

```
...
"an" => $author || "",
"tn" => $title  || "",
...
```

Moreover, if we wanted to allow the search to specify that only first editions should be shown, some experimentation with *formpairs.pl* and our local copy of the form shows that checking the "First Edition" checkbox produces a new form pair fe=on, between the bi= and prl= pairs, where previously there was nothing. This jibes with the HTML source code:

```
<INPUT TYPE=CHECKBOX NAME=fe><B>First Edition</B>
```

This could be modeled in our program with a variable $first_edition, which, if set to a true value, produces that form pair; otherwise, it produces nothing:

```
...
"bi" => "",
$first_edition ? ("fe" => "on") : (),
"prl" => "",
...
```

This can all be bundled up in a single routine that runs a search based on three given parameters: author, title, and whether only first editions should be shown:

```
sub run_search {
  my($author, $title, $first_edition) = @_;
  my $response = $browser->post(
    'http://dogbert.abebooks.com/abe/BookSearch',
    [
      "ph" => "2",
      "an" => $author || "",
      "tn" => $title  || "",
      "pn" => "",
      "sn" => "",
      "gpnm" => "All Book Stores",
      "cty" => "All Countries",
      "bi" => "Any Binding",
      $first_edition ? ("fe" => "on") : (),
      "prl" => "",
      "prh" => "",
      "sortby" => "0",
      "ds" => "100",
      "bu" => "Start Search",
    ]
  );
  return $response;
}
```

That run_search( ) routine takes all we know about how any new-books query to ABEBooks needs to be performed and puts it all in a single place. From here, we need only apply initialization code and code to call the run_search routine, and do whatever needs doing with it:

```
use strict;
use LWP;
my $browser = LWP::UserAgent->new;
do_stuff();

sub do_stuff {
  my $response = run_search( # author, title, first edition
    '', 'Codex Seraphinianus', ''
  );
  process_search($response, 'result_seraph.html');
}
```

```
sub process_search {
  my($response, $out_file) = @_;
  die "Error: ", $response->status_line, "\n"
   unless $response->is_success;
  open(OUT, ">$out_file") || die "Can't write-open $out_file: $!";
  binmode(OUT);
  print OUT $response->content;
  close(OUT);
  print "Bytes saved: ", -s $out_file, " in $out_file\n";
  return;
}
```

Generalizing the Program

This program still just runs an ABEBooks search for books with the title "Codex Seraphinianus", and saves the results to *result_seraph.html*. But the benefit of reshuffling the code as we did is that now, by just changing do_stuff slightly, we change our program from being dedicated to running one search, to being a generic tool for running any number of searches:

```
my @searches = (  # outfile, author, title, first_edition
  ['result_seraph.html',      '', 'Codex Seraphinianus', ''],
  ['result_vidal_1green.html', 'Gore Vidal', 'Dark Green Bright Red', 1],
  ['result_marchand.html',    'Hans Marchand', 'Categories', ''],
  ['result_origins.html',     'Eric Partridge', 'Origins', ''],
  ['result_navajo.html',      '', 'Navajo',   ''],
  ['result_navaho.html',      '', 'Navaho',   ''],
  ['result_iroq.html',        '', 'Iroquois', ''],
  ['result_tibetan.html',     '', 'Tibetan',  ''],
);
do_stuff();

sub do_stuff {
  foreach my $search (@searches) {
    my $out_file = shift @$search;
    my $resp = run_search(@$search);
    sleep 3; # Don't rudely query the ABEbooks server too fast!
    process_search($resp, $out_file);
  }
}
```

Running this program saves each of those searches in turn:

```
% perl -w abesearch03.pl
Bytes saved: 15452 in result_seraph.html
Bytes saved: 57693 in result_vidal_1green.html
Bytes saved: 8009 in result_marchand.html
Bytes saved: 25322 in result_origins.html
Bytes saved: 125337 in result_navajo.html
Bytes saved: 128665 in result_navaho.html
Bytes saved: 127475 in result_iroq.html
Bytes saved: 130941 in result_tibetan.html
```

The user can then open each file and skim it for interesting new titles. Each book listed there comes with a working absolute URL to a book detail page on the ABEBooks server, which can be used for buying the book. For some of the queries that generate large numbers of results, it would be particularly convenient to have do_stuff( ) actually track which books it has seen before (using the book-detail URL of each) and report only on new ones:

```
my $is_first_time;
my (%seen_last_time, %seen_this_time, @new_urls);
sub do_stuff {
  if (-e 'seen_last_time.dat') {
    # Get URLs seen last time.
    open(LAST_TIME, "<seen_last_time.dat") || die $!;
    while (<LAST_TIME>) { chomp; $seen_last_time{$_} = 1 };
    close(LAST_TIME);
  } else {
    $is_first_time = 1;
  }

  foreach my $search (@searches) {
    my $out_file = shift @$search;
    my $resp = run_search(@$search);
    process_search($resp, $out_file);

    foreach my $url ($resp->content =~
      # Extract URLs of book-detail pages:
      m{"(http://dogbert.abebooks.com/abe/BookDetails\?bi=[^\s\"]+)"}g
    ){
      push @new_urls, $url unless $seen_last_time{$url}
        or $seen_this_time{$url};
      $seen_this_time{$url} = 1;
    }
  }

  # Save URLs for comparison next time.
  open(LAST_TIME, ">seen_last_time.dat") || die $!;
  for (keys %seen_this_time) { print LAST_TIME $_, "\n" }
  close(LAST_TIME);

  if($is_first_time) {
    print "(This was the first time this program was run.)\n";
  } elsif (@new_urls) {
    print "\nURLs of new books:\n";
    for (@new_urls) { print $_, "\n" }
  } else {
    print "No new books to report.\n";
  }
}
```

A typical run of this will produce output as above, but with this addendum:

```
URLs of new books:
http://dogbert.abebooks.com/abe/BookDetails?bi=24017010
http://dogbert.abebooks.com/abe/BookDetails?bi=4766571
http://dogbert.abebooks.com/abe/BookDetails?bi=110543730
```

```
http://dogbert.abebooks.com/abe/BookDetails?bi=58703369
http://dogbert.abebooks.com/abe/BookDetails?bi=93298753
http://dogbert.abebooks.com/abe/BookDetails?bi=93204427
http://dogbert.abebooks.com/abe/BookDetails?bi=24086008
```

File Uploads

So far we've discussed users entering text data that they type (or paste) into forms. But there's another way to submit data: with a type=file form element, which allows users to select a file on their local systems to upload when the form is submitted.

Currently, three things have to happen for a user to upload a file via a form. First, the program that will be processing the form has to be expecting a file to be uploaded (you can't just alter the HTML for any form and stick a type=file field into it). Second, the form has to have an <input type=**file** name=*whatever*> element. And third, the form element has to have its attributes set like so:

```
<form method=post enctype="multipart/form-data" action="url">
```

This is necessary because file-upload fields can't be conveyed by the normal form-data encoding system, but instead have to use the "multipart/form-data" encoding system (which, incidentally, can be conveyed only across POST requests, not across GET requests).

Suppose, for example, that you were automating interaction with an HTML form that looked like this:

```
<form enctype="multipart/form-data" method=post
  action="http://pastel.int/feedback.pl">
Subject:            <input name="subject" type="text">
<br>File to process -- <input name="saywhat" type="file">
<br>Your Name --     <input name="user"    type="text">
<input type="submit" value="Send!"></form>
```

Modeling the first and third fields is as we've seen before—a simple matter of $browser->post($url, ['subject'=>..., 'user'=>...]). But the file-upload part involves some doing. First off, you have to add a header line of 'Content_Type' => 'form-data' to mean that yes, you really mean this to be a "multipart/form-data" POSTing. And secondly, where you would have a string in 'saywhat'=>*text*, you instead have an array reference where the first array item is the path to the file you want to upload. So it ends up looking like this:

```
my $response = $browser->post(
  'http://pastel.int/feedback.pl',
  [ 'subject' => 'Demand for pie.',
    'saywhat' => ["./today/earth_pies1.dml"],
    'user'    => 'Adm. Kang',
  ],
  'Content_Type' => 'form-data',
  ...any other header lines...
);
```

Assume that *./today/earth_pies1.dml* looks like this:

```
<?xml version="1.0" encoding='iso-8859-1' standalone="yes"?>
<Demand xml:lang="i-klingon">
  DaH chabmeyraj tunob!
</Demand>
```

The request that the above program actually sends will look like this:

```
--xYzZY
Content-Disposition: form-data; name="subject"

Demand for pie.
--xYzZY
Content-Disposition: form-data; name="saywhat"; filename="earth_pies1.dml"
Content-Length: 131
Content-Type: text/plain

<?xml version="1.0" encoding='iso-8859-1' standalone="yes"?>
<Demand xml:lang="i-klingon">
  DaH chabmeyraj tunob!
</Demand>

--xYzZY
Content-Disposition: form-data; name="user"

Adm. Kang
--xYzZY--
```

Note that each form-field is like a little HTTP message of its own, with its own set of headers and its own body. For the "normal" fields (the first and third fields), the header basically expresses that this is ordinary data for a particular field name, and the body expresses the form data. But for the type=file field, we get the file's content as the body. Take a look at the header again:

```
Content-Disposition: form-data; name="saywhat"; filename="earth_pies1.dml"
Content-Length: 131
Content-Type: text/plain
```

The name="saywhat" expresses what the name="..." attribute was on the <input type=file ...> element to which this corresponds, which we coded into our program in the saywhat=>[...] line. But note that LWP also tells the remote host the basename of the file we're uploading by default (i.e., the filename minus directory names) as well as its best guess at the MIME type for that file. Because LWP (specifically, the LWP::MediaTypes module) has never heard of the *.dml* extension, it falls back on text/plain. (If this file had clearly been a binary file, LWP would call it application/octet-stream, the MIME type for general binary files.) In case you want to change the name that LWP presents to the remote server, you can provide that name as a second item in the arrayref:

```
fieldname => [local_filespec => as_what_name],
```

So if you change the saywhat line in the above program to this:

```
'saywhat' => ["./today/earth_pies1.dml" => "allyourpie.xml"],
```

Then the resulting headers on its part of the POST request would look like this:

```
Content-Disposition: form-data; name="saywhat"; filename="allyourpie.xml"
Content-Length: 131
Content-Type: text/plain
```

Although most applications that take file uploads across the Web pay no attention to the MIME types (because so many browsers get them wrong), if you want to specify a MIME type for a particular file upload, you could do so with a third item in the array reference:

```
fieldname => [local_filespec => as_what_name => MIME_type],
```

Like so:

```
'saywhat' => ["./today/earth_pies1.dml" => "allyourpie.xml"
            => "application/angry-ultimatum"],
```

Then the resulting headers on its part of the POST request would look like this:

```
Content-Disposition: form-data; name="saywhat"; filename="allyourpie.xml"
Content-Length: 131
Content-Type: application/angry-ultimatum
```

All these file-upload options work just as well for binary files (such as JPEGs) as for text files. Note, however, that when LWP constructs and sends the request, it currently has to read into memory all files you're sending in this request. If you're sending a 20-megabyte MP3 file, this might be a problem! You can tell LWP not to read the files into memory by setting $HTTP::Request::Common::DYNAMIC_FILE_UPLOAD = 1 (it bears explaining that HTTP::Request::Common is the library that LWP uses for creating these file-upload requests), but unfortunately, at the time of this writing, many servers and CGIs do not understand the resulting HTTP POST request.

One especially neat trick is that you don't even need to have a file to upload to send a "file upload" request. To send content from a string in memory instead of from a file on disk, use this syntax:

```
fieldname => [
    undef,   # yes, undef!
    as_what_name,
    'Content_Type' => MIME_type,
    'Content' => data_to_send
],
```

For example, we could change our saywhat line in the above program to read:

```
'saywhat' => [
    undef,
    'allyourpie.xml',
    'Content_Type' => 'application/angry-ultimatum',
    'Content' => "All your pies are belong to me!\nGNAR!"
],
```

The resulting request will contain this chunk of data for the saywhat field:

```
Content-Disposition: form-data; name="saywhat"; filename="allyourpie.xml"
Content-Type: application/angry-ultimatum

All your pies are belong to me!
GNAR!
```

Limits on Forms

The examples in this chapter use approaches to form-data submission that work well for almost all form systems that you'd run into, namely, systems where the form data is meant to be keyed into HTML forms that do not change. Some form systems can't be treated with that approach because they contain JavaScript code that can do just about anything, such as manipulate the form data in arbitrary ways before sending it to the server. The best one can do in such cases is write Perl code that replicates what the JavaScript code does, as needed.

Some form systems are problematic not because of JavaScript, but because the forms into which users are meant to key data are not always the same each time they're loaded. In most cases, the extent of change is merely a hidden form variable containing a session ID. These you can code around by using LWP to download the form, extracting the session ID or other hidden fields, and submitting those along with your other values.

In a few remaining cases where the form in question is predictable enough for a program to manipulate it, but unpredictable enough that your program needs to carefully scrutinize its contents each time before choosing what form data to submit, you may be able put to good use either of the two CPAN modules that provide an abstracted interface to forms and the fields in them, HTML::Form and HTTP::Request::Form.

HTML::Form is an LWP class for objects representing HTML forms. That is, it parses HTML source that you give it and builds an object for the form, each form containing an object for each input element in the form. HTTP::Request::Form is quite similar, except it takes as input an HTML::TreeBuilder tree, not HTML source text. In practice, however, those modules are needed in very few cases, and the simpler strategies in this chapter will be enough for submitting just about any form on the Web and processing the result.

## CHAPTER 6

Simple HTML Processing with Regular Expressions

The preceding chapters have been about getting things from the Web. But once you get a file, you have to process it. If you get a GIF, you'll use some module or external program that reads GIFs and likewise if you get a PNG, an RSS file, an MP3, or whatever. However, most of the interesting processable information on the Web is in HTML, so much of the rest of this book will focus on getting information out of HTML specifically.

In this chapter, we will use a rudimentary approach to processing HTML source: Perl regular expressions. This technique is powerful and most web sites can be mined in this fashion. We present the techniques of using regular expressions to extract data and show you how to debug those regular expressions. Examples from Amazon, the O'Reilly Network, Netscape bookmark files, and the Weather Underground web site demonstrate the techniques.

Automating Data Extraction

Suppose we want to extract information from an Amazon book page. The first problem is getting the HTML. Browsing Amazon shows that the URL for a book page is *http://www.amazon.com/exec/obidos/ASIN/ISBN*, where *ISBN* is the book's unique International Standard Book Number. So to fetch the *Perl Cookbook*'s page, for example:

```
#!/usr/bin/perl -w
use strict;
use LWP::Simple;

my $html = get("http://www.amazon.com/exec/obidos/ASIN/1565922433")
   or die "Couldn't fetch the Perl Cookbook's page.";
```

The relevant piece of HTML looks like this:

```
<br clear="left">
<FONT FACE="Arial,Helvetica" size=2>
<b>Paperback</b>
```

```
- 794 pages (August 1998)
<br></font>
<font face="Arial,Helvetica" size=-2>
O'Reilly &amp; Associates; </font>
<font face="Arial,Helvetica" size=-2>
ISBN: 1565922433
; Dimensions (in inches): 1.55 x 9.22 x 7.08
<br>
<FONT FACE="Arial,Helvetica" size=2>
</font><br>
</font>
</span>
<font face=verdana,arial,helvetica size=-1>
<b>Amazon.com Sales Rank: </b> 4,070 </font><br>
<font face=verdana,arial,helvetica size=-1>
```

The easiest way to extract information here is to use regular expressions. For example:

```
$html =~ m{Amazon\.com Sales Rank: </b> ([\d,]+) </font><br>};
$sales_rank = $1;
$sales_rank =~ tr[,][]d;      # 4,070 becomes 4070
```

This regular expression describes the information we want (a string of digits and commas), as well as the text around the text we're after (Amazon.com Sales Rank: and </font>
). We use curly braces to delimit the regular expression to avoid problems with the slash in </font>, and we use parentheses to capture the desired information. We save that information to $sales_rank, then modify the variable's value to clean up the data we extracted.

The final program appears in Example 6-1.

Example 6-1. cookbook-rank

```
#!/usr/bin/perl -w
# cookbook-rank - find rank of Perl Cookbook on Amazon

use LWP::Simple;

my $html = get("http://www.amazon.com/exec/obidos/ASIN/1565922433")
  or die "Couldn't fetch the Perl Cookbook's page.";
$html =~ m{Amazon\.com Sales Rank: </b> ([\d,]+) </font><br>} || die;
my $sales_rank = $1;
$sales_rank =~ tr[,][]d;      # 4,070 becomes 4070
print "$sales_rank\n";
```

It's then straightforward to generalize the program by allowing the user to provide the ISBN on the command line, as shown in Example 6-2.

Example 6-2. amazon-rank

```
#!/usr/bin/perl -w
# amazon-rank: fetch Amazon rank given ISBN on cmdline

use LWP::Simple;
```

Example 6-2. amazon-rank (continued)

```
my $isbn = shift
  or die "usage:\n$0 ISBN\n";
my $html = get("http://www.amazon.com/exec/obidos/ASIN/$isbn");
$html =~ m{Amazon\.com Sales Rank: </b> ([\d,]+) </font><br>} || die;
my $sales_rank = $1;
$sales_rank =~ tr[,][]d;     # 4,070 becomes 4070
print "$sales_rank\n";
```

We could take this program in any direction we wanted. For example, it would be a simple enhancement to take a list of ISBNs from the command line or from STDIN, if none were given on the command line. It would be trickier, but more useful, to have the program accept book titles instead of just ISBNs. A more elaborate version of this basic program is one of O'Reilly's actual market research tools.

Regular Expression Techniques

Web pages are designed to be easy for humans to read, not for programs. Humans are very flexible in what they can read, and they can easily adapt to a new look and feel of the web page. But if the underlying HTML changes, a program written to extract information from the page will no longer work. Your challenge when writing a data-extraction program is to get a feel for the amount of natural variation between pages you'll want to download.

The following are a set of techniques for you to use when creating regular expressions to extract data from web pages. If you're an experienced Perl programmer, you probably know most or all of them and can skip ahead to the "Troubleshooting" section.

Anchor Your Match

An important decision is how much surrounding text you put into your regular expression. Put in too much of this context and you run the risk of being too specific—the natural variation from page to page causes your program to fail to extract some information it should have been able to get. Similarly, put in too little context and you run the risk of your regular expression erroneously matching elsewhere on the page.

Whitespace

Many HTML pages have whitespace added to make the source easier to read or as a side effect of how they were produced. For example, notice the spaces around the number in this line:

```
<b>Amazon.com Sales Rank: </b> 4,070 </font><br>
```

Without checking, it's hard to guess whether every page has that space. You could check, or you could simply be flexible in what you accept:

```
$html =~ m{Amazon\.com Sales Rank: </b>\s*([\d,]+)\s*</font><br>} || die;
```

Now we can match the number regardless of the amount of whitespace around it. The \s wildcard matches any whitespace character.

Embedded Newlines

Beware of using \s when you are matching across multiple lines, because \s matches newlines. You can construct a character class to represent "any whitespace but newlines":

```
[^\S\n]
```

As a further caveat, the regexp dot "." normally matches any character *except* a newline. To make the dot match newlines as well, use the /s option. Now you can say m{<b>.*?</b>}s and find the bold text even if it includes newlines. But this /s option doesn't change the meaning of ^ and $ from their usual "start of string" and "end of string, or right before the newline at the end of the string if present." To change that, use the /m option, which makes ^ and $ match the beginning and end of lines within the string. That is, with /m, a ^ matches the start of the string or right after any newline in the string; and a $ then matches the end of the string, or right before any newline in the string.

For example, to match the ISBN that starts out a line while ignoring any other occurrences of "ISBN" in the page, you might say:

```
m{^ISBN: ([-0-9A-Za-z]+)}m
```

Incidentally, you might expect that because an ISBN is called a number, we'd use \d+ to match it. However, ISBNs occasionally have letters in them and are sometimes shown with dashes; hence the [-0-9A-Za-z] range instead of the overly restrictive \d+ range, which would fail to match an ISBN such as 038079439X or 0-8248-1898-9.

Minimal and Greedy Matches

If you want to extract everything between two tags, there are two approaches:

```
m{<b>(.*?)</b>}i
m{<b>([^<]*)</b>}i
```

The former uses minimal matching to match as little as possible between the <b> and the </b>. The latter uses greedy matching to match as much text that doesn't contain a greater-than sign as possible between <b> and </b>. The latter is marginally faster but won't successfully match text such as <b><i>hi</i></b>, whereas the former will.

Capture

To extract information from a regular expression match, surround part of the regular expression in parentheses. This causes the regular expression engine to set the $1, $2, etc. variables to contain the portions of the string that match those parts of the pattern. For example:

```
$string = '<a href="there.html">go here now!</a>';
$string =~ m{ href="(.*?)"}i;        # extract destination of link
$url = $1;
```

A match in scalar context returns true or false depending on whether the regular expression matched the string. A match in list context returns a list of $1, $2, ... captured text.

```
$matched = $string =~ m{RE};
@matches = $string =~ m{RE};
```

To group parts of a regular expression together without capturing, use the (?:RE) construct:

```
$string = '<a href="jumbo.html"><img src="big.gif"></a>';
@links = $string =~ m{(?:href|src)="(.*?)"}g;
print "Found @links\n";
Found jumbo.html big.gif
```

Repeated Matches

The /g modifier causes the match to be repeated. In scalar context, the match continues from where the last match left off. Use this to extract information *one* match at a time. For example:

```
$string = '<img src="big.gif"><img src="small.gif">';
while ($string =~ m{src="(.*?)"}g) {
  print "Found: $1\n";
}
Found: big.gif
Found: small.gif
```

In list context, /g causes *all* matching captured strings to be returned. Use this to extract all matches at once. For example:

```
$string = '<img src="big.gif"><img src="small.gif">';
@pix = $string =~ m{src="(.*?)"}g;
print "Found @pix\n";
Found big.gif small.gif
```

If your regular expression doesn't use capturing parentheses, the entire text that matches is returned:

```
$string = '<img src="big.gif"><img src="small.gif">';
@gifs = $string =~ m{\w+\.gif}g;
print "Found @gifs\n";
Found big.gif small.gif
```

Develop from Components

There are many reasons to break regular expressions into components—it makes them easier to develop, debug, and maintain. Use the qr// operator to compile a chunk of a regular expression, then interpolate it into a larger regular expression without sacrificing performance:

```
$string = '<a href="jumbo.html"><img src="big.gif"></a>';
$ATTRIBUTE = qr/href|src/;
$INSIDE_QUOTES = qr/.*?/;
@files = $string =~ m{(?:$ATTRIBUTE)="($INSIDE_QUOTES)"}g;
print "Found @files\n";
Found jumbo.html big.gif
```

Use Multiple Steps

A common conceit in programmers is to try to do everything with one regular expression. Don't be afraid to use two or more. This has the same advantages as building your regular expression from components: by only attempting to solve one part of the problem at each step, the final solution can be easier to read, debug, and maintain.

For example, the front page of *http://www.oreillynet.com/* has several articles on it. Inspecting the HTML with View Source on the browser shows that each story looks like this:

```
<!-- itemtemplate -->
<p class="medlist"><b><a href="http://www.oreillynet.com/pub/a/dotnet/2002/03/04
/rotor.html">Uncovering Rotor -- A Shared Source CLI</a></b> ^M
 Recently, David Stutz and Stephen Walli hosted an informal, unannounced BOF at
BSDCon 2002 about Microsoft's Shared Source implementation of the ECMA CLI, also
known as Rotor. Although the source code for the Shared Source CLI wasn't yet
available, the BOF offered a preview of what's to come, as well as details about its
implementation and the motivation behind it.  [<a href="http://www.oreillynet.
com/dotnet/">.NET DevCenter</a>]</p>
```

That is, the article starts with the itemtemplate comment and ends with the </p> tag. This suggests a main loop of:

```
while ($html =~ m{<!-- itemtemplate -->(.*?)</p>}gs) {
  $chunk = $1;
  # extract URL, title, and summary from $chunk
}
```

It's surprisingly common to see HTML comments indicating the structure of the HTML. Most dynamic web sites are generated from templates, the comments help the people who maintain the templates keep track of the various sections.

Extracting the URL, title, and summary is straightforward. It's even a simple matter to use the standard Text::Wrap module to reformat the summary to make it easy to read:

```
    use Text::Wrap;

    while ($html =~ m{<!-- itemtemplate -->(.*?)</p>}gs) {
      $chunk = $1;
      ($URL, $title, $summary) =
        $chunk =~ m{href="(.*?)">(.*?)</a></b>\s* \s*(.*?)\[}i
        or next;
      $summary =~ s{ }{ }g;
      print "$URL\n$title\n", wrap("  ", "  ", $summary), "\n\n";
    }
```

Running this, however, shows HTML still in the summary. Remove the tags with:

```
    $summary =~ s{<.*?>}{}sg;
```

The complete program is shown in Example 6-3.

Example 6-3. orn-summary

```
#!/usr/bin/perl -w

use LWP::Simple;
use Text::Wrap;

$html = get("http://www.oreillynet.com/") || die;

while ($html =~ m{<!-- itemtemplate -->(.*?)</p>}gs) {
  $chunk = $1;
  ($URL, $title, $summary) =
    $chunk =~ m{href="(.*?)">(.*?)</a></b>\s* \s*(.*?)\[}i
    or next;
  $summary =~ s{ }{ }g;
  $summary =~ s{<.*?>}{}sg;
  print "$URL\n$title\n", wrap("  ", "  ", $summary), "\n\n";
}
```

Troubleshooting

Both when developing and maintaining data extraction programs, things can go wrong. Suddenly, instead of an article summary, you see a huge mass of HTML, or you don't get any output at all. Several things might cause this. For example, the web site's HTML changed, or your program wasn't flexible enough to deal with all the naturally occurring variations in the HTML.

There are two basic types of problems: false positives and false negatives. A false positive is when your regular expression identifies something it thinks is the information you're after, but it isn't really. For example, if the O'Reilly Network used the itemtemplate and summary format for things that aren't articles, the summary extraction program in Example 6-3 would report headlines that aren't really headlines.

There are two ways to deal with false positives. You can tighten your regular expression to prevent the uninteresting piece of HTML from matching. For example, matching text with /[^<]*/ instead of /.*?/ ensures the text has no HTML. The other way to prevent a false positive is to inspect the results of the match to ensure they're relevant to your search. For example, in Example 6-3, we checked that the URL, title, and summary were found when we decomposed the chunk.

A false negative is where your program fails to find information for which it is looking. There are also two ways to fix this. The first is to relax your regular expression. For example, replace a single space with /\s*/ to allow for any amount of whitespace. The second way is to make another pass through the document with a separate regular expression or processing technique, to catch the data you missed the first time around. For example, extract into an array all the things that look like news headlines, then remove the first element from the array if you know it's always going to be an advertisement instead of an actual headline.

Often the hardest part of debugging a regular expression is locating which part isn't matching or is matching too much. There are some simple steps you can take to identify where your regular expression is going wrong.

First, print the text you're matching against. Print it immediately before the match, so you are totally certain what the regular expression is being applied to. You'd be surprised at the number of subtle ways the page your program fetches can differ from the page for which you designed the regular expression.

Second, put capturing parentheses around every chunk of the regular expression to see what's matching. This lets you find runaway matches, i.e., places where a quantifier matches too much. For example, the /.*/ intended to skip just the formatting HTML might instead skip the formatting HTML, three entries, and another piece of formatting HTML. In such situations, it's typically because either the thing being quantified was too general (e.g., instead of the dot, we should have had /[^<]/ to avoid matching HTML), or because the literal text after the quantifier wasn't enough to identify the stop point. For example, /<font/ instead of /<font size=-1/ might make a minimal quantifier stop too soon (at the first font tag, instead of the correct font tag) or a greedy quantifier match too much (at the last font tag, instead of the last size=-1 font tag).

If the regular expression you've created isn't matching at all, repeatedly take the last chunk off the regular expression until it does match. The last bit you removed was causing the match to fail, so inspect it to see why.

For example, let's find out why this isn't matching:

```
$text = qq(<a href="file.html"><b>Dog</b></a>Woof\nWoof</p>);
($file, $title, $summary) =
    $text =~ m{<a href="(.*?)"><b>(.*?)</b></a>\s*(.*?)</p>};
```

Taking the last piece off yields this regular expression:

```
<a href="(.*?)"><b>(.*?)</b></a>\s*(.*?)
```

This matches. This tells us that /</p>/ wasn't being found after /(.*?)/ matched. We're not going to see much if we print $3 at this point, as we're matching minimally, and without something forcing the quantifier to match more than 0, it'll be happy to match nothing.

The way around this is to remove the minimal matching—how much could it match?

```
<a href="(.*?)"><b>(.*?)</b></a>\s*(.*)
```

Printing $3 now show us that /.*/ is matching only Woof, instead of Woof\nWoof. The newline should be the giveaway—we need to add the /s modifier to the original regular expression (be sure to change the /.*/ back to /.*?/!) to ensure that summaries with embedded newlines are correctly located.

When Regular Expressions Aren't Enough

Regular expressions are powerful, but they can't describe everything. In particular, nested structures (for example, lists containing lists, with any amount of nesting possible) and comments are tricky. While you can use regular expressions to extract the components of the HTML and then attempt to keep track of whether you're in a comment or to which nested array you're adding elements, these types of programs rapidly balloon in complexity and become maintenance nightmares.

The best thing to do in these situations is to use a real HTML tokenizer or parser such as HTML::Parser, HTML::TokeParser, and HTML::TreeBuilder (all demonstrated in the next chapter), and forego your regular expressions.

Example: Extracting Links from a Bookmark File

Suppose we want to delegate to a Perl program the task of checking URLs in my Netscape bookmark file. I'm told that this isn't the same format as is used in newer Netscapes. But, antiquarian that I am, I still use Netscape 4.76, and this is what the file looks like:

```
<!DOCTYPE NETSCAPE-Bookmark-file-1>
<!-- This is an automatically generated file.
It will be read and overwritten.
Do Not Edit! -->
<TITLE>Bookmarks for Sean M. Burke</TITLE>
<H1>Bookmarks for Sean M. Burke</H1>

<DL><p>
    <DT><H3 ADD_DATE="911669103">Personal Toolbar Folder</H3>
    <DL><p>
        <DT><A HREF="http://libros.unm.edu/" ADD_DATE="908672224" ...
```

```
<DT><A HREF="http://www.melvyl.ucop.edu/" ADD_DATE="900184542" ...
<DT><A HREF="http://www.guardian.co.uk/" ADD_DATE="935897798" ...
<DT><A HREF="http://www.booktv.org/schedule/" ADD_DATE="935897798" ...
<DT><A HREF="http://www.suck.com/" ADD_DATE="942604862" ...
...and so on...
```

There are three important things we should note here:

- Each bookmark item is on a line of its own. This means we can use the handy Perl idioms for line-at-a-time processing such as while(<IN>) {...} or @lines = <IN>.

- Every URL is absolute. There are no relative URLs such as HREF="../stuff.html". That means we don't have to bother with making URLs absolute (not yet, at least).

- The only thing we want from this file is the URL in the HREF="...*url*..." part of the line—and if there is no HREF on the line, we can ignore this line. This practically begs us to use a Perl regexp!

So we scan the file one line at a time, find URLs in lines that have a HREF="...*url*..." in them, then check those URLs. Example 6-4 shows such a program.

Example 6-4. bookmark-checker

```perl
#!/usr/bin/perl -w
# bookmark-checker - check URLs in Netscape bookmark file

use strict;
use LWP;
my $browser;
my $bmk_file = $ARGV[0]
  || 'c:/Program Files/Netscape/users/sburke/bookmark.htm';
open(BMK, "<$bmk_file") or die "Can't read-open $bmk_file: $!";

while (<BMK>) {
  check_url($1) if m/ HREF="([^"\s]+)" /;
}

print "# Done after ", time - $^T, "s\n";
exit;

my %seen;  # for tracking which URLs we've already checked

sub check_url {
  # Try to fetch the page and report failure if it can't be found
  # This routine even specially reports if the URL has changed
  # to be on a different host.

  my $url = URI->new( $_[0] )->canonical;

  # Skip mailto: links, and in fact anything not http:...
  return unless $url->scheme() eq 'http';

  # Kill anything like '#staff' in 'http://luddites.int/them.txt#staff'
  $url->fragment(undef);
```

Example 6-4. bookmark-checker (continued)

```perl
  # Kill anything like the currently quite useless but
  # occasionally occurring 'jschmo@' in
  #  'http://jschmo@luddites.int/them.txt'
  # (It's useless because it doesn't actually show up
  # in the request to the server in any way.)
  $url->userinfo(undef);

  return if $seen{$url};  # silently skip duplicates
  $seen{$url} = 1;

  init_browser() unless $browser;
  my $response = $browser->head($url);
  my $found = URI->new( $response->request->url )->canonical;
  $seen{$found} = 1; # so we don't check it later.

  # If the server complains that it doesn't understand "HEAD",
  #  (405 is "Method Not Allowed"), then retry it with "GET":
  $response = $browser->get($found) if $response->code == 405;

  if($found ne $url) {
    if($response->is_success) {
      # Report the move, only if it's a very different URL.
      # That is, different schemes, or different hosts.
      if(
        $found->scheme ne $url->scheme
       or
        lc( $found->can('host') ? $found->host : '' )
         ne
        lc(    $url->can('host') ?    $url->host : '' )
      ) {
        print "MOVED: $url\n    -> $found\n",
      }

    } else {
      print "MOVED: $url\n    -> $found\n",
        "        but that new URL is bad: ",
        $response->status_line( ), "\n"
    }
  } elsif($response->is_success) {
    print "## okay: $url\n";
  } else {
    print "$url is bad! ", $response->status_line, "\n";
  }
  return;
}

sub init_browser {
  $browser = LWP::UserAgent->new;

  # Speak only HTTP - no mailto or FTP or anything.
  $browser->protocols_allowed( [ 'http' ] );
```

Example 6-4. bookmark-checker (continued)

```
  # And any other initialization we might need to do.

  return $browser;
}
```

And for this rigidly formatted input file, our line-at-a-time regexp-based approach works just fine; our simple loop:

```
    while (<BMK>) { check_url($1) if m/ HREF="([^"\s]+)" / }
```

really does catch every URL in my Netscape bookmark file.

Example: Extracting Links
from Arbitrary HTML

Suppose that the links we want to check are in a remote HTML file that's not quite as rigidly formatted as my local bookmark file. Suppose, in fact, that a representative section looks like this:

```
    <p>Dear Diary,
    <br>I was listening to <a href="http://www.freshair.com">Fresh
    Air</a> the other day and they had <a href
    ="http://www.cs.Helsinki.FI/u/torvalds/">Linus Torvalds</a> on,
    and he was going on about how he wrote some kinda
    <a href="http://www.linux.org/">program</a> or something.  If
    he's so smart, why didn't he write something useful, like <a
    href="why_I_love_tetris.html">Tetris</a> or <a href="../minesweeper_hints/"
    >Minesweeper</a>, huh?
```

In the case of the bookmarks, we noted that links were each alone on a line, all absolute, and each capturable with m/ HREF="([^"\s]+)" /. But none of those things are true here! Some links (such as href="why_I_love_tetris.html") are relative, some lines have more than one link in them, and one link even has a newline between its href attribute name and its ="..." attribute value.

Regexps are still usable, though—it's just a matter of applying them to a whole document (instead of to individual lines) and also making the regexp a bit more permissive:

```
    while ( $document =~ m/\s+href\s*=\s*"([^"\s]+)"/gi ) {
      my $url = $1;
      ...
    }
```

(The /g modifier ("g" originally for "globally") on the regexp tries to match the pattern as many times as it can, each time picking up where the last match left off.)

Example 6-5 shows this basic idea fleshed out to include support for fetching a remote document, matching each link in it, making each absolute, and calling a checker routine (currently a placeholder) on it.

Example 6-5. diary-link-checker

```perl
#!/usr/bin/perl -w
# diary-link-checker - check links from diary page

use strict;
use LWP;

my $doc_url = "http://chichi.diaries.int/stuff/diary.html";
my $document;
my $browser;
init_browser();

{  # Get the page whose links we want to check:
  my $response = $browser->get($doc_url);
  die "Couldn't get $doc_url: ", $resp->status_line
    unless $response->is_success;
  $document = $response->content;
  $doc_url = $response->request->base;
  # In case we need to resolve relative URLs later
}

while ($document =~ m/href\s*=\s*"([^"\s]+)"/gi) {
  my $absolute_url = absolutize($1, $doc_url);
  check_url($absolute_url);
}

sub absolutize {
  my($url, $base) = @_;
  use URI;
  return URI->new_abs($url, $base)->canonical;
}

sub init_browser {
  $browser = LWP::UserAgent->new;
  # ...And any other initialization we might need to do...
  return $browser;
}

sub check_url {
  # A temporary placeholder...
  print "I should check $_[0]\n";
}
```

When run, this prints:

```
I should check http://www.freshair.com/
I should check http://www.cs.Helsinki.FI/u/torvalds/
I should check http://www.linux.org/
I should check http://chichi.diaries.int/stuff/why_I_love_tetris.html
I should check http://chichi.diaries.int/minesweeper_hints/
```

So our while (*regexp*) loop is indeed successfully matching all five links in the document. (Note that our absolutize routine is correctly making the URLs absolute, as with turning *why_I_love_tetris.html* into *http://chichi.diaries.int/stuff/why_I_love_tetris.html* and *../minesweeper_hints/* into *http://chichi.diaries.int/minesweeper_hints/* by using the URI class that we explained in Chapter 4.)

Now that we're satisfied that our program is matching and absolutizing links correctly, we can drop in the check_url routine from the Example 6-4, and it will actually check the URLs that the our placeholder check_url routine promised we'd check.

Example: Extracting Temperatures from Weather Underground

The Weather Underground web site (*http://www.wunderground.com*) is a great source of meteorological information. Let's write a program to tell us which of the two O'Reilly offices, Cambridge and Sebastopol, is warmer and by how many degrees.

First, we fetch the pages with the temperatures. A quick look around the Weather Underground site indicates that the best way to get the temperature for a place is to fetch a URL like:

```
http://www.wunderground.com/cgi-bin/findweather/getForecast?query=95472
```

95472 is the Zip Code for the Sebastopol office, while 02140 is the Zip Code for the Cambridge office. The program begins by fetching those pages:

```
#!/usr/bin/perl -w

use strict;
use LWP::Simple;

my $url = "http://www.wunderground.com/cgi-bin/findweather/getForecast?query=";
my $ca = get("${url}95472"); # Sebastopol, California
my $ma = get("${url}02140"); # Cambridge, Massachusetts
```

Next, we need to extract the temperature from the HTML. Viewing the source to one of the pages reveals the relevant portion as:

```
<tr ><td>Temperature</td>
<td><b>52&#176;</b> F</td></tr>
```

Because we need to extract the temperature from multiple pages, we define a subroutine that takes the HTML string and returns the temperature:

```
sub current_temp {
  local $_ = shift;
  m{<tr ><td>Temperature</td>\s+<td><b>(\d+)} || die "No temp data?";
  return $1;
}
```

Now all that's left to do is extract the temperatures and display the message:

```
my $ca_temp = current_temp($ca);
my $ma_temp = current_temp($ma);
my $diff = $ca_temp - $ma_temp;

print $diff > 0 ? "California" : "Massachusetts";
print " is warmer by ", abs($diff), " degrees F.\n";
```

When you run the program, you see something like:

```
% ora-temps
California is warmer by 21 degrees F.
```

The complete program is shown in Example 6-6.

Example 6-6. ora-temps

```perl
#!/usr/bin/perl -w

use strict;
use LWP::Simple;

my $url = "http://www.wunderground.com/cgi-bin/findweather/getForecast?"
        . "query=";
my $ca = get("${url}95472"); # Sebastopol, California
my $ma = get("${url}02140"); # Cambridge, Massachusetts

my $ca_temp = current_temp($ca);
my $ma_temp = current_temp($ma);
my $diff = $ca_temp - $ma_temp;

print $diff > 0 ? "California" : "Massachusetts";
print " is warmer by ", abs($diff), " degrees F.\n";

sub current_temp {
  local $_ = shift;
  m{<tr ><td>Temperature</td>\s+<td><b>(\d+)} || die "No temp data?";
  return $1;
}
```

## CHAPTER 7

HTML Processing with Tokens

Regular expressions are powerful, but they're a painfully low-level way of dealing with HTML. You're forced to worry about spaces and newlines, single and double quotes, HTML comments, and a lot more. The next step up from a regular expression is an HTML tokenizer. In this chapter, we'll use HTML::TokeParser to extract information from HTML files. Using these techniques, you can extract information from any HTML file, and never again have to worry about character-level trivia of HTML markup.

HTML as Tokens

Your experience with HTML code probably involves seeing raw text such as this:

```
<p>Dear Diary,
<br>I'm gonna be a superstar, because I'm learning to play
the <a href="http://MyBalalaika.com">balalaika</a> &amp; the <a
href='http://MyBazouki.com'>bazouki</a>!!!
```

The HTML::TokeParser module divides the HTML into units called *tokens*, which means units of parsing. The above source code is parsed as this series of tokens:

start-tag token
> p with no attributes

text token
> Dear Diary,\n

start-tag token
> br with no attributes

text token
> I'm gonna be a superstar, because I'm learning to play\nthe

start-tag token
> a, with attribute href whose value is http://MyBalalaika.com

text token
> balalaika

end-tag token

> a

text token

> & the , which means & the

start-tag token

> a, with attribute href equals http://MyBazouki.com

text token

> bazouki

end-tag token

> a

text token

> !!!\n

This representation of things is more abstract, focusing on markup concepts and not individual characters. So whereas the two <a> tags have different types of quotes around their attribute values in the raw HTML, as tokens each has a start-tag of type a, with an href attribute of a particular value. A program that extracts information by working with a stream of tokens doesn't have to worry about the idiosyncrasies of entity encoding, whitespace, quotes, and trying to work out where a tag ends.

Basic HTML::TokeParser Use

The HTML::TokeParser module is a class for accessing HTML as tokens. An HTML::TokeParser object gives you one token at a time, much as a filehandle gives you one line at a time from a file. The HTML can be tokenized from a file or string. The tokenizer decodes entities in attributes, but not entities in text.

Create a token stream object using one of these two constructors:

```
my $stream = HTML::TokeParser->new($filename)
  || die "Couldn't read HTML file $filename: $!";
```

or:

```
my $stream = HTML::TokeParser->new( \$string_of_html );
```

Once you have that stream object, you get the next token by calling:

```
my $token = $stream->get_token();
```

The $token variable then holds an array reference, or undef if there's nothing left in the stream's file or string. This code processes every token in a document:

```
my $stream = HTML::TokeParser->new($filename)
  || die "Couldn't read HTML file $filename: $!";

while(my $token = $stream->get_token) {
  # ... consider $token ...
}
```

The $token can have one of six kinds of values, distinguished first by the value of $token->[0], as shown in Table 7-1.

Table 7-1. Token types

Token	Values
Start-tag	["S", $tag, $attribute_hashref, $attribute_order_arrayref, $source]
End-tag	["E", $tag, $source]
Text	["T", $text, $should_not_decode]
Comment	["C", $source]
Declaration	["D", $source]
Processing instruction	["PI", $content, $source]

Start-Tag Tokens

If $token->[0] is "S", the token represents a start-tag:

```
["S",  $tag, $attribute_hash, $attribute_order_arrayref, $source]
```

The components of this token are:

$tag
> The tag name, in lowercase.

$attribute_hashref
> A reference to a hash encoding the attributes of this tag. The (lowercase) attribute names are the keys of the hash.

$attribute_order_arrayref
> A reference to an array of (lowercase) attribute names, in case you need to access elements in order.

$source
> The original HTML for this token.

The first three values are the most interesting ones, for most purposes.

For example, parsing this HTML:

```
<IMG SRC="kirk.jpg" alt="Shatner in r&ocirc;le of Kirk" WIDTH=352 height=522>
```

gives this token:

```
[
  'S',
  'img',
  { 'alt' => 'Shatner in rôle of Kirk',
    'height' => '522', 'src' => 'kirk.jpg', 'width' => '352'
  },
  [ 'src', 'alt', 'width', 'height' ],
  '<IMG SRC="kirk.jpg" alt="Shatner in r&ocirc;le of Kirk" WIDTH=352 height=522>'
]
```

Notice that the tag and attribute names have been lowercased, and the ô entity decoded within the alt attribute.

End-Tag Tokens

When $token->[0] is "E", the token represents an end-tag:

```
[ "E", $tag, $source ]
```

The components of this tag are:

$tag
> The lowercase name of the tag being closed.

$source
> The original HTML for this token.

Parsing this HTML:

```
</A>
```

gives this token:

```
[ 'E', 'a', '</A>' ]
```

Text Tokens

When $token->[0] is "T", the token represents text:

```
["T", $text, $should_not_decode]
```

The elements of this array are:

$text
> The text, which may have entities.

$should_not_decode
> A Boolean value true indicating that you should not decode the entities in $text.

Tokenizing this HTML:

```
&amp; the
```

gives this token:

```
[ 'T',
  ' &amp; the',
  ''
]
```

The empty string is a false value, indicating that there's nothing stopping us from decoding $text with decode_entities( ) from HTML::Entities:

```
decode_entities($token->[1]) if $token->[2];
```

Text inside <script>, <style>, <xmp>, <listing>, and <plaintext> tags is not supposed to be entity-decoded. It is for such text that $should_not_decode is true.

Comment Tokens

When $token->[0] is "C", you have a comment token:

```
["C", $source]
```

The $source component of the token holds the original HTML of the comment. Most programs that process HTML simply ignore comments.

Parsing this HTML

```
<!-- Shatner's best known r&ocirc;le -->
```

gives us this $token value:

```
[ 'C',                              #0: we're a comment
  '<!-- Shatner's best known r&ocirc;le -->'  #1: source
]
```

Markup Declaration Tokens

When $token->[0] is "D", you have a declaration token:

```
["D", $source]
```

The $source element of the array is the HTML of the declaration. Declarations rarely occur in HTML, and when they do, they are rarely of any interest. Almost all programs that process HTML ignore declarations.

This HTML:

```
<!DOCTYPE HTML PUBLIC "-//W3C//DTD HTML 3.2 Final//EN">
```

gives this token:

```
[ 'D',
  '<!DOCTYPE HTML PUBLIC "-//W3C//DTD HTML 3.2 Final//EN">'
]
```

Processing Instruction Tokens

When $token->[0] is "PI", the token represents a processing instruction:

```
[ "PI", $instruction, $source ]
```

The components are:

$instruction
> The processing instruction stripped of initial <? and trailing >.

$source
> The original HTML for the processing instruction.

A processing instruction is an SGML construct rarely used in HTML. Most programs extracting information from HTML ignore processing instructions. If you do handle processing instructions, be warned that in SGML (and thus HTML) a processing instruction ends with a greater-than (>), but in XML (and thus XHTML), a processing instruction ends with a question mark and a greater-than sign (?>).

Tokenizing:

```
<?subliminal message>
```

gives:

```
[ 'PI', 'subliminal message', '<?subliminal message>' ]
```

Individual Tokens

Now that you know the composition of the various types of tokens, let's see how to use HTML::TokeParser to write useful programs. Many problems are quite simple and require only one token at a time. Programs to solve these problems consist of a loop over all the tokens, with an if statement in the body of the loop identifying the interesting parts of the HTML:

```
use HTML::TokeParser;
my $stream = HTML::TokeParser->new($filename)
  || die "Couldn't read HTML file $filename: $!";
# For a string: HTML::TokeParser->new( \$string_of_html );

while (my $token = $stream->get_token) {
   if ($token->[0] eq 'T') { # text
     # process the text in $text->[1]

   } elsif ($token->[0] eq 'S') { # start-tag
     my($tagname, $attr) = @$token[1,2];
     # consider this start-tag...

   } elsif ($token->[0] eq 'E') {
     my $tagname = $token->[1];
     # consider this end-tag
   }

   # ignoring comments, declarations, and PIs
}
```

Checking Image Tags

Example 7-1 complains about any img tags in a document that are missing alt, height, or width attributes:

Example 7-1. Check <img> tags

```
while(my $token = $stream->get_token) {
  if($token->[0] eq 'S' and $token->[1] eq 'img') {
    my $i = $token->[2]; # attributes of this img tag
```

Example 7-1. Check <img> tags (continued)

```
    my @lack = grep !exists $i->{$_}, qw(alt height width);
    print "Missing for ", $i->{'src'} || "????", ": @lack\n" if @lack;
  }
}
```

When run on an HTML stream (whether from a file or a string), this outputs:

```
Missing for liza.jpg: height width
Missing for aimee.jpg: alt
Missing for laurie.jpg: alt height width
```

Identifying images has many applications: making HEAD requests to ensure the URLs are valid, or making a GET request to fetch the image and using Image::Size from CPAN to check or insert the height and width attributes.

HTML Filters

A similar while loop can use HTML::TokeParser as a simple code filter. You just pass through the $source from each token you don't mean to alter. Here's one that passes through every tag that it sees (by just printing its source as HTML::TokeParser passes it in), except for img start-tags, which get replaced with the content of their alt attributes:

```
while (my $token = $stream->get_token) {
  if ($token->[0] eq 'S') {
    if ($token->[1] eq 'img') {
      print $token->[2]{'alt'} || '';
    } else {
      print $token->[4];
    }
  }
  elsif($token->[0] eq 'E' ) { print $token->[2] }
  elsif($token->[0] eq 'T' ) { print $token->[1] }
  elsif($token->[0] eq 'C' ) { print $token->[1] }
  elsif($token->[0] eq 'D' ) { print $token->[1] }
  elsif($token->[0] eq 'PI') { print $token->[2] }
}
```

So, for example, a document consisting just of this:

```
<!-- new entry -->
<p>Dear Diary,
<br>This is me &amp; my balalaika, at BalalaikaCon 1998:
<img src="mybc1998.jpg" src="BC1998! WHOOO!"> Rock on!</p>
```

is then spat out as this:

```
<!-- new entry -->
<p>Dear Diary,
<br>This is me &amp; my balalaika, at BalalaikaCon 1998:
BC1998! WHOOO! Rock on!</p>
```

Token Sequences

Some problems cannot be solved with a single-token approach. Often you need to scan for a sequence of tokens. For example in Chapter 4, we extracted the Amazon sales rank from HTML like this:

```
<b>Amazon.com Sales Rank: </b> 4,070 </font><br>
```

Here we're looking for the text Amazon.com Sales Rank: , an end-tag for b, and the next token as a text token with the sales rank. To solve this, we need to check the next few tokens while being able to put them back if they're not what we expect.

To put tokens back into the stream, use the unget_token( ) method:

```
$stream->unget_token(@next);
```

The tokens stored in @next will be returned to the stream. For example, to solve our Amazon problem:

```
while (my $token = $stream->get_token()) {
  if ($token->[0] eq 'T' and
    $token->[1] eq 'Amazon.com Sales Rank: ') {
    my @next;
    push @next, $stream->get_token();
    my $found = 0;
    if ($next[0][0] eq 'E' and $next[0][1] eq 'b') {
      push @next, $stream->get_token();
      if ($next[1][0] eq 'T') {
        $sales_rank = $next[1][1];
        $found = 1;
      }
    }
    $stream->unget_token(@next) unless $found;
  }
}
```

If it's the text we're looking for, we cautiously explore the next tokens. If the next one is a </b> end-tag, check the next token to ensure that it's text. If it is, then that's the sales rank. If any of the tests fail, put the tokens back on the stream and go back to processing.

Example: BBC Headlines

Suppose, for example, that your morning ritual is to have the help come and wake you at about 11 a.m. as they bring two serving trays to your bed. On one tray there's a croissant, some *pain au chocolat*, and of course some *café au lait*, and on the other tray, your laptop with a browser window already open on each story from BBC News's front page (*http://news.bbc.co.uk*). However, the help have been getting mixed up lately and opening the stories on *The Guardian*'s web site, and that's a bit awkward, since clearly *The Guardian* is an after-lunch paper. You'd say something about it, but one doesn't want to make a scene, so you just decide to write a program that the help can run on the laptop to find all the BBC story URLs.

So you look at the source of *http://news.bbc.co.uk* and discover that each headline link is wrapped in one of two kinds of code. There are lots of headlines in code such as these:

```
<B CLASS="h3"><A href="/hi/english/business/newsid_1576000/1576290.stm">Bank
of England mulls rate cut</A></B><BR>

<B CLASS="h3"><A href="/hi/english/uk_politics/newsid_1576000/1576541.stm">Euro
battle revived by Blair speech</A></B><BR>
```

and also some headlines in code like this:

```
<A href="/hi/english/business/newsid_1576000/1576636.stm">
  <B class="h2"> Swissair shares wiped out</B><BR>
</A>

<A href="/hi/english/world/middle_east/newsid_1576000/1576113.stm">
  <B class="h1">Mid-East blow to US anti-terror drive</B><BR>
</A>
```

(Note that the a start-tag's class value can be h1 or h2.)

Studying this, you realize that this is how you find the story URLs:

- Every time there's a B start-tag with class value of h3, and then an A start-tag with an href value, save that href.
- Every time there's an A start-tag with an href value, a text token consisting of just whitespace, and then a B start-tag with a class value of h1 or h2, save the first token's href value.

Translating the Problem into Code

We can take some shortcuts when translating this into `$stream->unget_token($token)` code. The following HTML is typical:

```
<B CLASS="h3">Top Stories</B><BR>
...
<B CLASS="h3"><A href="/hi/english/business/newsid_1576000/1576290.stm">Bank
of England mulls rate cut</A></B><BR>
```

When we see the first B-h3 start-tag token, we think it might be the start of a B-h3-A-href pattern. So we get another token and see if it's an A-href token. It's not (it's the text token Top Stories), so we put it back into the stream (useful in case some other pattern we're looking for involves that being the first token), and we keep looping. Later, we see another B-h3, we get another token, and we inspect it to see if it's an A-href token. This time it is, so we process its href value and resume looping. There's no reason for us to put that a-href back, so the next iteration of the loop will resume with the next token being Bank of England mulls rate cut.

```
sub scan_bbc_stream {
  my($stream, $docbase) = @_;

  Token:
  while(my $token = $stream->get_token) {

    if ($token->[0] eq 'S'  and  $token->[1] eq 'b'  and
        ($token->[2]{'class'} || '') eq 'h3') {
      # The href we want is in the NEXT token... probably.
      # Like: <B CLASS="h3"><A href="magic_url_here">

      my(@next) = ($stream->get_token);

      if ($next[0] and $next[0][0] eq 'S'  and  $next[0][1] eq 'a'  and
          defined $next[0][2]{'href'} ) {
        # We found <a href="...">!  This rule matches!
        print URI->new_abs($next[0][2]{'href'}, $docbase), "\n";
        next Token;
      }
      # We get here only if we've given up on this rule:
      $stream->unget_token(@next);
    }

    # fall thru to subsequent rules here...

  }
  return;
}
```

The general form of the rule above is this: if the current token looks promising, pull
off a token and see if that looks promising too. If, at any point, we see an unex-
pected token or hit the end of the stream, we restore what we've pulled off (held in
the temporary array @next), and continue to try other rules. But if all the expecta-
tions in this rule are met, we make it to the part that processes this bunch of tokens
(here it's just a single line, which prints the URL), and then call next Token to start
another iteration of this loop *without* restoring the tokens that have matched this
pattern. (If you are disturbed by this use of a named block and lasting and nexting
around, consider that this could be written as a giant if/else statement at the risk of
potentially greater damage to what's left of your sanity.)

Each such rule, then, can pull from the stream however many tokens it needs to
either match or reject the pattern it's after. Either it matches and starts another iteration of this loop, or it restores the stream to exactly the way it was before this rule
started pulling from it. This business of a temporary @next list may seem like overkill
when we only have to look one token ahead, only ever looking at $next[0]. How-
ever, the if block for the next pattern (which requires looking two tokens ahead)
shows how the same framework can be accommodating:

```
# Add this right after the first if-block ends.
if($token->[0] eq 'S'  and  $token->[1] eq 'a'  and
    defined $token->[2]{'href'} ) {
  # Like: <A href="magic_url_here"> <B class="h2">
```

```
my(@next) = ($stream->get_token);
if ($next[0] and $next[0][0] eq 'T' and $next[0][1] =~ m/^\s+/s ) {
  # We found whitespace.
  push @next, $stream->get_token;
  if ($next[1] and $next[1][0] eq 'S'  and  $next[1][1] eq 'b'  and
      ($next[1][2]{'class'} || '') =~ m/^h[12]$/s ) {
    # We found <b class="h2">!  This rule matches!
    print URI->new_abs( $token->[2]{'href'}, $docbase ), "\n";
    next Token;
  }
}
# We get here only if we've given up on this rule:
$stream->unget_token(@next);
}
```

Bundling into a Program

With all that wrapped up in a pure function scan_bbc_stream( ), we can test it by first saving the contents of *http://news.bbc.co.uk* locally as *bbc.html* (which we probably already did to scrutinize its source code and figure out what HTML patterns surround headlines), and then calling this:

```
use strict;
use HTML::TokeParser;
use URI;

scan_bbc_stream(
  HTML::TokeParser->new('bbc.html') || die($!),
  'http://news.bbc.co.uk/' # base URL
);
```

When run, this merrily scans the local copy and say:

```
http://news.bbc.co.uk/hi/english/world/middle_east/newsid_1576000/1576113.stm
http://news.bbc.co.uk/hi/english/world/south_asia/newsid_1576000/1576186.stm
http://news.bbc.co.uk/hi/english/uk_politics/newsid_1576000/1576051.stm
http://news.bbc.co.uk/hi/english/uk/newsid_1576000/1576379.stm
http://news.bbc.co.uk/hi/english/business/newsid_1576000/1576636.stm
http://news.bbc.co.uk/sport/hi/english/in_depth/2001/england_in_zimbabwe/newsid_
1574000/1574824.stm
http://news.bbc.co.uk/hi/english/business/newsid_1576000/1576546.stm
http://news.bbc.co.uk/hi/english/uk/newsid_1576000/1576313.stm
http://news.bbc.co.uk/hi/english/uk_politics/newsid_1576000/1576541.stm
http://news.bbc.co.uk/hi/english/business/newsid_1576000/1576290.stm
http://news.bbc.co.uk/hi/english/entertainment/music/newsid_1576000/1576599.stm
http://news.bbc.co.uk/hi/english/sci/tech/newsid_1574000/1574048.stm
http://news.bbc.co.uk/hi/english/health/newsid_1576000/1576776.stm
http://news.bbc.co.uk/hi/english/in_depth/uk_politics/2001/conferences_2001/labour/
newsid_1576000/1576086.stm
```

At least that's what the program said once I got scan_bbc_stream( ) in its final working state shown above. As I was writing it and testing bits of it, I could run and re-run the program, scanning the same local file. Then once it's working on the local file (or files, depending on how many test cases you have), you can write the routine that gets what's at a URL, makes a stream pointing to its content, and runs a given scanner routine (such as scan_bbc_stream( )) on it:

```
my $browser;
BEGIN {
  use LWP::UserAgent;
  $browser = LWP::UserAgent->new;
  # and any other $browser initialization code here
}

sub url_scan {
  my($scanner, $url) = @_;
  die "What scanner function?" unless $scanner and ref($scanner) eq 'CODE';
  die "What URL?" unless $url;
  my $resp = $browser->get( $url );
  die "Error getting $url: ", $resp->status_line
    unless $resp->is_success;
  die "It's not HTML, it's ", $resp->content_type
    unless $resp->content_type eq 'text/html';

  my $stream = HTML::TokeParser->new( $resp->content_ref )
    || die "Couldn't make a stream from $url\'s content!?";
  # new( ) on a string wants a reference, and so that's what
  #  we give it!  HTTP::Response objects just happen to
  #  offer a method that returns a reference to the content.
  $scanner->($stream, $resp->base);
}
```

If you thought the contents of $url could be very large, you could save the contents to a temporary file, and start the stream off with HTML::TokeParser->new($tempfile). With the above url_scan( ), to retrieve the BBC main page and scan it, you need only replace our test statement that scans the input stream, with this:

```
url_scan(\&scan_bbc_stream, 'http://news.bbc.co.uk/');
```

And then the program outputs the URLs from the live BBC main page (or will die with an error message if it can't get it). To actually complete the task of getting the printed URLs to each open a new browser instance, well, this depends on your browser and OS, but for my MS Windows laptop and Netscape, this Perl program will do it:

```
my $ns = "c:\\program files\\netscape\\communicator\\program\\netscape.exe";
die "$ns doesn't exist" unless -e $ns;
die "$ns isn't executable" unless -x $ns;
while (<>) { chomp; m/\S/ and system($ns, $_) and die $!; }
```

This is then called as:

```
C:\perlstuff> perl bbc_urls.pl | perl urls2ns.pl
```

Under Unix, the correct system( ) command is:

```
system("netscape '$url' &")
```

More HTML::TokeParser Methods

Example 7-1 illustrates that often you aren't interested in every kind of token in a stream, but care only about tokens of a certain kind. The HTML::TokeParser interface supports this with three methods, get_tag( ), get_text( ), and get_trimmed_text( ) that do something other than simply get the next token.

```
$text_string = $stream->get_text( );
```
    If the next token is text, return its value.

```
$text_string = $stream->get_text('foo');
```
    Return all text up to the next foo start-tag.

```
$text_string = $stream->get_text('/bar');
```
    Return all text up to the next /bar end-tag.

```
$text = $stream->get_trimmed_text( );
$text = $stream->get_trimmed_text('foo');
$text = $stream->get_trimmed_text('/bar');
```
    Like get_text( ) calls, except with initial and final whitespace removed, and all other whitespace collapsed.

```
$tag_ref = $stream->get_tag( );
```
    Return the next start-tag or end-tag token.

```
$tag_ref = $stream->get_tag('foo', '/bar', 'baz');
```
    Return the next foo start-tag, /bar end-tag, or baz start-tag.

We will explain these methods in detail in the following sections.

The get_text( ) Method

The get_text( ) syntax is:

```
$text_string = $stream->get_text( );
```

If $stream's next token is text, this gets it, resolves any entities in it, and returns its string value. Otherwise, this returns an empty string.

For example, if you are parsing this snippet:

```
<h1 lang='en-GB'>Shatner Reprises Kirk R&ocirc;le</h1>
```

and have just parsed the token for h1, $stream->get_text( ) returns "Shatner Reprises Kirk Rôle." If you call it again (and again and again), it will return the empty string, because the next token waiting is not a text token but an h1 end-tag token.

The get_text( ) Method with Parameters

The syntax for get_text( ) with parameters is:

```
$text_string = $stream->get_text('foo');
$text_string = $stream->get_text('/bar');
```

Specifying a foo or /bar parameter changes the meaning of get_text( ). If you specify a tag, you get all the text up to the next time that tag occurs (or until the end of the file, if that tag never occurs).

For however many text tokens are found, their text values are taken, entity sequences are resolved, and they are combined and returned. (All the other sorts of tokens seen along the way are just ignored.)

Note that the tag name that you specify (whether foo or /bar) must be in lowercase.

This sounds complex, but it works out well in real use. For example, imagine you've got this snippet:

```
<h1 lang='en-GB'>Star of <cite>Star Trek</cite> in New R&ocirc;le</h1>
    <cite>American Psycho II</cite> in Production.
    <!-- I'm not making this up, folks. -->
    <br>Shatner to play FBI profiler.
```

and that you've just parsed the token for h1. Calling $stream->get_text( ), simply gets Star of . If, however, the task you're performing is the extraction of the text content of <h1> elements, then what's called for is:

```
$stream->get_text('/h1')
```

This returns Star of Star Trek in New Rôle.

Calling:

```
$stream->get_text('br')
```

returns:

```
"Star of Star Trek in New Rôle\n  American Psycho II in Production.\n   \n  "
```

And if you instead called $stream->get_text('schlock') and there is no <schlock...> in the rest of the document, you will get Star of Star Trek in New Rôle\n American Psycho II in Production.\n \n Shatner to play FBI profiler.\n, plus whatever text there is in the rest of the document.

Note that this never introduces whitespace where it's not there in the original. So if you're parsing this:

```
<table>
<tr><th>Height<th>Weight<th>Shoe Size</tr>
<tr><th>6' 2"<th>180lbs<th>n/a</tr>
</table>
```

and you've just parsed the table token, if you call:

```
$stream->get_text('/table')
```

you'll get back:

```
"\nHeightWeightShoe Size\n6' 2"180lbsn/a\n"
```

Not all nontext tokens are ignored by $stream->get_text( ). Some tags receive special treatment: if an img or applet tag is seen, it is treated as if it were a text token; if it has an alt attribute, its value is used as the content of the virtual text token; otherwise, you get just the uppercase tag name in brackets: [IMG] or [APPLET]. For further information on altering and expanding this feature, see perldoc HTML::TokeParser in the documentation for the get_text method, and possibly even the surprisingly short HTML::TokeParser source code.

If you just want to turn off such special treatment for all tags:

```
$stream->{'textify'} = {}
```

This is the only case of the $object->{'thing'} syntax we'll discuss in this book. In no other case does an object require us to access its internals directly like this, because it has no method for more normal access. For more information on this particular syntax, see perldoc perlref's documentation on hash references.

The get_trimmed_text( ) Method

The syntax for the get_trimmed_text( ) method is:

```
$text = $stream->get_trimmed_text( );
$text = $stream->get_trimmed_text('foo');
$text = $stream->get_trimmed_text('/bar');
```

These work exactly like the corresponding $stream->get_text( ) calls, except any leading and trailing whitespace is removed and each sequence of whitespace is replaced with a single space.

Returning to our news example:

```
$html = <<<EOF ;
<h1 lang='en-GB'>Star of <cite>Star Trek</cite> in New R&ocirc;le</h1>
    <cite>American Psycho II</cite> in Production.
    <!-- I'm not making this up, folks. -->
    <br>Shatner to play FBI profiler.
EOF
$stream = HTML::TokeParser->new(\$html);
$stream->get_token( );                      # skip h1
```

The get_text( ) method would return Star of (with the trailing space), while the get_trimmed_text( ) method would return Star of (no trailing space).

Similarly, $stream->get_text('br') would return:

```
"Star of Star Trek in New Rôle\n  American Psycho II in Production.\n  \n  "
```

whereas $stream->get_trimmed_text ('br') would return:

```
"Star of Star Trek in New Rôle American Psycho II in Production."
```

Notice that the medial newline-space-space became a single space, and the final newline-space-space-newline-space-space was simply removed.

The caveat that get_text( ) does not introduce any new whitespace applies also to get_trimmed_text( ). So where, in the last example in get_text( ), you would have gotten \nHeightWeightShoe Size\n6' 2"180lbsn/a\n, get_trimmed_text( ) would return HeightWeightShoe Size 6' 2"180lbsn/a.

The get_tag( ) Method

The syntax for the get_tag( ) method is:

```
$tag_reference = $stream->get_tag( );
```

This returns the next start-tag or end-tag token (throwing out anything else it has to skip to get there), except while get_token( ) would return start and end-tags in these formats:

```
['S', 'hr', {'class','Ginormous'}, ['class'], '<hr class=Ginormous>']
['E', 'p' , '</P>']
```

get_tag( ) instead returns them in this format:

```
['hr', {'class','Ginormous'}, ['class'], '<hr class=Ginormous>']
['/p' , '</P>']
```

That is, the first item has been taken away, and end-tag names start with /.

Start-tags

Unless $tag->[0] begins with a /, the tag represents a start-tag:

```
[$tag, $attribute_hash, $attribute_order_arrayref, $source]
```

The components of this token are:

$tag
> The tag name, in lowercase.

$attribute_hashref
> A reference to a hash encoding the attributes of this tag. The (lowercase) attribute names are the keys of the hash.

$attribute_order_arrayref
> A reference to an array of (lowercase) attribute names, in case you need to access elements in order.

$source
> The original HTML for this token.

The first two values are the most interesting ones, for most purposes.

For example, parsing this HTML with $stream->get_tag( ) :

```
<IMG SRC="kirk.jpg" alt="Shatner in r&ocirc;le of Kirk" WIDTH=352 height=522>
```

gives this tag:

```
[
  'img',
  { 'alt' => 'Shatner in rôle of Kirk',
      'height' => '522', 'src' => 'kirk.jpg', 'width' => '352'
  },
  [ 'src', 'alt', 'width', 'height' ],
  '<IMG SRC="kirk.jpg" alt="Shatner in r&ocirc;le of Kirk" WIDTH=352 height=522>'
]
```

Notice that the tag and attribute names have been lowercased, and the ô entity decoded within the alt attribute.

End-tags

When $tag->[0] does begin with a /, the token represents an end-tag:

```
[ "/$tag", $source ]
```

The components of this tag are:

$tag
: The lowercase name of the tag being closed, with a leading /.

$source
: The original HTML for this token.

Parsing this HTML with $stream->get_tag( ) :

```
</A>
```

gives this tag:

```
[ '/a', '</A>' ]
```

Note that if get_tag( ) reads to the end of the stream and finds no tag tokens, it will return undef.

The get_tag( ) Method with Parameters

Pass a list of tags, to skip through the tokens until a matching tag is found:

```
$tag_reference = $stream->get_tag('foo', '/bar', 'baz');
```

This returns the next start-tag or end-tag that matches any of the strings you provide (throwing out anything it has to skip to get there). Note that the tag name(s) that you provide as parameters must be in lowercase.

If get_tag( ) reads to the end of the stream and finds no matching tag tokens, it will return undef. For example, this code's get_tag( ) looks for img start-tags:

```
while (my $img_tag = $stream->get_tag('img')) {
    my $i = $img_tag->[1];          # attributes of this img tag
    my @lack = grep !exists $i->{$_}, qw(alt height width);
    print "Missing for ", $i->{'src'} || "????", ": @lack\n" if @lack;
}
```

Using Extracted Text

Consider the BBC story-link extractor introduced earlier. Its task was to find links to stories, in either of these kinds of patterns:

```
<B CLASS="h3"><A href="/hi/english/business/newsid_1576000/1576290.stm">Bank
  of England mulls rate cut</A></B><BR>

<A href="/hi/english/world/middle_east/newsid_1576000/1576113.stm">
  <B class="h1">Mid-East blow to US anti-terror drive</B><BR>
</A>
```

and then to isolate the URL, absolutize it, and print it. But it ignores the actual link text, which starts with the next token in the stream. If we want that text, we could get the next token by calling get_text( ):

```
print $stream->get_text( ), "\n  ",
  URI->new_abs($next[0][2]{'href'}, $docbase), "\n";
```

That prints the text like this:

```
Bank
 of England mulls rate cut
  http://news.bbc.co.uk/hi/english/business/newsid_1576000/1576290.stm
```

Note that the newline (and any indenting, if there was any) in the source hasn't been filtered out. For some applications, this makes no difference, but for neatness sake, let's keep headlines to one line each. Changing get_text( ) to get_trimmed_text( ) makes that happen:

```
print $stream->get_trimmed_text( ), "\n  ",
  URI->new_abs($next[0][2]{'href'}, $docbase), "\n";
Bank of England mulls rate cut
  http://news.bbc.co.uk/hi/english/business/newsid_1576000/1576290.stm
```

If the headlines are potentially quite long, we can pass them through Text::Wrap, to wrap them at 72 columns.

There's a trickier problem that occurs often with get_text( ) or get_trimmed_text( ). What if the HTML we're parsing looks like this?

```
<B CLASS="h3"><A href="/unlikely/2468.stm">Shatner &amp; Kunis win Oscars
  for <cite>American Psycho II</cite> r&ocirc;les</A></B><BR>
```

If we've just parsed the b and the a, the next token in the stream is a text token, Shatner & Kunis win Oscars for , that's what get_text( ) returns (get_trimmed_text( ) returns the same thing, minus the final space). But we don't want only the first text token in the headline, we want the whole headline. So instead of defining the headline as "the next text token," we could define it as "all the text tokens until the next </a>." So the program changes to:

```
print $stream->get_trimmed_text('/a'), "\n  ",
  URI->new_abs($next[0][2]{'href'}, $docbase), "\n";
```

That happily prints:

```
Shatner & Kunis win Oscars for American Psycho II rôles
   http://news.bbc.co.uk/unlikely/2468.stm
```

Note that the & and ô entity references were resolved to & and ô. If you were using such a program to spit out something other than plain text (such as XML or RTF), a bare & and/or a bare high-bit character such as ô might be unacceptable, and might need escaping in some fashion. Even if you are emitting plain text, the \xA0 (nonbreaking space) or \xAD (soft hyphen) characters may not be happily interpreted by whatever application you're reading the text with, in which case a tr/\xA0/ / and tr/\xAD//d are called for. If you're taking the output of get_text( ) or get_trimmed_text( ) and sending it to a system that understands only U.S. ASCII, then passing the text through a module such as Text::Unidecode might be called for to turn the ô into an o. This is not really an HTML or HTML::TokeParser matter at all, but is the sort of problem that commonly arises when extracting content from HTML and putting it into other formats.

## CHAPTER 8

Tokenizing Walkthrough

So far, I've been showing examples of data in a particular format, then presenting code for extracting the data out of that format, as an illustration of newly introduced HTML::TokeParser methods. But in real life, you do not proceed tidily from the problem to an immediate and fully formed solution. And ideally, the task of data extraction is simple: identify patterns surrounding the data you're after and write a program that matches those patterns and extracts the embedded data.

In practice, however, you write programs bit by bit and in fits and starts, and with data extraction specifically; this involves a good amount of trying one pattern, finding that its matching is too narrow or too broad, trying to amend it, possibly having to backtrack and try another pattern, and so on. Moreover, even equally effective patterns are not equal; some patterns are easier to capture in code than others, and some patterns are more temporary than others.

In this section, I'll try to make these points by walking though the implementation of a data extraction task, with all alternatives considered, and even a misstep or two.

The Problem

As a starting point, consider the task of harvesting a month's worth of listings and corresponding RealAudio URLs from the web site of the National Public Radio program *Fresh Air*, at *http://freshair.npr.org*. *Fresh Air* is on NPR stations each weekday, and on every show, different guests are interviewed. The show's web site lists which guests appear on the show each day and has links to the RealAudio files for each segment of each show. If your particular weekday schedule doesn't have you listening to *Fresh Air* every night or afternoon, you would find it useful to have a program tell you who had been on in the past month, so you could make a point of listening to the RealAudio files for the guests you find interesting. Such a data-extraction program could be scheduled with crontab to run on the first or second day of every month, to harvest the past month's program data.

Getting the Data

The first step is to figure out what web pages we need to request to get the data in any form. With the BBC extractor, it was just a matter of requesting the single page *http://news.bbc.co.uk*, but here there's no one page that lists all the data we want. Instead, you can view the program description for each show, one day at a time. Moreover, the URL for each such page looks like this, which displays the program info for July 2, 2001:

```
http://freshair.npr.org/dayFA.cfm?todayDate=07%2F02%2F2001
```

It's relatively clear that the format for the bit after the equal sign is the two-digit month, %2F, the two-digit day, %2F, and the four-digit year. (It's even more clear when you consider that %2F is the / character encoded, so that the above means 07/02/2001.) Harvesting all the data is a simple matter of iterating over all the days of the month (or whatever period you want to cover), skipping weekends (because the program listings are only for weekdays), substituting the proper date numbers into that URL. Once each page is harvested, the data can be extracted from it.

Already the outlines of the program's design are becoming clear: there needs to be a loop that harvests the contents of a URL based on each date, then scans the returned content. Scanning the content isn't a distinct enough task that it has to be part of the same block of code as the code that actual harvests the URL. Instead, it can simply be a routine that is given a new stream from which it is expected to extract data. Moreover, that is the hard part of the program, so we might as well do that first (the stuff with date handling and URL interpolation is much less worrisome, and can be put off until last).

So, to figure out the format of the data we want to harvest, consider a typical program listing page in its rendered form in a browser. We establish that this is a "typical" page (shown in Figure 8-1) by flipping through the listings and finding that they all pretty much look like that. (That stands to reason, as the URL tells us that they're being served dynamically, and all through the same *.cfm*—Cold Fusion—file, such that having each day's bit of content poured into a common template is the easy way for the web site's designers to have implemented this.) So we have good reason to hope that whatever code we work up to extract successfully from one typical page, would hopefully work for all of them. The only remarkable difference is in the number of segments per show: here there's two, but there could be one, or four, or even more. Also, the descriptions can be several paragraphs, sometimes much shorter.

What we want to extract here is the link text that says "Monday - July 2, 2001," "Editor and writer Walter Kirn," and "Casting director and actress Joanna Merlin," and for each we also want the link URL as an absolute URL. We don't want the "Listen to" part, since it'd be pointlessly repetitive to have a whole month's worth of listings where every line starts with "Listen to".

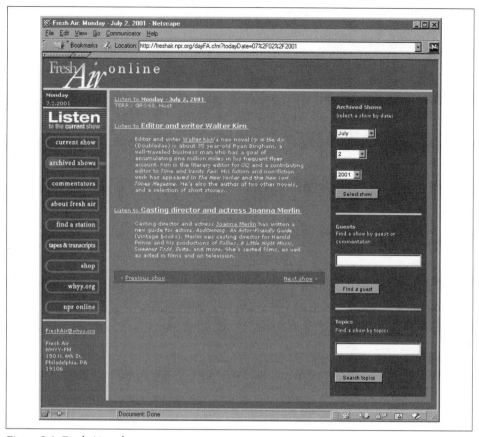

Figure 8-1. Fresh Air web page

Inspecting the HTML

The first step to getting some code working is to save a file locally. This is so you can look at the source in an editor, and secondly so you can initially test your data extractor on that local file. It may take a good deal of hit-and-miss before you get it working right, and there's no point in making each trial run go and get the same page across the network, especially to *Fresh Air*'s occasionally quite busy server. Saving the above URL as *fresh1.html* gives us a 12K file. While there's only about 1K of text shown on the screen, the other 11K are mostly whitespace that indents the HTML, some JavaScript, plus all the table code needed to make the navigation bar on the left and the search form on the right. We can completely ignore all that code and just try to figure out how to extract the "Listen..." links. Sifting through the HTML source, we see that those links are represented with this code (note that most lines begin with at least two spaces):

```
...
<A HREF="http://www.npr.org/ramfiles/fa/20010702.fa.ram">
```

```
  <FONT FACE="Verdana, Charcoal, Sans Serif" COLOR="#FFCC00" SIZE="2">
    Listen to <B>Monday - July 2, 2001</B>
  </FONT>
 </A>

...

 <A HREF="http://www.npr.org/ramfiles/fa/20010702.fa.01.ram">Listen to
 <FONT FACE="Verdana, Charcoal, Sans Serif" COLOR="#ffffff" SIZE="3">
 <B> Editor and writer Walter Kirn                    </B>
 </FONT></A>

<BR>
<FONT FACE="Verdana, Charcoal, Sans Serif" COLOR="#ffffff" SIZE="2">
<BLOCKQUOTE>Editor and writer <A
HREF="http://freshair.npr.org/guestInfoFA.cfm?name=walterkirn">Walter
Kirn</A>'s new novel <I>Up in the Air</I> (Doubleday) is about
...
</BLOCKQUOTE></FONT>
<BR>

 <A HREF="http://www.npr.org/ramfiles/fa/20010702.fa.02.ram">Listen to
 <FONT FACE="Verdana, Charcoal, Sans Serif" COLOR="#ffffff" SIZE="3">
 <B> Casting director and actress Joanna Merlin          </B>
 </FONT></A>

<BR>
<FONT FACE="Verdana, Charcoal, Sans Serif" COLOR="#ffffff" SIZE="2">
<BLOCKQUOTE>Casting director and actress <A
HREF="http://freshair.npr.org/guestInfoFA.cfm?name=joannamerlin">Joanna
Merlin</A> has written a new guide for actors, <I>Auditioning: An
...
</BLOCKQUOTE></FONT>
<BR>
...
```

First Code

Because we want links, let's get links, like this:

```
use strict;
use HTML::TokeParser;
parse_fresh_stream(
  HTML::TokeParser->new('fresh1.html') || die $!
);

sub parse_fresh_stream {
  my($stream) = @_;
  while(my $a_tag = $stream->get_tag('a')) {
    my $text = $stream->get_trimmed_text('/a');
    printf "%s\n  %s\n", $text, $a_tag->[1]{'href'} || '??';
  }
  return;
}
```

But this outputs:

```
Fresh Air Online
  index.cfm
Listen to Current Show
  http://www.npr.org/ramfiles/fa/20011011.fa.ram
[...]
NPR Online
  http://www.npr.org
FreshAir@whyy.org
  mailto:freshair@whyy.org
Listen to Monday - July 2, 2001
  http://www.npr.org/ramfiles/fa/20010702.fa.ram
Listen to Editor and writer Walter Kirn
  http://www.npr.org/ramfiles/fa/20010702.fa.01.ram
Walter Kirn
  http://freshair.npr.org/guestInfoFA.cfm?name=walterkirn
Listen to Casting director and actress Joanna Merlin
  http://www.npr.org/ramfiles/fa/20010702.fa.02.ram
Joanna Merlin
  http://freshair.npr.org/guestInfoFA.cfm?name=joannamerlin
Previous show
  dayFA.cfm?todayDate=06%2F29%2F2001
Next show
  dayFA.cfm?todayDate=07%2F03%2F2001
```

We got what we wanted (those three "Listen to" links are in there), but it's buried in other stuff. You see, the navigation bar on the left does consist of image links, whose ALT content shows up when we call get_trimmed_text( ) or get_text( ). We also get the mailto: link from the bottom of the navigation bar, the bio links for the guests from the paragraphs describing each segment, and the "Previous Show" and "Next Show" links.

Narrowing In

Now, we could try excluding every kind of thing we know we don't want. We could exclude the mailto: link by excluding all URLs that start with *mailto:*; we could exclude the guest bio URLs by excluding URLs that contain *guestinfo*; we could exclude the "Previous" and "Next" links by ignoring any URLs with *dayFA* in them; and we could think of a way to exclude the image URLs. However, tomorrow the people at *Fresh Air* might add this to their general template:

```
<a href="buynow.html"><img alt="Buy the Terry Gross mug"
  src="/mug.jpg" width=450 weight=90></a>
```

Because that isn't explicitly excluded, it would make its way through and appear as a segment link in every program listed.

It is a valid approach to come up with criteria for the kinds of things we *don't* want to see, but it's usually easier to come up with criteria to capture what we *do* want to see. So this is what we'll do.

We could characterize the links we're after in several ways:

1. These links all contain a `<font...>` ... `</font>` sequence and a `<b>` ... `</b>` sequence.

2. They all have an `<a ...>` tag with an `href` attribute pointing to a URL.

3. The URL they point to looks like *http://www.npr.org/ramfiles/fa/20010702.fa.ram*.

4. Notably, the URL's scheme is `http`, it's on the server `www.npr.org`, its path includes `ramfiles`, and it ends in `.ram`.

5. The (trimmed) link text up to `/a` always begins with `Listen to `.

Now, of these, the first criterion is most reminiscent of the sort of things we did earlier with the BBC news extractor. But in this case, it's actually sort of a bother, because we can't specify that the next token after the `<a ...>` start-tag is a `<font...>` tag.

If, by this first criterion, we simply mean that calling `$x->get_tag('/a', 'font', 'b')` should give you `<font...>` or `<b>` before you hit `</a>`, well, this is true. But in either case, you'll have skipped over all the tokens between the current point in the stream and the next tag you find, and once you've skipped them, you can't get them back. In this case, we can get away with throwing out the content of `<a ...>...</a>` sequences that don't meet this one criterion, but in many situations you run into, you won't have that luxury. Moreover, in jumping from the `<a ...>` start-tag to the first `<font...>` tag, we may be jumping over text that we want but will never be able to get.

We could try implementing this all with the same approach we used with the BBC extractor in Chapter 7, where we cook up several patterns (such as an `<a href...>` start-tag, a text token `Listen to `, a `<font...>` start-tag, some whitespace, and a `<b>` start-tag) and base our pattern matcher on `get_token()` so we can always call `unget_token()` on tokens that don't match the pattern. This is feasible, but it's sounding like the hardest of the criteria to formalize, at least under HTML::TokeParser. (But testing whether a tag sequence contains another is easy with HTML::TreeBuilder, as we see in later chapters.) So we'll try to make do without this one criterion and consider it a last resort.

Winding irrevocably past things is a problem not just with `get_tag()`. It's also a problem with `get_text()` and `get_trimmed_text()`. Once you use any of these methods to skip past tags and/or comments, they're gone for good. Unless you did something particularly perverse, such as read a huge chunk of the stream with `get_token()` and then stuffed it back in with `unget_token()` while still keeping a copy around. If you're even contemplating something like that, it's a definite sign that your program is outgrowing what you can do with HTML::TokeParser, and you should either write a new searcher method that's like `get_text()` but that can restore tokens to the buffer, or more likely move on to a parsing model based on HTML::TreeBuilder.

The next criteria (numbers 3 and 4 in the list above) are easy to formalize. These involve characteristics of the URL. We simply add a line to our `while` loop, like so:

```
while(my $a_tag = $stream->get_tag('a')) {
  my $url = $a_tag->[1]{'href'} || next;
  next unless $url =~ m{^http:}s and $url =~ m/www\.npr\.org/i
```

```
    and $url =~ m{/ramfiles/} and $url =~ m/\.ram$/;
    # (There's many other ways of doing the above.)
    my $text = $stream->get_trimmed_text('/a');
    printf "%s\n  %s\n", $text, $url;
}
```

But this raises a point on which many programmers will, legitimately, diverge. Currently, we can say "it's interesting only if the URL ends in *.ram*," like so:

```
next unless $url =~ m/\.ram$/;
```

It works! But what if, tomorrow, some code like the following is added to the normal template?

```
<a href="/stuff/holiday_greets.ram">Happy Holidays
 from Terry Gross!</a>
<!-- just a short RA file of Terry saying "Happy NATO Day!" -->
```

We'll be annoyed we didn't make our link extractor check $url =~ m/www\.npr\.org/i and $url =~ m{/ramfiles/}. On the other hand, if we do check those additional facts about the URL, and tomorrow all the *.ram* files are moved off of *www.npr.org* and onto *archive.npr.org*, or onto *terrygross.com* or whatever, then it'll look like there were no links for this program! Then we'll be annoyed that we did make our link extractor check those additional things about the URL. Moreover, tomorrow NPR could switch to a better audio format than RealAudio, and all the *.ram* files could turn into something else, such that even m/\.ram$/ is no longer true. It could even be something served across a protocol other than HTTP! In other words, no part of the URL is reliably stable. On one hand, National Public Radio is not normally characterized by lavish budgets for web design (and redesign, and re-redesign), so you can expect some measure of stability. But on the other hand, you never know!

Rewrite for Features

My core approach in these cases is to pick some set of assumptions and stick with it, but also to assume that they will fail. So I write the code so that when it does fail, the point of failure will be easy to isolate. I do this is with *debug levels*, also called *trace levels*. Consider this expanded version of our code:

```
use strict;
use constant DEBUG => 0;

use HTML::TokeParser;
parse_fresh_stream(
  HTML::TokeParser->new('fresh1.html') || die($!),
  'http://freshair.npr.org/dayFA.cfm?todayDate=07%2F02%2F2001'
);

sub parse_fresh_stream {
  use URI;
  my($stream, $base_url) = @_;
  DEBUG and print "About to parse stream with base $base_url\n";
```

```
    while(my $a_tag = $stream->get_tag('a')) {
      DEBUG > 1 and printf "Considering {%s}\n", $a_tag->[3];
      my $url = URI->new_abs( ($a_tag->[1]{'href'} || next), $base_url);
      unless($url->scheme eq 'http') {
        DEBUG > 1 and print "Scheme is no good in $url\n";
        next;
      }
      unless($url->host =~ m/www\.npr\.org/) {
        DEBUG > 1 and print "Host is no good in $url\n";
        next;
      }
      unless($url->path =~ m{/ramfiles/.*\.ram$}) {
        DEBUG > 1 and print "Path is no good in $url\n";
        next;
      }
      DEBUG > 1 and print "IT'S GOOD!\n";
      my $text = $stream->get_trimmed_text('/a') || "??";
      printf "%s\n  %s\n", $text, $url;
    }
    DEBUG and print "End of stream\n";
    return;
  }
```

Among the notable changes here, I'm making a URI object for each URL I'm scruti-
nizing, and to make a new absolute URI object out of each potentially relative URL, I
have to pass the base URL as a parameter to the parse_fresh_stream( ) function.
Once I do that, I get to isolate parts of URLs the proper way, using URI methods
such as host( ) and path( ), instead of by applying regexp matches to the bare URL.

Debuggability

The greatest change is the introduction of all the links with "DEBUG" in them.
Because the DEBUG constant is declared with value 0, all the tests of whether
DEBUG is nonzero are obviously always false, and so all these lines are never run; in
fact, the Perl compiler removes them from the parse tree of this program, so they're
discarded the moment they're parsed. (Incidentally, there's nothing magic about the
name "DEBUG"; you can call it "TRACE" or "Talkytalky" or "_mumbles" or whatever you want. However, using all caps is a matter of convention.) So, with a DEBUG
value of 0, when you run this program, it simply prints this:

```
Listen to Current Show
  http://www.npr.org/ramfiles/fa/20011011.fa.ram
Listen to Monday - July 2, 2001
  http://www.npr.org/ramfiles/fa/20010702.fa.ram
Listen to Editor and writer Walter Kirn
  http://www.npr.org/ramfiles/fa/20010702.fa.01.ram
Listen to Casting director and actress Joanna Merlin
  http://www.npr.org/ramfiles/fa/20010702.fa.02.ram
```

(That first link is superfluous, but we'll deal with that in a bit; otherwise, it all works
okay.) So these DEBUG lines do nothing. And when we deploy the above program
with some code that harvests the pages instead of working from the local test page, the

DEBUG lines will continue to do nothing. But suppose that, months later, the program just stops working. That is, it runs, but prints nothing, and we don't know why. Did NPR change the Fresh Air site so much that the old program listings' URLs are no longer serve any content? Or has some part of the format changed? If we just change DEBUG => 0 to DEBUG => 1 and rerun the program, we can see that parse_fresh_stream( ) is definitely being called on a stream from an HTML page, because we see the messages from the print statements in that routine:

```
About to parse stream with base
http://freshair.npr.org/dayFA.cfm?todayDate=07%2F02%2F2001
End of stream
```

Change the DEBUG level to 2, and we get more detailed output:

```
About to parse stream with base
http://freshair.npr.org/dayFA.cfm?todayDate=07%2F02%2F2001
Considering {<A HREF="index.cfm">}
Host is no good in http://freshair.npr.org/index.cfm
Considering {<A HREF="http://www.npr.org/ramfiles/fa/20011011.fa.prok">}
Path is no good in http://www.npr.org/ramfiles/fa/20011011.fa.prok
Considering {<A HREF="dayFA.cfm?todayDate=current">}
[...]
Considering {<A HREF="http://www.npr.org/ramfiles/fa/20010702.fa.prok">}
Path is no good in http://www.npr.org/ramfiles/fa/20010702.fa.prok
Considering {<A HREF="http://www.npr.org/ramfiles/fa/20010702.fa.01.prok">}
Path is no good in http://www.npr.org/ramfiles/fa/20010702.fa.01.prok
Considering {<A HREF="http://freshair.npr.org/guestInfoFA.cfm?name=walterkirn">}
Host is no good in http://freshair.npr.org/guestInfoFA.cfm?name=walterkirn
Considering {<A HREF="http://www.npr.org/ramfiles/fa/20010702.fa.02.prok">}
Path is no good in http://www.npr.org/ramfiles/fa/20010702.fa.02.prok
Considering {<A HREF="http://freshair.npr.org/guestInfoFA.cfm?name=joannamerlin">}
Host is no good in http://freshair.npr.org/guestInfoFA.cfm?name=joannamerlin
Considering {<A HREF="dayFA.cfm?todayDate=06%2F29%2F2001">}
Host is no good in http://freshair.npr.org/dayFA.cfm?todayDate=06%2F29%2F2001
Considering {<A HREF="dayFA.cfm?todayDate=07%2F03%2F2001">}
Host is no good in http://freshair.npr.org/dayFA.cfm?todayDate=07%2F03%2F2001
End of stream
```

Our parse_fresh_stream( ) routine is still correctly rejecting *index.cfm* and the like, for having a "no good" host (i.e., not *www.npr.org*). And we can see that it's happening on those "ramfiles" links, and it's not rejecting their host, because they are on *www.npr.org*. But it rejects their paths. When we look back at the code that triggers rejection based on the path, it kicks in only when the path fails to match m{/ramfiles/.*\.ram$}. Why don't our ramfiles paths match that regexp anymore? Ah ha, because they don't end in *.ram* anymore; they end in *.prok*, some new audio format that NPR has switched to! This is evident at the end of the lines beginning "Path is no good." Change our regexp to accept *.prok*, rerun the program, and go about our business. Similarly, if the audio files moved to a different server, we'd be alerted to their host being "no good" now, and we could adjust the regexp that checks that.

We had to make some fragile assumptions to tell interesting links apart from uninteresting ones, but having all these DEBUG statements means that when the assumptions no longer hold, we can quickly isolate the problem.

Images and Applets

Speaking of assumptions, what about the fact that (back to our pre-.*prok* local test file and setting DEBUG back to 0) we get an extra link at the start of the output here?

```
Listen to Current Show
   http://www.npr.org/ramfiles/fa/20011011.fa.ram
Listen to Monday - July 2, 2001
   http://www.npr.org/ramfiles/fa/20010702.fa.ram
Listen to Editor and writer Walter Kirn
   http://www.npr.org/ramfiles/fa/20010702.fa.01.ram
Listen to Casting director and actress Joanna Merlin
   http://www.npr.org/ramfiles/fa/20010702.fa.02.ram
```

If we go to our browser and use the "Find in Page" function to see where "Listen to Current Show" appears in the rendered page, we'll probably find no match. So where's it coming from? Try the same search on the source, and you'll see:

```
<A HREF="http://www.npr.org/ramfiles/fa/20011011.fa.ram">
   <IMG SRC="images/listen.gif" ALT="Listen to Current Show"
     WIDTH="124" HEIGHT="47" BORDER="0" HSPACE="0" VSPACE="0">
</A>
```

Recall that get_text( ) and get_text_trimmed( ) give special treatment to img and applet elements; they treat them as virtual text tags with contents from their alt values (or in the absence of any alt value, the strings [IMG] or [APPLET]). That might be a useful feature normally, but it's bothersome now. So we turn it off by adding this line just before our while loop starts reading from the stream:

```
$stream->{'textify'} = {};
```

We know that's the line to use partly because I mentioned it as an aside much earlier, and partly because it's in the HTML::TokeParser manpage (where you can also read about how to do things with the textify feature other than just turn it off). With that change made, our program prints this:

```
??
   http://www.npr.org/ramfiles/fa/20011011.fa.ram
Listen to Monday - July 2, 2001
   http://www.npr.org/ramfiles/fa/20010702.fa.ram
Listen to Editor and writer Walter Kirn
   http://www.npr.org/ramfiles/fa/20010702.fa.01.ram
Listen to Casting director and actress Joanna Merlin
   http://www.npr.org/ramfiles/fa/20010702.fa.02.ram
```

That ?? is there because when the first link had no link text (and we're no longer counting alt text), it caused get_trimmed_text( ) to return an empty string. That is a false value in Perl, so it causes the fallthrough to ?? here:

```
my $text = $stream->get_trimmed_text('/a') || "??";
```

If we want to explicitly skip things with no link text, we change that to:

```
my $text = $stream->get_trimmed_text('/a');
unless(length $text) {
  DEBUG > 1 and print "Skipping link with no link-text\n";
  next;
}
```

That makes the program give this output, as we wanted it:

```
Listen to Monday - July 2, 2001
  http://www.npr.org/ramfiles/fa/20010702.fa.ram
Listen to Editor and writer Walter Kirn
  http://www.npr.org/ramfiles/fa/20010702.fa.01.ram
Listen to Casting director and actress Joanna Merlin
  http://www.npr.org/ramfiles/fa/20010702.fa.02.ram
```

Link Text

Now that everything else is working, remember that we didn't want all this "Listen to" stuff starting every single link. Moreover, remember that the presence of a "Listen to" at the start of the link text was one of our prospective criteria for whether it's an interesting link. We didn't implement that, but we can implement it now:

```
unless($text =~ s/^Listen to //) {
  DEBUG > 1 and print "Odd, \"$text\" doesn't start with \"Listen to\"...\n";
  next;
}
Monday - July 2, 2001
  http://www.npr.org/ramfiles/fa/20010702.fa.ram
Editor and writer Walter Kirn
  http://www.npr.org/ramfiles/fa/20010702.fa.01.ram
Casting director and actress Joanna Merlin
  http://www.npr.org/ramfiles/fa/20010702.fa.02.ram
```

In other words, unless the link next starts with a "Listen to" that we can strip off, this link is rejected. And incidentally, you might notice that with all these little changes we've made, our program now works perfectly!

Live Data

All it needs to actually pull data from the Fresh Air web site, is to comment out the code that calls the local test file and substitute some simple code to get the data for a block of days. Here's is the whole program source, with those changes and additions:

```
use strict;
use constant DEBUG => 0;
use HTML::TokeParser;

#parse_fresh_stream(
#  HTML::TokeParser->new('fresh1.html') || die($!),
#  'http://freshair.npr.org/dayFA.cfm?todayDate=07%2F02%2F2001'
#);
```

```
  scan_last_month( );

sub scan_last_month {
  use LWP::UserAgent;
  my $browser = LWP::UserAgent->new( );
  foreach my $date_mdy (weekdays_last_month( )) {
    my $url = sprintf(
     'http://freshair.npr.org/dayFA.cfm?todayDate=%02d%%2f%02d%%2f%04d',
     @$date_mdy
    );
    DEBUG and print "Getting @$date_mdy URL $url\n";
    sleep 3; # Don't hammer the NPR server!
    my $response = $browser->get($url);
    unless($response->is_success) {
      print "Error getting $url: ", $response->status_line, "\n";
      next;
    }
    my $stream = HTML::TokeParser->new($response->content_ref)
     || die "What, couldn't make a stream?!";
    parse_fresh_stream($stream, $response->base);
  }
}

sub weekdays_last_month { # Boring date handling. Feel free to skip.
  my($now) = time;
  my $this_month = (gmtime $now)[4];
  my(@out, $last_month, $that_month);

  do { # Get to end of last month.
    $now -= (24 * 60 * 60); # go back a day
    $that_month = (gmtime $now)[4];
  } while($that_month == $this_month);
  $last_month = $that_month;

  do { # Go backwards thru last month
    my(@then) = (gmtime $now);
    unshift @out, [$then[4] + 1 , $then[3], $then[5] + 1900] # m,d,yyyy
      unless $then[6] == 0 or $then[6] == 6;
    $now -= (24 * 60 * 60); # go back one day
    $that_month = (gmtime $now)[4];
  } while($that_month == $last_month);
  return @out;
}

# Unchanged since you last saw it:
sub parse_fresh_stream {
  use URI;
  my($stream, $base_url) = @_;
  DEBUG and print "About to parse stream with base $base_url\n";

  while(my $a_tag = $stream->get_tag('a')) {
    DEBUG > 1 and printf "Considering {%s}\n", $a_tag->[3];
    my $url = URI->new_abs( ($a_tag->[1]{'href'} || next), $base_url);
    unless($url->scheme eq 'http') {
```

```
      DEBUG > 1 and print "Scheme is no good in $url\n";
      next;
    }
    unless($url->host =~ m/www\.npr\.org/) {
      DEBUG > 1 and print "Host is no good in $url\n";
      next;
    }
    unless($url->path =~ m{/ramfiles/.*\.ram$}) {
      DEBUG > 1 and print "Path is no good in $url\n";
      next;
    }
    DEBUG > 1 and print "IT'S GOOD!\n";
    my $text = $stream->get_trimmed_text('/a') || "??";
    printf "%s\n  %s\n", $text, $url;
  }
  DEBUG and print "End of stream\n";
  return;
}
```

Alternatives

Now, with the sort of 20/20 hindsight that is always in abundance in such cases, we can see that there were other ways it could have been done. For example, instead of using the various tricks to keep the first image-ALT link from printing, we could simply have kept a count of the good links seen so far in the current stream and ignored the first one. Our actual solution is more proper in this case, but sometimes counting items is the best or only way to get a problem solved.

More importantly, we could have done without all the code that tests the link URL and used one regexp to implement our last criterion, i.e., that the link text begin with "Listen to". But, as with our earlier consideration of how much of the URL to check, it comes down to the question: do you want something that's more careful (i.e., enforcing more assumptions on the input data, and so more prone to reject appropriate links in the future) or more forgiving (i.e., enforcing fewer assumptions, but more likely to match inappropriate links in the future)?

The answer depends on how concise you want the code to be, how much time you want to spend thinking up assumptions, and, most importantly, what happens if it breaks. If I've crontabbed this program to harvest Fresh Air listings every month and mail me the results, if it breaks, I'll get some sort of anomalous output mailed to me (whether with too few links, or too many) and it's no big deal because, working or not, it's just so I can listen to interesting radio programs. But your data extraction program may instead serve many people who will be greatly inconvenienced if it stops working properly. You have to decide on a case-by-case basis whether your program should be more likely to clam up and miss interesting data in new formats, or pass through new kinds of data despite the risk that they might be irrelevant or just plain wrong.

## CHAPTER 9

HTML Processing with Trees

Treating HTML as a stream of tokens is an imperfect solution to the problem of extracting information from HTML. In particular, the token model obscures the hierarchical nature of markup. Nested structures such as lists within lists or tables within tables are difficult to process as just tokens. Such structures are best represented as trees, and the HTML::Element class does just this.

This chapter teaches you how to use the HTML::TreeBuilder module to construct trees from HTML, and how to process those trees to extract information. Chapter 10 shows how to modify HTML using trees.

Introduction to Trees

The HTML in Example 9-1 can be represented by the tree in Figure 9-1.

Example 9-1. Simple HTML

```
<ul>
  <li>Ice cream.</li>
  <li>Whipped cream.
  <li>Hot apple pie <br>(mmm pie)</li>
</ul>
```

In the language of trees, each part of the tree (such as html, li, Ice cream., and br) is a *node*. There are two kinds of nodes in an HTML tree: *text nodes*,which are strings with no tags, and *elements*, which symbolize not mere strings, but things that can have attributes (such as align=left), and which generally came from an open tag (such as <li>), and were possibly closed by an end-tag (such as </li>).

When several nodes are contained by another, as the li elements are contained by the ul element, the contained ones are called *children*. Children of the same element are called *siblings*. For example, head and body are siblings, as they are both children of the html element. Text nodes can't have children; only elements can have children.

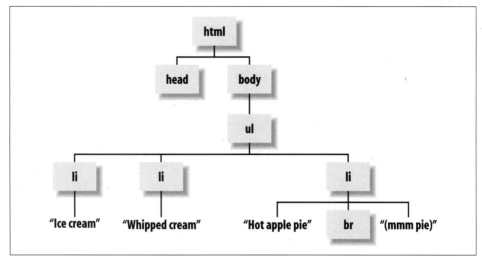

Figure 9-1. HTML tree

Example 9-1 shows the difference between a *tag* and an *element*. A tag is a piece of markup source, such as the string <li>. An element is a feature of the tree that you get by parsing the source that contains tags. The relationship between the two isn't always easy to figure out by just looking at the source, because HTML lets you omit closing tags (such as </li>) and in some cases omit entire groups of tags (such as <html><head></head><body>...</body></html>, as were omitted above but showed up in the tree anyway). This is unlike XML, where there are exactly as many elements in the tree as there are <foo>...</foo> tag pairs in the source.

Trees let you work with elements and ignore the way the HTML was marked up. If you're processing the tree shown in Figure 9-1, you don't need to worry about whether the </li> tag was or was not present.

In LWP, each element in a tree is an HTML::Element object. The HTML::TreeBuilder module parses HTML and constructs a tree for you. The parsing options in a given HTML::TreeBuilder object control the nature of the final tree (for example, whether comments are ignored or represented in the tree). Once you have a tree, you can call methods on it that search for bits of content and emit parts of it as HTML or text. In the next chapter, we even see how to move nodes around within the tree, and from tree to tree.

HTML::TreeBuilder

There are five steps to an HTML::TreeBuilder program:

1. Create the HTML::TreeBuilder object.
2. Set the parse options.

3. Parse the HTML.

4. Process it according to the needs of your problem.

5. Delete the HTML::TreeBuilder object.

Example 9-2 is a simple HTML::TreeBuilder program.

Example 9-2. Simple HTML::TreeBuilder program

```perl
#!/usr/bin/perl -w
use strict;
use HTML::TreeBuilder 3;  # make sure our version isn't ancient
my $root = HTML::TreeBuilder->new;
$root->parse(  # parse a string...
q{
  <ul>
    <li>Ice cream.</li>
    <li>Whipped cream.
    <li>Hot apple pie <br>(mmm pie)</li>
  </ul>
});
$root->eof();  # done parsing for this tree
$root->dump;    # print() a representation of the tree
$root->delete; # erase this tree because we're done with it
```

Four of the five steps are shown here. The HTML::TreeBuilder class's new( ) constructor creates a new object. We don't set parse options, preferring instead to use
the defaults. The parse( ) method parses HTML from a string. It's designed to let
you supply HTML in chunks, so you use the eof( ) method to tell the parser when
there's no more HTML. The dump( ) method is our processing here, printing a string
form of the tree (the output is given in Example 9-3). And finally we delete( ) the
tree to free the memory it used.

Example 9-3. Output of Example 9-2

```
<html> @0 (IMPLICIT)
  <head> @0.0 (IMPLICIT)
  <body> @0.1 (IMPLICIT)
    <ul> @0.1.0
      <li> @0.1.0.0
        "Ice cream."
      <li> @0.1.0.1
        "Whipped cream. "
      <li> @0.1.0.2
        "Hot apple pie "
        <br> @0.1.0.2.1
        "(mmm pie)"
```

Each line in the dump represents either an element or text. Each element is identified by a dotted sequence of numbers (e.g., 0.1.0.2). This sequence identifies the
position of the element in the tree (2nd child of the 0th child of the 1st child of the
0th child of the root of the tree). The dump also identifies some nodes as (IMPLICIT),

meaning they weren't present in the HTML fragment but have been inferred to make a valid document parse tree.

Constructors

To create a new empty tree, use the new( ) method:

```
$root = HTML::TreeBuilder->new();
```

To create a new tree and parse the HTML in one go, pass one or more strings to the new_from_content( ) method:

```
$root = HTML::TreeBuilder->new_from_content([string, ...]);
```

To create a new HTML::TreeBuilder object and parse HTML from a file, pass the filename or a filehandle to the new_from_file( ) method:

```
$root = HTML::TreeBuilder->new_from_file(filename);
$root = HTML::TreeBuilder->new_from_file(filehandle);
```

If you use new_from_file( ) or new_from_content( ), the parse is carried out with the default parsing options. To parse with any nondefault options, you must use the new( ) constructor and call parse file( ) or parse( ).

Parse Options

Set options for the parse by calling methods on the HTML::TreeBuilder object. These methods return the old value for the option and set the value if passed a parameter. For example:

```
$comments = $root->strict_comment();
print "Strict comment processing is ";
print $comments ? "on\n" : "off\n";
$root->strict_comments(0);      # disable
```

Some options affect the way the HTML standard is ignored or obeyed, while others affect the internal behavior of the parser. The full list of parser options follows.

$root->strict_comments([boolean]);
> The HTML standard says that a comment is terminated by an even number of --s between the opening < and the closing >, and there must be nothing but whitespace between even and odd --s. That part of the HTML standard is little known, little understood, and little obeyed. So most browsers simply accept any --> as the end of a comment. If enabled via a true value, this option makes the HTML::TreeBuilder recognize *only* those comments that obey the HTML standard. By default, this option is off, so that HTML::TreeBuilder will parse comments as normal browsers do.

$root->strict_names([boolean]);
> Some HTML has unquoted attribute values that include spaces, e.g., <img alt=big dog! src="dog.jpg">. If this option is enabled, that tag would be reported as text, because it doesn't obey the standard (dog! is not a valid

attribute name). If the option is disabled, as it is by default, source such as this is parsed as a tag, with a Boolean attribute called dog! set.

`$root->implicit_tags([`*`boolean`*`]);`

Enabled by default, this option makes the parser create nodes for missing start- or end-tags. If disabled, the parse tree simply reflects the input text, which is rarely useful.

`$root->implicit_body_p_tag([`*`boolean`*`]);`

This option controls what happens to text or phrasal tags (such as <i>...</i>) that are directly in a <body>, without a containing <p>. By default, the text or phrasal tag nodes are children of the <body>. If enabled, an implicit <p> is created to contain the text or phrasal tags.

`$root->ignore_unknown([`*`boolean`*`]);`

By default, unknown tags, such as <footer>, are ignored. Enable this to create nodes in the parse tree for unknown tags.

`$root->ignore_text([`*`boolean`*`]);`

By default, text in elements appears in the parse tree. Enable this option to create parse trees without the text from the document.

`$root->ignore_ignorable_whitespace([`*`boolean`*`]);`

Whitespace between most tags is ignorable, and multiple whitespace characters are collapsed to one. If you want to preserve the whitespace present in the original HTML, enable this option.

Parsing

There are two ways of parsing HTML: from a file or from strings.

Pass the parse_file( ) method a filename or filehandle to parse the HTML in that file:

```
$success = $root->parse_file(filename);
$success = $root->parse_file(filehandle);
```

For example, to parse HTML from STDIN:

```
$root->parse_file(*STDIN) or die "Can't parse STDIN";
```

The parse_file( ) method returns the HTML::TreeBuilder object if successful or undef if an error occurred.

The parse( ) method takes a chunk of HTML and parses it. Call parse( ) on each chunk, then call the eof( ) method when there's no more HTML to come.

```
$success = $root->parse(chunk);
$success = $root->eof( );
```

This method is designed for situations where you are acquiring your HTML one chunk at a time. It's also useful when you're extracting HTML from a larger file and can't simply parse the entire file with parse_file( ). In many cases, you could use new_from_content( ), but recall that new_from_content( ) doesn't give you an opportunity to set nondefault parsing options.

Cleanup

The delete( ) method frees the tree and its elements, giving the memory it used back to Perl:

```
$root->delete( );
```

Use this method in persistent environments such as mod_perl or when your program will parse a lot of HTML files. It's not enough to simply have $root be a private variable that goes out of scope, or to assign a new value to $root. Perl's current memory-management system fails on the kinds of data structures that HTML::Element uses.

Processing

Once you have parsed some HTML, you need to process it. Exactly what you do will depend on the nature of your problem. Two common models are extracting information and producing a transformed version of the HTML (for example, to remove banner advertisements).

Whether extracting or transforming, you'll probably want to find the bits of the document you're interested in. They might be all headings, all bold italic regions, or all paragraphs with class="blinking". HTML::Element provides several functions for searching the tree.

Methods for Searching the Tree

In scalar context, these methods return the first node that satisfies the criteria. In list context, all such nodes are returned. The methods can be called on the root of the tree or any node in it.

$node->find_by_tag_name(*tag* [, ...])

Return node(s) for tags of the names listed. For example, to find all h1 and h2 nodes:

```
@headings = $root->find_by_tag_name('h1', 'h2');
```

$node->find_by_attribute(*attribute, value*)

Returns the node(s) with the given attribute set to the given value. For example, to find all nodes with class="blinking":

```
@blinkers = $root->find_by_attribute("class", "blinking");
```

$node->look_down(...)
$node->look_up(...)

These two methods search $node and its children (and children's children, and so on) in the case of look_down, or its parent (and the parent's parent, and so on) in the case of look_up, looking for nodes that match whatever criteria you specify. The parameters are either attribute => value pairs (where the special attribute _tag represents the tag name), or a subroutine that is passed a current node and returns true to indicate that this node is of interest.

For example, to find all h2 nodes in the tree with class="blinking":

```
@blinkers = $root->look_down(_tag => 'h2', class => 'blinking');
```

We'll discuss look_down in greater detail later.

Attributes of a Node

Four methods give access to the basic information in a node:

$node->tag( )

The tag name string of this element. Example values: html, img, blockquote. Note that this is always lowercase.

$node->parent( )

This returns the node object that is the parent of this node. If $node is the root of the tree, $node->parent( ) will return undef.

$node->content_list( )

This returns the (potentially empty) list of nodes that are this node's children.

$node->attr(*attributename*)

This returns the value of the HTML *attributename* attribute for this element. If there is no such attribute for this element, this returns undef. For example: if $node is parsed from <img src="x1.jpg" alt="Looky!">, then $node->attr("src") will return the string x1.jpg.

Four more methods convert a tree or part of a tree into another format, such as HTML or text.

$node->as_HTML([*entities* [, *indent_char* [, *optional_end_tags*]]]);

Returns a string consisting of the node and its children as HTML. The *entities* parameter is a string containing characters that should be entity escaped (if empty, all potentially unsafe characters are encoded as entities; if you pass just <>&, just those characters will get encoded—a bare minimum for valid HTML). The *indent_char* parameter is a string used for indenting the HTML. The *optional_end_tags* parameter is a reference to a hash that has a true value for every key that is the name of a tag whose closing tag is optional. The most common value for this parameter is {} to force all tags to be closed:

```
$html = $node->as_HTML("", "", {});
```

For example, this will emit </li> tags for any li nodes under $node, even though </li> tags are technically optional, according to the HTML specification.

Using $node->as_HTML( ) with no parameters should be fine for most purposes.

$node->as_text( )

Returns a string consisting of all the text nodes from this element and its children.

$node->starttag([*entities*])

Returns the HTML for the start-tag for this node. The *entities* parameter is a string of characters to entity escape, as in the as_HTML( ) method; you can omit this. For example, if this node came from parsing <TD class=loud>Hooboy</TD>, then $node->starttag( ) returns `<td class="loud">`. Note that the original source text is not reproduced exactly, because insignificant differences, such as the capitalization of the tag name or attribute names, will have been discarded during parsing.

$node->endtag( )

> Returns the HTML for the end-tag for this node. For example, if this node came from parsing `<TD class=loud>Hooboy</TD>`, then $node->endtag( ) returns `</td>`.

These methods are useful once you've found the desired content. Example 9-4 prints all the bold italic text in a document.

Example 9-4. Bold-italic headline printer

```
#!/usr/bin/perl -w

use HTML::TreeBuilder;
use strict;

my $root = HTML::TreeBuilder->new_from_content(<<"EOHTML");
<b><i>Shatner wins Award!</i></b>
Today in <b>Hollywood</b> ...
<b><i>End of World Predicted!</i></b>
Today in <b>Washington</b> ...
EOHTML
$root->eof( );

# print contents of <b><i>...</i></b>
my @bolds = $root->find_by_tag_name('b');
foreach my $node (@bolds) {
  my @kids = $node->content_list( );
  if (@kids and ref $kids[0] and $kids[0]->tag( ) eq 'i') {
    print $kids[0]->as_text( ), "\n";
  }
}
```

Example 9-4 is fairly straightforward. Having parsed the string into a new tree, we get a list of all the bold nodes. Some of these will be the headlines we want, while others will simply be bolded text. In this case, we can identify headlines by checking that the node that it contains represents `<i>...</i>`. If it is an italic node, we print its text content.

The only complicated part of Example 9-4 is the test to see whether it's an interesting node. This test has three parts:

@kids

> True if there are children of this node. An empty `<b></b>` would fail this test.

ref $kids[0]

> True if the first child of this node is an element. This is false in cases such as `<b>Washington</b>`, where the first (and here, only) child is text. If we fail to

check this, the next expression, $kids[0]->tag( ), would produce an error when $kids[0] isn't an object value.

$kids[0]->tag( ) eq 'i'

True if the first child of this node is an i element. This would weed out anything like <img src="shatner.jpg">, where $kids[0]->tag( ) would return img, or Yes, Shatner!, where $kids[0]->tag( ) would return strong.

Traversing

For many tasks, you can use the built-in search functions. Sometimes, though, you'd like to visit every node of the tree. You have two choices: you can use the existing traverse( ) function or write your own using either recursion or your own stack.

The act of visiting every node in a tree is called a *traversal*. Traversals can either be *preorder* (where you process the current node before processing its children) or *postorder* (where you process the current node after processing its children). The traverse( ) method lets you both:

```
$node->traverse(callbacks [, ignore_text]);
```

The traverse( ) method calls a callback before processing the children and again afterward. If the *callbacks* parameter is a single function reference, the same function is called before and after processing the children. If the *callbacks* parameter is an array reference, the first element is a reference to a function called before the children are processed, and the second element is similarly called after the children are processed, unless this node is a text segment or an element that is prototypically empty, such as br or hr. (This last quirk of the traverse( ) method is one of the reasons that I discourage its use.)

Callbacks get called with three values:

```
sub callback
  my ($node, $startflag, $depth,
      $parent, $my_index) = @_;
  # ...
}
```

The current node is the first parameter. The next is a Boolean value indicating whether we're being called before (true) or after (false) the children, and the third is a number indicating how deep into the traversal we are. The fourth and fifth parameters are supplied only for text elements: the parent node object and the index of the current node in its parent's list of children.

A callback can return any of the following values:

HTML::Element::OK *(or any true value)*

Continue traversing.

HTML::Element::PRUNE *(or any false value)*

> Do not go into the children. The postorder callback is not called. (Ignored if returned by a postorder callback.)

HTML::Element::ABORT

> Abort the traversal immediately.

HTML::Element::PRUNE_UP

> Do not go into this node's children or into its parent node.

HTML::Element::PRUNE_SOFTLY

> Do not go into the children, but do call this node's postorder callback.

For example, to extract text from a node but not go into table elements:

```
my $text;
sub text_no_tables {
  return if ref $_[0] && $_[0]->tag eq 'table';
  $text .= $_[0] unless ref $_[0];   # only append text nodex
  return 1;                          # all is copacetic
}

$root->traverse([\&text_no_tables]);
```

This prevents descent into the contents of tables, while accumulating the text nodes in $text.

It can be hard to think in terms of callbacks, though, and the multiplicity of return values and calling parameters you get with traverse( ) makes for confusing code, as you will likely note when you come across its use in existing programs that use HTML::TreeBuilder.

Instead, it's usually easier and clearer to simply write your own recursive subroutine, like this one:

```
my $text = '';
sub scan_for_non_table_text {
  my $element = $_[0];
  return if $element->tag eq 'table';   # prune!
  foreach my $child ($element->content_list) {
    if (ref $child) {  # it's an element
      scan_for_non_table_text($child);  # recurse!
    } else {           # it's a text node!
      $text .= $child;
    }
  }
  return;
}
scan_for_non_table_text($root);
```

Alternatively, implement it using a stack, doing the same work:

```
my $text = '';
my @stack = ($root);   # where to start
```

```
while (@stack) {
  my $node = shift @stack;
  next if ref $node and $node->tag eq 'table';  # skip tables
  if (ref $node) {
    unshift @stack, $node->content_list;        # add children
  } else {
    $text .= $node;                             # add text
  }
}
```

The while( ) loop version can be faster than the recursive version, but at the cost of being much less clear to people who are unfamiliar with this technique. If speed is a concern, you should always benchmark the two versions to make sure you really need the speedup and that the while( ) loop version actually delivers. The speed difference is sometimes insignificant. The manual page perldoc HTML::Element::traverse discusses writing more complex traverser routines, in the rare cases where you might find this necessary.

Example: BBC News

In Chapter 7, we considered the task of extracting the headline link URLs from the BBC News main page, and we implemented it in terms of HTML::TokeParser. Here, we'll consider the same problem from the perspective of HTML::TreeBuilder.

To review the problem: when you look at the source of *http://news.bbc.co.uk*, you discover that each headline link is wrapped in one of two kinds of code. There are a lot of headlines expressed with code like this:

```
<B CLASS="h3"><A href="/hi/english/business/newsid_1576000/1576290.stm">Bank
of England mulls rate cut</A></B><BR>

<B CLASS="h3"><A href="/hi/english/uk_politics/newsid_1576000/1576541.stm">Euro
battle revived by Blair speech</A></B><BR>
```

and some headlines expressed with code like this:

```
<A href="/hi/english/business/newsid_1576000/1576636.stm">
  <B class="h2"> Swissair shares wiped out</B><BR>
</A>

<A href="/hi/english/world/middle_east/newsid_1576000/1576113.stm">
  <B class="h1">Mid-East blow to US anti-terror drive</B><BR>
</A>
```

(Note that in this second case, the B element's class value can be h1 or h2.)

In both cases, we can find what we want by first looking for B elements. We then look for the href attribute either on the A element that's a child of this B element, or on the A element that's this B element's parent. Whether we look for a parent A node or a child A node depends on the class attribute of the B element. To make sure we're on the right track, we can code up something to formalize our idea of what sorts of nodes we want, and call the dump method on each of them.

```
use strict;
use HTML::TreeBuilder 3;

my $tree = HTML::TreeBuilder->new();
$tree->parse_file('bbc.html') || die $!;  # the saved source from BBC News
scan_bbc_tree( $tree, 'http://news.bbc.co.uk/' );
$tree->delete();

sub scan_bbc_tree {
  my($root, $docbase) = @_;
    # $docbase will be needed if we want to absolutize the URL
  foreach my $b ($root->find_by_tag_name('b')) {
    my $class = $b->attr('class') || next;
    if($class eq 'h3') {
      # expect one 'a' element as a child
      print "Found a b-h3.  Dumping it:\n";
      $b->dump;
    } elsif($class eq 'h1' or $class eq 'h2') {
      # expect the parent to be an 'a'
      print "Found a b-h[1-2].  Dumping its parent:\n";
      $b->parent->dump;
    }
  }
  return;
}
```

When run on the full file, that program produces this output:

```
Found a b-h3.  Dumping it:
<b class="h3"> @0.1.2.2.0.0.3.2.0.3.0.0.0.0.6
  <a href="/sport/hi/english/in_depth/2001/england_in_zimbabwe/newsid_1574000/
1574824.stm"> @0.1.2.2.0.0.3.2.0.3.0.0.0.0.6.0
    "Zimbabwe suffer treble blow"

Found a b-h3.  Dumping it:
<b class="h3"> @0.1.2.2.0.0.3.2.0.6.1.0
  <a href="/hi/english/business/newsid_1576000/1576546.stm"> @0.1.2.2.0.0.3.2.0.6.1.
0.0
    "UK housing market stalls"

Found a b-h[1-2].  Dumping its parent:
<a href="/hi/english/uk_politics/newsid_1576000/1576051.stm"> @0.1.2.2.0.0.1.2.0.14.2
  " "
  <b class="h1"> @0.1.2.2.0.0.1.2.0.14.2.1
    "UK hate crime laws to be tightened"
  <br> @0.1.2.2.0.0.1.2.0.14.2.2

Found a b-h[1-2].  Dumping its parent:
<a href="/hi/english/uk/newsid_1576000/1576379.stm"> @0.1.2.2.0.0.1.2.0.18.2
  " "
  <b class="h2"> @0.1.2.2.0.0.1.2.0.18.2.1
    "Leeds footballers' trial begins"
  <br> @0.1.2.2.0.0.1.2.0.18.2.2
```

[...and others just like those...]

This output shows all the sorts of nodes from which we'll want to extract data and contains no other kinds of nodes. With the situation we see in the first two cases, the b element with the class="h3" attribute indeed has only one child node, which is an a element whose href we want, and in the latter two cases, we need only look to the href attribute on the parent of the b element (which has a class="h1" or class="h2" attribute). So because we're identifying things correctly, we can go ahead and change our code so that instead of dumping nodes, it will actually pull the hrefs out, absolutize them, and print them:

```
sub scan_bbc_tree {
  my($root, $docbase) = @_;
  foreach my $b ($root->find_by_tag_name('b')) {
    my $class = $b->attr('class') || next;
    if($class eq 'h3') {
      # Expect one 'a' element as a child
      my @children = $b->content_list;
      if(@children == 1 and ref $children[0] and $children[0]->tag eq 'a')
        print URI->new_abs(
          $children[0]->attr('href') || next,
          $docbase
        ), "\n";
      }
    } elsif($class eq 'h1' or $class eq 'h2') {
      # Expect an 'a' element as a parent
      my $parent = $b->parent;
      if($parent and $parent->tag eq 'a') {
        print URI->new_abs(
          $parent->attr('href') || next,
          $docbase
        ), "\n";
      }
    }
  }
  return;
}
```

When run, this correctly reports all the URLs in the document:

```
http://news.bbc.co.uk/sport/hi/english/in_depth/2001/england_in_zimbabwe/newsid_
1574000/1574824.stm
http://news.bbc.co.uk/hi/english/business/newsid_1576000/1576546.stm
http://news.bbc.co.uk/hi/english/uk_politics/newsid_1576000/1576051.stm
http://news.bbc.co.uk/hi/english/uk/newsid_1576000/1576379.stm
[...etc...]
```

If we want to make our program also capture the text inside the link, that's straightforward too; we need only change each occurrence of:

```
print URI->new_abs(...
```

to:

```
print $b->as_text( ), "\n  ", URI->new_abs(...
```

Then you'll get output like this:

```
UK housing market stalls
  http://news.bbc.co.uk/hi/english/business/newsid_1576000/1576546.stm
UK hate crime laws to be tightened
  http://news.bbc.co.uk/hi/english/uk_politics/newsid_1576000/1576051.stm
Leeds footballers' trial begins
  http://news.bbc.co.uk/hi/english/uk/newsid_1576000/1576379.stm
 Swissair shares wiped out
  http://news.bbc.co.uk/hi/english/business/newsid_1576000/1576636.stm
[...]
```

Notice that in the fourth link there, we have a space at the start. Wanting to *not* have whitespace at the start or end of as_text() is common enough that there's a method just for that: as_trimmed_text(), which wraps around as_text(), removes any whitespace at the start or end, and collapses any whitespace nodes on the inside.* When we replace our calls to get_text() with calls to get_trimmed_text(), that last link changes to this:

```
[...]
Swissair shares wiped out
  http://news.bbc.co.uk/hi/english/business/newsid_1576000/1576636.stm
[...]
```

that is, without the space at the start of the line.

Example: Fresh Air

Another HTML::TokeParser problem (in Chapter 8) was extracting relevant links from the program descriptions from the Fresh Air web site. There were aspects of the task that we will not review here (such as how to request a month's worth of weekday listings at a time), but we will instead focus on the heart of the program, which is how to take HTML source from a local file, feed it to HTML::TreeBuilder, and pull the interesting links out of the resulting tree.

If we save the HTML source of a program description page as *fresh1.html* and sift through its source, we get a 12-KB file. Only about one 1 KB of that is real content, like this:

```
...
<A HREF="http://www.npr.org/ramfiles/fa/20010702.fa.ram">
  <FONT FACE="Verdana, Charcoal, Sans Serif" COLOR="#FFCC00" SIZE="2">
    Listen to <B>Monday - July 2, 2001</B>
  </FONT>
</A>

...
```

---

* This is exactly the same as the $stream->get_text() versus $stream->get_trimmed_text() distinction in HTML::TokeParser.

```
<A HREF="http://www.npr.org/ramfiles/fa/20010702.fa.01.ram">Listen to
<FONT FACE="Verdana, Charcoal, Sans Serif" COLOR="#ffffff" SIZE="3">
<B> Editor and writer Walter Kirn                          </B>
</FONT></A>

<BR>
<FONT FACE="Verdana, Charcoal, Sans Serif" COLOR="#ffffff" SIZE="2">
<BLOCKQUOTE>Editor and writer <A
HREF="http://freshair.npr.org/guestInfoFA.cfm?name=walterkirn">Walter
Kirn</A>'s new novel <I>Up in the Air</I> (Doubleday) is about
...
</BLOCKQUOTE></FONT>
<BR>

<A HREF="http://www.npr.org/ramfiles/fa/20010702.fa.02.ram">Listen to
<FONT FACE="Verdana, Charcoal, Sans Serif" COLOR="#ffffff" SIZE="3">
<B> Casting director and actress Joanna Merlin          </B>
</FONT></A>

<BR>
<FONT FACE="Verdana, Charcoal, Sans Serif" COLOR="#ffffff" SIZE="2">
<BLOCKQUOTE>Casting director and actress <A
HREF="http://freshair.npr.org/guestInfoFA.cfm?name=joannamerlin">Joanna
Merlin</A> has written a new guide for actors, <I>Auditioning: An
...
</BLOCKQUOTE></FONT>
<BR>
...
```

The rest of the file is mostly taken up by some JavaScript, some search box forms, and code for a button bar, which contains image links like this:

```
...
<A HREF="dayFA.cfm?todayDate=archive"><IMG SRC="images/nav_archived_on.gif"
ALT="Archived Shows" WIDTH="124" HEIGHT="36" BORDER="0" HSPACE="0" VSPACE="0"></A>
<A HREF="commFA.cfm"><IMG SRC="images/nav_commentators_off.gif" ALT="Commentators"
WIDTH="124" HEIGHT="36" BORDER="0" HSPACE="0" VSPACE="0"></A>
<A HREF="aboutFA.cfm"><IMG SRC="images/nav_about_off.gif" ALT="About Fresh Air"
WIDTH="124" HEIGHT="36" BORDER="0" HSPACE="0" VSPACE="0"></A>
<A HREF="stationsFA.cfm"><IMG SRC="images/nav_stations_off.gif" ALT="Find a Station"
WIDTH="124" HEIGHT="36" BORDER="0" HSPACE="0" VSPACE="0"></A>
...
```

Then, after the real program description text, there is code that links to the description pages for the previous and next shows:

```
...
<TD WIDTH="50%" ALIGN="left" BGCOLOR="#4F4F85">
  <FONT FACE="Verdana, Charcoal, Sans Serif" SIZE="2" COLOR="#FFCC00">
      &#171; 
  </FONT>
  <A HREF="dayFA.cfm?todayDate=06%2F29%2F2001">
    <FONT FACE="Verdana, Charcoal, Sans Serif" SIZE="2" COLOR="#FFCC00">
    Previous show
    </FONT>
```

```
    </A>
  </TD>
  <TD WIDTH="50%" ALIGN="right" BGCOLOR="#4F4F85">
    <A HREF="dayFA.cfm?todayDate=07%2F03%2F2001">
      <FONT FACE="Verdana, Charcoal, Sans Serif" SIZE="2" COLOR="#FFCC00">
        Next show
      </FONT>
    </A>
    <FONT FACE="Verdana, Charcoal, Sans Serif" SIZE="2" COLOR="#FFCC00">
       &#187;  
    </FONT>
  </TD>
  ...
```

The trick is in capturing the URLs and link text from each program link in the main text, while ignoring the button bar links and the "Previous Show" and "Next Show" links. Two criteria distinguish the links we want from the links we don't: First, each link that we want (i.e., each a element with an href attribute) has a font element as a child; and secondly, the text content of the a element starts with "Listen to" (which we incidentally want to leave out when we print the link text). This is directly implementable with calls to HTML::Element methods:

```perl
use HTML::TreeBuilder;
my $tree = HTML::TreeBuilder->new;
$tree->parse_file( 'fresh1.html' ) || die $!;
my $base_url = 'http://www.freshair.com/whatever';
  # for resolving relative URLs

foreach my $a ( $tree->find_by_tag_name('a') ) {

  my $href = $a->attr('href') || next;
    # Make sure it has an href attribute

  next unless grep ref($_) && $_->tag eq 'font', $a->content_list;
    # Make sure (at least) one of its children is a font element

  my $text_content = $a->as_text;
  next unless $text_content =~ s/^\s*Listen to\s+//s;
    # Make sure its text content starts with that (and remove it)

  # It's good!  Print it:
  use URI;
  print "$text_content\n  ", URI->new_abs($href, $base_url), "\n";
}

$tree->delete;  # Delete tree from memory
```

CHAPTER 10

Modifying HTML with Trees

In Chapter 9, we saw how to extract information from HTML trees. But that's not the only thing you can use trees for. HTML::TreeBuilder trees can be altered and can even be written back out as HTML, using the as_HTML( ) method. There are four ways in which a tree can be altered: you can alter a node's attributes; you can delete a node; you can detach a node and reattach it elsewhere; and you can add a new node. We'll treat each of these in turn.

Changing Attributes

Suppose that in your new role as fixer of large sets of HTML documents, you are given a bunch of documents that have headings like this:

```
<h3 align=center>Free Monkey</h3>
<h3 color=red>Inquire Within</h3>
```

that need to be changed like this:

```
<h2 class=scream>Free Monkey</h2>
<h4 class=mutter>Inquire Within</h4>
```

Before you start phrasing this in terms of HTML::Element methods, you should consider whether this can be done with a search-and-replace operation in an editor. In this case, it cannot, because you're not just changing every <h3 align=center> to <h2 class=scream> and every <h4 color=red> to <h3 class=mutter> (which are apparently simple search-and-replace operations), you also have to change </h3> to </h2> or to </h4>, depending on what you did to the element that it closes. That sort of context dependency puts this well outside the realm of simple search-and-replace operations. One could try to implement this with HTML::TokeParser, reading every token and printing it back out, after having possibly altered it. In such a program, every time we see an <h3...> and maybe alter it, we'd have to set a flag indicating what the next </h3> should be changed to.

So far, you've seen the method $element->attr(*attrname*) to get the value of an attribute (returning undef if there is no such attribute). To alter attribute values, you need only two additional syntaxes: $element->attr(*attrname, newval*) sets a value (regardless of whether that attribute had a previous value), and $element-> attr(*attrname,* undef) deletes an attribute. That works even for changing the _tag attribute (for which the $element->tag method is a shortcut).

That said, it's just a matter of knowing what nodes to change and then changing them, as in Example 10-1.

Example 10-1. Modifying attributes

```
use strict;
use HTML::TreeBuilder;
my $root = HTML::TreeBuilder->new;
$root->parse_file('rewriters1/in1.html') || die $!;

print "Before:\n";
$root->dump;

my @h3_center = $root->look_down('_tag', 'h3', 'align', 'center');
my @h3_red    = $root->look_down('_tag', 'h3', 'color', 'red');
foreach my $h3c (@h3_center) {
  $h3c->attr('_tag', 'h2');
  $h3c->attr('style', 'scream');
  $h3c->attr('align', undef);
}

foreach my $h3r (@h3_red) {
  $h3r->attr('_tag', 'h4');
  $h3r->attr('style', 'mumble');
  $h3r->attr('color', undef);
}

print "\n\nAfter:\n";
$root->dump;
```

Suppose that the input file consists of this:

```
<html><body>

<h3 align=center>Free Monkey</h3>
<h3 color=red>Inquire Within</h3>
<p>It's a monkey!  <em>And it's free!</em></html>
```

When we run the program, we can see the tree dump before and after the modifications happen:

```
Before:
<html> @0
  <head> @0.0 (IMPLICIT)
  <body> @0.1
    <h3 align="center"> @0.1.0
      "Free Monkey"
```

```
        <h3 color="red">  @0.1.1
          "Inquire Within"
        <p>  @0.1.2
          "It's a monkey! "
          <em>  @0.1.2.1
            "And it's free!"
    After:
    <html>  @0
      <head>  @0.0 (IMPLICIT)
      <body>  @0.1
        <h2 style="scream">  @0.1.0
          "Free Monkey"
        <h4 style="mumble">  @0.1.1
          "Inquire Within"
        <p>  @0.1.2
          "It's a monkey! "
          <em>  @0.1.2.1
            "And it's free!"
```

The changes applied correctly, so we can go ahead and add this code to the end of the program, to dump the tree to disk:

```
open(OUT, ">rewriters1/out1.html") || die "Can't write: $!";
print OUT $root->as_HTML;
close(OUT);
$root->delete; # done with it, so delete it
```

Whitespace

Examining the output file shows it to be one single line, consisting of this (wrapped so it will fit on the page):

```
<html><head></head><body><h2 style="scream">Free Monkey</h2><h4
style="mumble">Inquire Within</h4><p>It's a monkey! <em>And it's
free!</em></body></html>
```

Where did all the nice whitespace from the original go, such as the newline after each </h3>?

Whitespace in HTML (except in pre elements and a few others) isn't contrastive. That is, any amount of whitespace is as good as just one space. So whenever HTML::TreeBuilder sees whitespace tokens as it is parsing the HTML source, it compacts each group into a single space. Furthermore, whitespace between some kinds of tags (such as between </h3> and <h3>, or between </h3> and <p>) isn't meaningful at all, so when HTML::TreeBuilder sees such whitespace, it just discards it.

This whitespace mangling is the default behavior of an HTML::TreeBuilder tree and can be changed by two options that you set before parsing from a file:

```
my $root = HTML::TreeBuilder->new;

$root->ignore_ignorable_whitespace(0);
```

```
  # Don't try to delete whitespace between block-level elements.

$root->no_space_compacting(1);
  # Don't smash every whitespace sequences into a single space.
```

With those lines added to our program, the parse tree output file ends up with the appropriate whitespace.

```
<html><head></head><body>

<h2 style="scream">Free Monkey</h2>
<h4 style="mumble">Inquire Within</h4>

<p>It's a monkey!  <em>And it's free!</em></body>

</html>
```

An alternative is to have the as_HTML( ) method try to indent the HTML as it prints it. This is achieved by calling as_HTML like so:

```
print OUT $root->as_HTML(undef, "  ");
```

This feature is still somewhat experimental, and its implementation might change, but at time of this writing, this makes the output file's code look like this:

```
<html>
  <head>
  </head>
  <body>
    <h2 style="scream">Free Monkey</h2>
    <h4 style="mumble">Inquire Within</h4>
    <p>It's a monkey! <em>And it's free!</em></body>
</html>
```

Other HTML Options

Besides this indenting option, there are further options to as_HTML( ), as described in Chapter 9. One option controls whether omissible end-tags (such as </p> and </li>) are printed.

Another controls what characters are escaped using &foo; sequences. Notably, by default, this encodes all characters over ASCII 126, so for example, as_HTML will print an é in the parse tree as é (whether it came from a literal é or from an é). This is always safe, but in cases where you're dealing with text with a lot of Latin-1 or Unicode characters, having every one of those characters encoded as a &*foo*; sequence might be bothersome to any people looking at the HTML markup output.

In that case, your call to as_HTML can consist of $root->as_HTML('<>&'), in which case only the minimum of characters (<, >, and &) will be escaped. There's no point is using these options (or in preserving whitespace with ignore_ignorable_whitespace and no_space_compacting) if you're reasonably sure nobody will ever be looking at the resulting HTML. But for cases where people might need to look at the HTML, these options will make the code more inviting than just one huge block of HTML.

Deleting Images

Instead of altering nodes or extracting data from them, it's common to want to just delete them. For example, consider that we have the task of taking normally complex and image-rich web pages and making unadorned text-only versions of them, such as one would print out or paste into email. Each document in question has one big table with three rows, like this:

```
<html>
<head><title>Shatner and Kunis Sweep the Oscars</title></head>
<body>
<table>
  <tr class="top_button_bar">
  ...appalling amounts of ad banners and button bars...
  </tr>
  <tr class="main">
    <td class="left_geegaws">
    ...yet more ads and button bars...
    </td>
    <td class="story">

    <h1>Shatner and Kunis Sweep the Oscars</h1>

    <img src="shatner_kunis_awards.jpg" align=left>

    <p>Stars of <cite>American Psycho II</cite> walked away with four
        Academy Awards...

    </td>
    <td class="right_geegaws">
    ...even more ads...
    </td>
  </tr>
  <tr class="top_button_bar">
  ...ads, always ads...
  </tr>
</table>
<hr>Copyright 2002, United Lies Syndicate
</html>
```

The simplified version of such a page should omit all images and elements of the class top_button_bar, bottom_button_bar, left_geegaws, and right_geegaws. This can be implemented with a simple call to look_down:

```
use HTML::TreeBuilder;
my $root = HTML::TreeBuilder->new;
$root->parse_file('rewriters1/in002.html') || die $!;

foreach my $d ($root->look_down(
  sub {
    return 1 if $_[0]->tag eq 'img';   # we're looking for images
    # no class means ignore it
    my $class = $_[0]->attr('class') || return 0;
```

```
        return 1 if $class eq 'top_button_bar' or $class eq 'right_geegaws'
                or $class eq 'bottom_button_bar' or $class eq 'left_geegaws';
        return 0;
      }
)) {
  $d->delete;
}

open(OUT, ">rewriters1/out002.html") || die "Can't write: $!";
print OUT $root->as_HTML(undef, '  '); # two-space indent in output
close(OUT);
$root->delete; # done with it, so delete it
```

The call to $d->delete detaches the node in $d from its parent, then destroys it along with all its descendant nodes. The resulting file looks like this:

```
<html>
  <head>
    <title>Shatner and Kunis Sweep the Oscars</title>
  </head>
  <body>
    <table>
      <tr class="main">
        <td class="story">
          <h1>Shatner and Kunis Sweep the Oscars</h1>
          <p>Stars of <cite>American Psycho II</cite> walked [...] </td>
      </tr>
    </table>
    <hr>Copyright 2002, United Lies Syndicate </body>
</html>
```

One pragmatic point here: the list returned by the look_down( ) call will contain the two tr and td elements, any images they contain, and also images elsewhere in the document. When we delete one of those tr or td nodes, we are also implicitly deleting every one of its descendant nodes, including some img elements that we are about to hit in a subsequent iteration through look_down( )'s return list.

This isn't a problem in this case, because deleting an already deleted node is a harmless no-operation. The larger point here is that when look_down( ) finds a matching node (as with a left_geegaws td node, in our example), that doesn't stop it from looking below that node for more matches. If you need that kind of behavior, you'll need to implement it in your own traverser, as discussed in Chapter 9.

Detaching and Reattaching

Suppose that the output of our above rewriter is not satisfactory. While its output contains an apparently harmless one-cell one-row table, this is somehow troublesome when the president of the company tries viewing that web page on his cellphone/PDA, which has a typically limited understanding of HTML. Some experimentation shows that any web pages with tables in them will deeply confuse the boss's PDA.

So your task should be changed to this: find the one interesting cell in the table (the td with class="story"), detach it, then replace the table with the td, and delete the table. This is a complex series of actions, but luckily every one of them is directly translatable into an HTML::Element method. The result is Example 10-2.

Example 10-2. Detaching and reattaching nodes

```
use strict;
use HTML::TreeBuilder;
my $root = HTML::TreeBuilder->new;
$root->parse_file('rewriters1/in002.html') || die $!;

my $good_td = $root->look_down( '_tag', 'td', 'class', 'story', );
die "No good td?!" unless $good_td;        # sanity checking
my $big_table = $root->look_down( '_tag', 'table' );
die "No big table?!" unless $big_table;   # sanity checking

$good_td->detach;
$big_table->replace_with($good_td);
  # Yes, there's even a method for replacing one node with another!

open(OUT, ">rewriters1/out002b.html") || die "Can't write: $!";
print OUT $root->as_HTML(undef, '  '); # two-space indent in output
close(OUT);
$root->delete; # done with it, so delete it
```

The resulting document looks like this:

```
<html>
  <head>
    <title>Shatner and Kunis Sweep the Oscars</title>
  </head>
  <body>
    <td class="story">
      <h1>Shatner and Kunis Sweep the Oscars</h1>
      <p>Stars of <cite>American Psycho II</cite> walked [...] </td>
    <hr>Copyright 2002, United Lies Syndicate </body>
</html>
```

One problem, though: we have a td outside of a table. Simply change it from a td element into something innocuous, such as a div, and while we're at it, delete that class attribute:

```
$good_td->tag('div');
$good_td->attr('class', undef);
```

That makes the output look like this:

```
<html>
  <head>
    <title>Shatner and Kunis Sweep the Oscars</title>
  </head>
  <body>
    <div>
```

```
    <h1>Shatner and Kunis Sweep the Oscars</h1>
      <p>Stars of <cite>American Psycho II</cite> walked [...] </div>
    <hr>Copyright 2002, United Lies Syndicate </body>
  </html>
```

An alternative is not to detach and save the td in the first place, but to detach and save only its content. That's simple enough:

```
my @good_content = $good_td->content_list;
foreach my $c (@good_content) {
  $c->detach if ref $c;
    # text nodes aren't objects, so aren't really "attached" anyhow
}
```

The detach_content( ) Method

The above task is so common that there's a method for it, called detach_content( ), which detaches and returns the content of the node on which it's called. So we can simply modify our program to read:

```
my @good_content = $good_td->detach_content;

$big_table->replace_with(@good_content);
$big_table->delete;
```

However you chose to express the node-moving operations, the parse tree looks like this:

```
<html>
  <head>
    <title>Shatner and Kunis Sweep the Oscars</title>
  </head>
  <body>
    <h1>Shatner and Kunis Sweep the Oscars</h1>
    <p>Stars of <cite>American Psycho II</cite> walked [...]
    <hr>Copyright 2002, United Lies Syndicate </body>
  </html>
```

In fact, every HTML::Element method that allows you to attach a node someplace (as replace_with does) will first detach that node if it's already attached elsewhere. So you could actually skip the whole detach_content( ) process step and just write this:

```
$big_table->replace_with( $good_td->content_list );
$big_table->delete;
```

It does the same thing and results in the same output.

Constraints

There are some constraints on what you can expect replace_with( ) to do, but these are just three constraints against fairly odd things that you would probably not try anyway. Namely, the documentation says you can't replace an element with multiple instances of itself; you can't replace an element with one (or more) of its siblings;

and you can't replace an element that has no parent, because replacing an element inherently means altering the content list of its parent.

Many methods in the HTML::Element documentation have similar constraints spelled out, although the typical programmer will never find them to be an obstacle in and of themselves. If one of those constraints is violated, it is typically a sign that something is conceptually wrong elsewhere in the program.

For example, if you try $element->replace_with(...) and are surprised by an error message that "the target node has no parent," it is almost definitely because you either already replaced the element with something (leaving it parentless) or deleted it (leaving it parentless, contentless, and attributeless). For example, that error message would result if our program had this:

```
$big_table->delete;
$big_table->replace_with( $good_td->content_list );
# Wrong!
```

instead of this:

```
$big_table->replace_with( $good_td->content_list );
$big_table->delete;
# Right.
```

Attaching in Another Tree

So far we've detached elements from one part of a tree and attached them elsewhere in the same tree. But there's nothing stopping you from attaching them in other trees.

For example, consider a case like the above example, where we extract the text in the <td class="story"> ... </td> element, but this time, instead of attaching it elsewhere in the same document tree, we're attaching it at a certain point in a different tree that we're using as a template. The template document looks like this:

```
<html><head><title>Put the title here</title></head>
<body><!-- printable version -->
<blockquote>
<font size="-1">
<!-- start -->
...put the content here...
<!-- end -->
<hr>Copyright 2002.  Printed from the United Lies Syndicate web site.
</font>
</blockquote>
</body></html>
```

You'll note that the web designers have helpfully inserted comments to denote where the inserted content should start and end. But when you have HTML::TreeBuilder parse the document with default parse options and dump the tree, you don't see any sign of the comments:

```
<html> @0
  <head> @0.0
    <title> @0.0.0
      "Put the title here"
  <body> @0.1
    <blockquote> @0.1.0
      <font size="-1"> @0.1.0.0
        "  ...put the content here...  "
        <hr> @0.1.0.0.1
        "Copyright 2002. Printed from the United Lies Syndicate web site. "
```

Retaining Comments

However, storing comments is controlled by an HTML::TreeBuilder parse option, store_comments( ), which is off by default. If we parse the file like so:

```
use strict;
use HTML::TreeBuilder;
my $template_root = HTML::TreeBuilder->new;
$template_root->store_comments(1);
$template_root->parse_file('rewriters1/template1.html')
  || dic "Can't read template file: $!";

$template_root->dump;
```

the comments now show up in the parse tree:

```
<html> @0
  <head> @0.0
    <title> @0.0.0
      "Put the title here"
  <body> @0.1
    <!-- printable version --> @0.1.0
    <blockquote> @0.1.1
      <font size="-1"> @0.1.1.0
        <!-- start --> @0.1.1.0.0
        " ...put the content here... "
        <!-- end --> @0.1.1.0.2
        <hr> @0.1.1.0.3
        "Copyright 2002. Printed from the United Lies Syndicate web site. "
```

Accessing Comments

What's left is to figure out how to take out what's between the <!-- start --> and <!-- end --> comments, to insert whatever content needs to be put in there, then to write out the document. First we need to find the comments, and to do that we need to figure out how comments are stored in the tree, because so far we've only dealt with elements and bits of text.

Mercifully, what we know about element objects in trees still applies, because that's how comments are stored: as element objects. But because comments aren't actual elements, the HTML::Element documentation refers to them as *pseudoelements*, and they are given a tag name that no real element could have: ~comment. The actual content of the comment (start) is stored as the value of the text attribute. In other words, <!-- start --> is stored as if it were <~comment text=' start '></~comment>. So finding comments is straightforward:

```
foreach my $c ($template_root->find_by_tag_name('~comment')) {
  print "A comment has text [", $c->attr('text'), "].\n";
}
```

That prints this:

```
A comment has text [ printable version ]
A comment has text [ start ]
A comment has text [ end ]
```

Finding the start and end comments is a matter of filtering those comments:

```
use strict;
use HTML::TreeBuilder;
my $template_root = HTML::TreeBuilder->new;
$template_root->store_comments(1);
$template_root->parse_file('rewriters1/template1.html')
 || die "Can't read template file: $!";

my($start_comment, $end_comment);
foreach my $c ($template_root->find_by_tag_name('~comment')) {
  if($c->attr('text') =~ m/^\s*start\s*$/) {
    $start_comment = $c;
  } elsif($c->attr('text') =~ m/^\s*end\s*$/) {
    $end_comment = $c;
  }
}
die "Couldn't find template's 'start' comment!" unless $start_comment;
die "Couldn't find template's 'end' comment!"  unless $end_comment;

die "start and end comments don't have the same parent?!"
  unless $start_comment->parent eq $end_comment->parent;
# Make sure things are sane.
```

Attaching Content

Once that's done, we need some way of taking some new content (which we'll get elsewhere) and putting that in place of what's between the "start" comment and the "end" comment. There are many ways of doing this, but this is the most straightforward in terms of the methods we've already seen in this chapter:

```
sub put_into_template {
  my @to_insert = @_;
  my $parent = $start_comment->parent;
  my @old_content = $parent->detach_content;
  my @new_content;

  # Copy everything up to the $start_comment into @new_content,
  # and then everything starting at $end_comment, and ignore
  # everything inbetween and instead drop in things from @to_insert.
```

```perl
my $am_saving = 1;
foreach my $node (@old_content) {
  if($am_saving) {
    push @new_content, $node;
    if($node eq $start_comment) {
      push @new_content, @to_insert;
      $am_saving = 0;    # and start ignoring nodes.
    }
  } else {  # I'm snipping out things to ignore
    if($node eq $end_comment) {
      push @new_content, $node;
      $am_saving = 1;
    } else {  # It's an element to ignore, and to destroy.
      $node->delete if ref $node;
    }
  }
}
$parent->push_content(@new_content);  # attach new children
return;
}
```

This seems a bit long, but it's mostly the work of just tracking whether we're in the mode of saving things from the old content list or ignoring (and in fact deleting) things from the old content list. With that subroutine in our program, we can test whether it works:

```perl
put_into_template("Testing 1 2 3.");
$template_root->dump;
put_into_template("Is this mic on?");
$template_root->dump;
```

That prints this:

```
<html> @0
  <head> @0.0
    <title> @0.0.0
      "Put the title here"
  <body> @0.1
    <!-- printable version --> @0.1.0
    <blockquote> @0.1.1
      <font size="-1"> @0.1.1.0
        <!-- start --> @0.1.1.0.0
        "Testing 1 2 3."
        <!-- end --> @0.1.1.0.2
        <hr> @0.1.1.0.3
        "Copyright 2002. Printed from the United Lies Syndicate web site. "
<html> @0
  <head> @0.0
    <title> @0.0.0
      "Put the title here"
  <body> @0.1
    <!-- printable version --> @0.1.0
    <blockquote> @0.1.1
      <font size="-1"> @0.1.1.0
```

```
<!-- start --> @0.1.1.0.0
"Is this mic on?"
<!-- end --> @0.1.1.0.2
<hr> @0.1.1.0.3
"Copyright 2002. Printed from the United Lies Syndicate web site. "
```

This shows that not only did we manage to replace the template's original ...put the content here... text node with a Testing 1 2 3. node, but also *another* call to replace it with Is this mic on? worked too. From there, it's just a matter of adapting the code from the last section, which found the content in a file. Except this time we use our new put_into_template( ) function on that content:

```perl
# Read an individual file for its content now.
my $content_file_root = HTML::TreeBuilder->new;
my $input_filespec = 'rewriters1/in002.html';   # or whatever input file
$content_file_root->parse_file($input_filespec)
 || die "Can't read input file $input_filespec: $!";

# Find its real content:
my $good_td = $content_file_root->look_down( '_tag', 'td',  'class', 'story', );
die "No good td?!" unless $good_td;

put_into_template( $good_td->content_list );
$content_file_root->delete;  # We don't need it anymore.

open(OUT, ">rewriters1/out003a.html") || die "Can't write: $!";
  # or whatever output filespec
print OUT $template_root->as_HTML(undef, '  '); # two-space indent in output
close(OUT);
```

When this runs, we see can see in the output file that the content was successfully inserted into the template and written out:

```html
<html>
  <head>
    <title>Put the title here</title>
  </head>
  <body>
    <!-- printable version -->
    <blockquote><font size="-1">
        <!-- start -->
        <h1>Shatner and Kunis Sweep the Oscars</h1>
        <p>Stars of <cite>American Psycho II</cite> walked away with four Academy
          Awards...
        <!-- end -->
        <hr>Copyright 2002. Printed from the United Lies Syndicate web site.
        </font></blockquote>
  </body>
</html>
```

All is well, except the title is no good. It still says "Put the title here". All that's left is to replace the content of the template's title with the content of the current file's title. We just find the title element in each, and swap content:

```
my $template_title = $template_root->find_by_tag_name('title')
  || die "No title in template?!";
$template_title->delete_content;
my $content_title = $content_file_root->find_by_tag_name('title');
if($content_title) {
  $template_title->push_content( $content_title->content_list );
    # This method, like all methods, automatically detaches
    #  elements from where they are currently, as necessary.
} else {
  $template_title->push_content( 'No title' );
}
```

We put that code in our program anywhere between when we read the file into $content_file_root and when we destroy it; it works happily and puts the right content into the output file's title element:

```
<html>
  <head>
    <title>Shatner and Kunis Sweep the Oscars</title>
  </head>
[...]
```

Because this works for a single given input file, and because we tested earlier to make sure our put_into_template( ) routine works for all subsequent invocations as well as for the first, that means we have the main building block for a system that does template extraction and insertion for any number of files. All we have to do is turn that into a function, and call it as many times as needed. For example:

```
# ...read in $template_root...
# ...get names of files to change into @input_files...
foreach my $input_filespec (@input_files) {
  template_redo($input_filespec, "../printables/$input_filespec");
}

sub template_redo {
  my($input_filespec, $output_filespec) = @_;
  my $content_file_root = HTML::TreeBuilder->new;
  $content_file_root->parse_file($input_filespec)
    || die "Can't read input file $input_filespec: $!";

  #  ...then extract content and put into the template tree, as above...

  $content_file_root->delete;  # We don't need it anymore.
  open(OUT, ">$output_filespec") || die "Can't write $output_file: $!";
  print OUT $template_root->as_HTML(undef, '  ');
  close(OUT);
}
```

Creating New Elements

So far we haven't directly created any new HTML::Element objects. All the elements that have appeared thus far were created by HTML::TreeBuilder as part of its delegated task of building whole trees. But suppose that we actually do need to add something to a tree that never existed elsewhere in that or any other tree. In the above section, we actually snuck in creating a new node in this statement:

```
$template_title->push_content( 'No title' );
```

But that's hardly an amazing feat, because that node isn't a real object. You can actually create a new object by calling HTML::Element->new('*tagname*'). So this would add an hr element to a given paragraph object:

```
my $hr = HTML::Element->new('hr');
$paragraph->push_content($hr);
```

And you could create a new img node with given attributes:

```
my $img = HTML::Element->new('img');
$img->attr('src', 'hooboy.png');
$img->attr('alt', 'Lookit that!');
$paragraph->push_content($img);
```

Incidentally, the setting of attributes can be done in the constructor call:

```
my $img = HTML::Element->new('img',    # plus any key,value pairs...
  'src' => 'hooboy.png',
  'alt' => 'Lookit that!',
);
$paragraph->push_content($img);
```

This is simple enough, but it becomes rather annoying when you want to construct several linked nodes. For example, suppose you wanted to construct objects equivalent to what you'd get if you parsed this:

```
<li>See <b><a href="page.html">here.</a></b>!</li>
```

Even this little treelet is fairly tedious to produce using normal constructor calls:

```
use HTML::Element;

my $li = HTML::Element->new('li');
my $b  = HTML::Element->new('b');
my $a  = HTML::Element->new('a', 'href' => 'page.html');
$a->push_content('here.');
$b->push_content($a);
$li->push_content("See ", $b, "!");

# Have a look:
print $li->as_HTML, "\n";
$li->dump;
```

That indeed shows us that we succeeded in constructing what we wanted:

```
<li>See <b><a href="page.html">here.</a></b>!

<li> @0
  "See "
  <b> @0.1
    <a href="page.html"> @0.1.0
      "here."
  "!"
```

Literals

If you try manually constructing and linking every element in a larger structure such as a table, the code will be maddening. One solution is not to create the elements at all, but to create a single element, called a ~literal pseudoelement, that contains the raw source you want to appear when that part of the tree is dumped. These sorts of objects are very much like the ~comment pseudoelements we saw in the last section; their real content is in their text attribute:

```
my $li = HTML::Element->new( '~literal',
  'text', '<li>See <b><a href="page.html">here.</a></b>!</li>'
);
```

This constructs something that will appear as that chunk of text when as_HTML( ) is called on it, but it's nothing like a normal HTML element—you can't put other elements or text under it, and you can't see it with look_down or find_by_tag_name( ) (unless you're looking for a ~literal element, which you're probably not).

New Nodes from Lists

Literals are fine for cases where you just want to drop arbitrarily large amounts of undigested HTML source into a tree right before you call as_HTML( ). But when you want to really make new, full-fledged elements, you can do that with a friendlier syntax with the new_from_lol( ) constructor.

With new_from_lol( ), you can specify an element with a list reference whose first item should be the tag name, which then specifies attributes with an optional hash reference, and then contains any other nodes, either as bits of text, preexisting element objects, or more list references. This is best shown by example:

```
my $li = HTML::Element->new_from_lol(
  [ 'li',
        "See ",
        [ 'b',
              [ 'a',
                    {'href' => 'page.html'},
                    "here."
              ]
        ],
        "!"
  ]
);    # or indent it however you prefer -- probably more concisely
```

And this produces exactly the same tree as when we called HTML::Element->new three times then linked up the resulting elements.

The benefits of the new_from_lol( ) approach are you can easily specify children at construction time, and it's very hard to produce mis-nested trees, because if the number of ['s above doesn't match the number of]'s, it won't parse as valid Perl.

Moreover, it can actually be a relatively concise format. The above code, with some whitespace removed, basically fits happily on one line:

```
my $li = HTML::Element->new_from_lol(
  ['li', "See ", ['b', ['a', {'href' => 'page.html'}, "here." ] ], "!" ]
);
```

So, for example, consider returning to the template-insertion problem in the previous section, and suppose that besides dumping the article's content into a template, we should also preface the content with something like this:

```
<p>The original version of the following story is to found at:
<br><a href="$orig_url">$orig_url</a></p>
<hr>
```

This can be done by replacing:

```
put_into_template( $good_td->content_list );
```

with this:

```
# Assuming $orig_url has been set somewhere...

put_into_template(
  HTML::Element->new_from_lol(
    ['p', "The original version of the following story is to found at:",
      ['a', {'href', $orig_url}, $orig_url],
    ]
  ),
  HTML::Element->new_from_lol(['hr']),
  $good_td->content_list,
);
```

If you find new_from_lol( ) notation to be an unnecessary elaboration, you can still manually construct each element with HTML::Element->new and link them up before passing them to put_into_template( ). Or you could just as well create a ~literal pseudoelement containing the raw source:

```
put_into_template(
  HTML::Element->new('~literal', 'text' => qq{
    <p>The original version of the following story is to found at:
    <br><a href="$orig_url">$orig_url</a></p>
    <hr>
  }),
  $good_td->content_list,
);
```

While the new_from_lol( ) syntax is an expressive shorthand for the general form of element construction, you may well prefer the directness of creating a single ~literal or the simplicity of normal ->new calls. As the Perl saying goes, there is more than one way to do it.

## CHAPTER 11

Cookies, Authentication, and Advanced Requests

Not every document can be fetched with a simple GET or POST request. Many pages require authentication before you can access them, some use cookies to keep track of the different users, and still others want special values in the Referer or User-Agent headers. This chapter shows you how to set arbitrary headers, manage cookies, and even authenticate using LWP. You'll be able to make your LWP programs appear to be Netscape or Internet Explorer, log in to a protected site, and work with sites that use cookies.

For example, suppose you're automating a web-based purchasing system. The server requires you to log in, then issues you a cookie to prove you've been authenticated. You must then send this cookie back to the server with every request you make.

Or, more mundanely, suppose you're extracting information from one of the many web sites that check the User-Agent header in your requests. If your User-Agent doesn't identify yours as a recent version of Netscape or Internet Explorer, the server sends you back an "Upgrade your browser" page. You need to set the User-Agent header to make it appear that you are using Netscape or Internet Explorer.

Cookies

HTTP was originally designed as a stateless protocol, meaning that each request is totally independent of other requests. But web site designers felt the need for something to help them identify the user of a particular session. The mechanism that does this is called a *cookie*. This section gives some background on cookies so you know what LWP is doing for you.

An HTTP cookie is a string that an HTTP server can send to a client, which the client is supposed to put in the headers of any future requests that it makes to that server. Suppose a client makes a request to a given server, and the response headers consist of this:

```
Date: Thu, 28 Feb 2002 04:29:13 GMT
Server: Apache/1.3.23 (Win32)
```

```
Content-Type: text/html
Set-Cookie: foo=bar; expires=Thu, 20 May 2010 01:23:45 GMT; path=/
```

This means that the server wants all further requests from this client to anywhere on this site (i.e., under /) to be accompanied by this header line:

```
Cookie: foo=bar
```

That header should be present in all this browser's requests to this site, until May 20, 2010 (at 1:23:45 in the morning), after which time the client should never send that cookie again.

A Set-Cookie line can fail to specify an expiration time, in which case this cookie ends at the end of this "session," where "session" is generally seen as ending when the user closes all browser windows. Moreover, the path can be something more specific than /. It can be, for example, */dahut/*, in which case a cookie will be sent only for URLs that begin *http://thishost/dahut/*. Finally, a cookie can specify that this site is not just on this one host, but also on all other hosts in this subdomain, so that if this host is *search.mybazouki.com*, cookies should be sent to any host-name under *mybazouki.com*, including *images.mybazouki.com*, *ads.mybazouki.com*, *extra.stuff.mybazouki.com*, and so on.

All those details are handled by LWP, and you need only make a few decisions for a given LWP::UserAgent object:

- Should it implement cookies at all? If not, it will just ignore any Set-Cookie: headers from the server and will never send any Cookie: headers.
- Should it load cookies when it starts up? If not, it will start out with no cookies.
- Should it save cookies to some file when the browser object is destroyed? If not, whatever cookies it has accumulated will be lost.
- What format should the cookies file be in? Currently the choices are either a format particular to LWP, or Netscape cookies files.

Enabling Cookies

By default, an LWP::UserAgent object doesn't implement cookies. To make an LWP::UserAgent object that implements cookies is as simple as this:

```
my $browser = LWP::UserAgent->new( );
$browser->cookie_jar( {} );
```

However, that browser object's cookie jar (as we call its HTTP cookie database) will start out empty, and its contents won't be saved anywhere when the object is destroyed. Incidentally, the above code is a convenient shortcut for what one previously had to do:

```
# Load LWP class for "cookie jar" objects
use HTTP::Cookies;
my $browser = LWP::UserAgent->new( );
my $cookie_jar = HTTP::Cookies->new( );
$browser->cookie_jar( $cookie_jar );
```

There's not much point to using the long form when you could use the short form instead, but the longer form becomes preferable when you're adding options to the cookie jar.

Loading Cookies from a File

To start the cookie jar by loading from a particular file, use the `file` option to the `HTTP::Cookies` new method:

```
use HTTP::Cookies;
my $cookie_jar = HTTP::Cookies->new(
    file    => "/some/where/cookies.lwp",
);
my $browser = LWP::UserAgent->new;
$browser->cookie_jar( $cookie_jar );
```

In that case, the file is read when the cookie jar is created, but it's never updated with any new cookies that the $browser object will have accumulated.

To read the cookies from a Netscape cookies file instead of from an LWP-format cookie file, use a different class, HTTP::Cookies::Netscape, which is just like HTTP::Cookies, except for the format that it reads and writes:

```
use HTTP::Cookies::Netscape;
my $cookie_jar = HTTP::Cookies::Netscape->new(
    file => "c:/program files/netscape/users/shazbot/cookies.txt",
);
my $browser = LWP::UserAgent->new;
$browser->cookie_jar( $cookie_jar );
```

Saving Cookies to a File

To make LWP write out its potentially changed cookie jar to a file when the object is no longer in use, add an `autosave => 1` parameter:

```
use HTTP::Cookies;
my $cookie_jar = HTTP::Cookies->new(
    file    => "/some/where/cookies.lwp",
    autosave => 1,
);
my $browser = LWP::UserAgent->new;
$browser->cookie_jar( $cookie_jar );
```

At time of this writing, using `autosave => 1` with HTTP::Cookies::Netscape has not been sufficiently tested and is not recommended.

Cookies and the New York Times Site

Suppose that you have felt personally emboldened and empowered by all the previous chapters' examples of pulling data off of news sites, especially the examples of simplifying HTML in Chapter 10. You decide that a great test of your skill would be to write

LWP code that downloads the stories off various newspapers' web sites and saves them all in a format (either plain text, highly simplified HTML, or even WML, if you have an html2wml tool around) that your ancient but trusty 2001-era PDA can read. Thus, you can spend your commute time on the train (or bus, tube, el, metro, jitney, T, etc.) merrily flipping through the day's news stories from papers all over the world.

Suppose also that you have the basic HTML-simplifying code in place (so we shall not discuss it further), and the LWP code that downloads stories from all the newspapers is working fine—except for the *New York Times* site. And you can't imagine why it's not working! You have a simple HTML::TokeParser program that gets the main page, finds all the URLs to stories in it, and downloads them one at a time. You verify that those routines are working fine. But when you look at the files that it claims to be successfully fetching and saving ($response->is_success returns true and everything!), all you see for each one is a page that says "Welcome to the New York Times on the Web! Already a member? Log in!" When you look at the exact same URL in Netscape, you don't see that page at all, but instead you see the news story that you want your LWP program to be accessing.

Then it hits you: years ago, the first time you accessed the *New York Times* site, it wanted you to register with an email address and a password. But you haven't seen that screen again, because of... HTTP cookies! You riffle through your Netscape HTTP cookies file, and lo, there you find:

```
.nytimes.com TRUE / FALSE 1343279235 RMID 809ac0ad1cff9a6b
```

Whatever this means to the *New York Times* site, it's apparently what differentiates your copy of Netscape when it's accessing a story URL, from your LWP program when it's accessing that URL.

Now, you could simply hardwire that cookie into the headers of the $browser->get( ) request's headers, but that involves recalling exactly how lines in Netscape cookie databases translate into headers in HTTP request. The optimally lazy solution is to simply enable cookie support in this LWP::UserAgent object and have it read your Netscape cookie database. So just after where you started off the program with this:

```
use LWP;
my $browser = LWP::UserAgent->new( );
```

Add this:

```
use HTTP::Cookies::Netscape;
my $cookie_jar = HTTP::Cookies::Netscape->new(
 'file' => 'c:/program files/netscape/users/me/cookies.txt'
);
$browser->cookie_jar($cookie_jar);
```

With those five lines of code added, your LWP program's requests to the *New York Times*'s server will carry the cookie that says that you're a registered user. So instead of giving your LWP program the "Log in!" page ad infinitum, the *New York Times*'s server now merrily serves your program the news stories. Success!

Adding Extra Request Header Lines

Here's some simplistic debugging advice: if your browser sees one thing at a given URL, but your LWP program sees another, first try just turning on cookie support, with an empty cookie jar. If that fails, have it read in your browser's cookie file.* And if *that* fails, it's time to start wondering what means the remote site is using for distinguishing your LWP program's requests from your browser's requests.

Every kind of browser sends different HTTP headers besides the very minimal headers that LWP::UserAgent typically sends. For example, whereas an LWP::UserAgent browser by default sends this header line:

```
User-Agent: libwww-perl/5.5394
```

Netscape 4.76 sends a header line like this:

```
User-Agent: Mozilla/4.76 [en] (Win98; U)
```

And also sends these header fields that an LWP::UserAgent browser doesn't send normally at all:

```
Accept: image/gif, image/x-xbitmap, image/jpeg, image/pjpeg, image/png, */*
Accept-Charset: iso-8859-1,*,utf-8
Accept-Encoding: gzip
Accept-Language: en-US
```

(That's assuming you've set your language preferences to U.S. English). That's on top of any Connection: keep-alive headers that may be sent, if the browser or any intervening firewall supports that feature (keep-alive) of HTTP.

Opera 5.12 is not much different:

```
User-Agent: Opera/5.12 (Windows 98; U)  [en]
Accept: text/html, image/png, image/jpeg, image/gif, image/x-xbitmap, */*
Accept-Language: en
Accept-Encoding: deflate, gzip, x-gzip, identity, *;q=0
```

But a recent version of Netscape gets rather more verbose:

```
User-Agent: Mozilla/5.0 (Macintosh; U; PPC Mac OS X; en-US;
   rv:0.9.4) Gecko/20011126 Netscape6/6.2.1
Accept: text/xml, application/xml, application/xhtml+xml, text/html;q=0.9,
   image/png, image/jpeg, image/gif;q=0.2, text/plain;q=0.8,
   text/css, */*;q=0.1
Accept-Charset: ISO-8859-1, utf-8;q=0.66, *;q=0.66
Accept-Encoding: gzip, deflate, compress;q=0.9
Accept-Language: en-us
```

Internet Explorer 5.12, in true Microsoft fashion, emits a few nonstandard headers:

```
Accept: */*
Accept-Language: en
```

---

* Currently there is support for only Netscape cookie files. But check CPAN; someone might write support for other browsers' cookie files.

```
Extension: Security/Remote-Passphrase
UA-CPU: PPC
UA-OS: MacOS
User-Agent: Mozilla/4.0 (compatible; MSIE 5.12; Mac_PowerPC)
```

Lynx can be verbose in reporting what MIME types my system's *etc/mailcap* tells it that it can handle:

```
Accept: text/html, text/plain, audio/mod, image/*, video/*, video/mpeg,
   application/pgp, application/pgp, application/pdf, message/partial,
   message/external-body, application/postscript, x-be2,
   application/andrew-inset, text/richtext, text/enriched
Accept: x-sun-attachment, audio-file, postscript-file, default,
   mail-file, sun-deskset-message, application/x-metamail-patch,
   text/sgml, */*;q=0.01
Accept-Encoding: gzip, compress
Accept-Language: en, es
User-Agent: Lynx/2.8.3dev.18 libwww-FM/2.14
```

This information can come in handy when trying to make your LWP program seem as much like a well-known interactive browser as possible

Pretending to Be Netscape

For example, suppose you're looking at *http://www.expreszo.nl/home.php* and you see that it has interesting headlines. You'd like to write a headline detector for this site to go with the other headline detectors we've been producing throughout the book. You look at the source in Netscape and see that each headline link looks like this:

```
<A class=pink href="headlines.php?id=749">...text...</A>
```

So you write something quite simple to capture those links:

```
use strict;
use warnings;
use LWP;
my $browser = LWP::UserAgent->new;

my $url = 'http://www.expreszo.nl/home.php';
my $response = $browser->get($url);
die "Can't get $url: ", $response->status_line
 unless $response->is_success;
$_ = $response->content;
my %seen;
while( m{href="(headlines.php[^"]+)">(.*?)</A>}sg ) {
  my $this = URI->new_abs($1,$response->base);
  print "$this\n   $2\n" unless $seen{$this}++;
}
print "NO HEADLINES?!  Source:\n", $response->content unless keys %seen;
```

And you run it, and it quite stubbornly says:

```
NO HEADLINES?!  Source:
<html><body>
 ...
```

```
Je hebt minimaal Microsoft Internet Explorer versie 4 of hoger, of
Netscape Navigator versie 4 of hoger nodig om deze site te bekijken.
...
</body></html>
```

That is, "you need MSIE 4 or higher, or Netscape 4 or higher, to view this site." It seems to be checking the `User-Agent` string of whatever browser visits the site and throwing a fit unless it's MSIE or Netscape! This is easily simulated, by adding this line right after `$browser` is created:

```
$browser->agent('Mozilla/4.76 [en] (Win98; U)');
```

With that one small change, the server sends the same page you saw in Netscape, and the headline extractor happily sees the headlines, and everything works:

```
http://www.expreszo.nl/headlines.php?id=752
  Meer syfilis en HIV bij homo's
http://www.expreszo.nl/headlines.php?id=751
  Imam hangt geldboete van € 1200 boven het hoofd
http://www.expreszo.nl/headlines.php?id=740
  SGP wil homohuwelijk terugdraaien
http://www.expreszo.nl/headlines.php?id=750
  Gays en moslims worden vaak gediscrimineerd
http://www.expreszo.nl/headlines.php?id=749
  Elton's gaydar rinkelt bij bruidegom Minnelli
http://www.expreszo.nl/headlines.php?id=746
  Lekkertje Drew Barrymore liever met een vrouw?
```

This approach works fine when the web site is looking only at the `User-Agent` line, as you can most easily control it with `$browser->agent(...)`. If you were dealing with some other site that insisted on seeing even more Netscape-like headers, that could be done, too:

```
my @netscape_like_headers = (
  'User-Agent' => 'Mozilla/4.76 [en] (Win98; U)',
  'Accept-Language' => 'en-US',
  'Accept-Charset' => 'iso-8859-1,*,utf-8',
  'Accept-Encoding' => 'gzip',
  'Accept' =>
  "image/gif, image/x-xbitmap, image/jpeg, image/pjpeg, image/png, */*",
);
my $response = $browser->get($url, @netscape_like_headers);
```

Referer

For some sites, that's not enough: they want to see that your `Referer` header value is something they consider appropriate. A `Referer` header line signals the URL of a page that either linked to the item you're requesting (as with `<a href="url">`) or inlines that image item (as with `<img src="url">`).

For example, I am a big fan of the comic strip *Dennis The Menace*. I find it to be the truest realization of deep satire, and I admire how its quality has kept up over the past 50 years, quite undeterred by the retirement and eventual death of its *auteur*, the comic genius Hank Ketcham. And nothing brightens my day more than laughing over the day's *Dennis The Menace* strip and hardcopying a really good one now and then, so I can pin it up on my office door to amuse my colleagues and to encourage them to visit the DTM web site. However, the server for the strip's image files doesn't want it to be inlined on pages that aren't authorized to do so, so they check the Referer line. Unfortunately, they have forgotten to allow for when there is no Referer line at all, such as happens when I try to hardcopy the day's image file using my browser. But LWP comes to the rescue:

```
my $response = $browser->get(
  # The URL of the image:
  'http://pst.rbma.com/content/Dennis_The_Menace',

  'Referer' =>   # The URL where I see the strip:

  'http://www.sfgate.com/cgi-bin/article.cgi?file=/comics/Dennis_The_Menace.dtl',
);
open(OUT, ">today_dennis.gif") || die $!;
binmode(OUT);
print OUT $response->content;
close(OUT);
```

By giving a Referer value that passes the image server's test for a good URL, I get to make a local copy of the image, which I can then print out and put on my office door.

Authentication

HTTP Basic Authentication is the most common type of authentication supported at the level of HTTP. The exchange works like this:

1. The browser makes a request for a URL.

2. The page is protected by Basic Authentication, so the server replies with a 401 Unauthorized status code. The response has a WWW-Authenticate header that specifies the authentication method ("basic") and the realm. "Realm" here is jargon for a string that identifies the locked-off area, which the browser is about to use in the next step.

3. The browser displays an "enter your username and password for *realm*" dialog box. Figure 11-1 shows the dialog box for a part of *www.unicode.org* whose realm name is "Unicode-MailList-Archives."

4. The browser requests the URL again, this time with an Authorization header that encodes the username and password.

5. If the username and password are verified, the server sends the document in a normal successful HTTP response. If the username and password aren't correct, we go back to step 2.

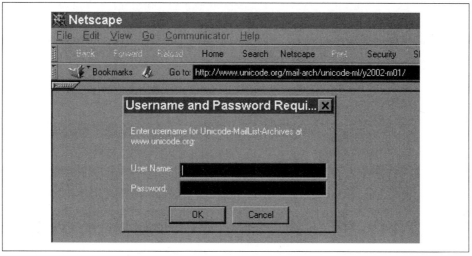

Figure 11-1. Authentication dialog box

Comparing Cookies with Basic Authentication

Like cookies, LWP implements HTTP Basic Authentication with attributes of an LWP::UserAgent object. There are basic differences, however.

There's no such thing as an explicit HTTP error message that means "you needed to send me a proper cookie, so try again!". The "Register Now!" page that the *New York Times* site returned is not an error in any HTTP sense; as far as the browser is concerned, it asked for something, and got it.

LWP's interface for HTTP cookies and HTTP Basic Authentication is different. To get an LWP::UserAgent browser object to implement cookies, one assigns it an object of class HTTP::Cookies (or a subclass), which represents a little database of cookies that this browser knows about. But there is no corresponding class for groups of username/password pairs, although I informally refer to the set of passwords that a user agent can consult as its "key ring."

Authenticating via LWP

To add a username and password to a browser object's key ring, call the `credentials` method on a user agent object:

```
$browser->credentials(
  'servername:portnumber',
  'realm-name',
  'username' => 'password'
);
```

In most cases, the port number is 80, the default TCP/IP port for HTTP. For example:

```
my $browser = LWP::UserAgent->new;
$browser->name('ReportsBot/1.01');

$browser->credentials(
  'reports.mybazouki.com:80',
  'web_server_usage_reports',
  'plinky' => 'banjo123'
);

my $response = $browser->get(
  'http://reports.mybazouki.com/this_week/'
);
```

One can call the `credentials` method any number of times, to add all the server-port-realm-username-password keys to the browser's key ring, regardless of whether they'll actually be needed. For example, you could read them all in from a datafile at startup:

```
my $browser = LWP::UserAgent->new( );
if(open(KEYS, "< keyring.dat")) {
  while(<KEYS>) {
    chomp;
    my @info = split "\t", $_, -1;
    $browser->credential(@info) if @info == 4;
  };
  close(KEYS);
}
```

Security

Clearly, storing lots of passwords in a plain text file is not terribly good security practice, but the obvious alternative is not much better: storing the same data in plain text in a Perl file. One could make a point of prompting the user for the information every time,* instead of storing it anywhere at all, but clearly this is useful only for interactive programs (as opposed to a programs run by *crontab*, for example).

In any case, HTTP Basic Authentication is not the height of security: the username and password are normally sent unencrypted. This and other security shortcomings with HTTP Basic Authentication are explained in greater detail in RFC 2617. See the Preface for information on where to get a copy of RFC 2617.

---

* In fact, Ave Wrigley wrote a module to do exactly that. It's not part of the LWP distribution, but it's available in CPAN as LWP::AuthenAgent. The author describes it as "a simple subclass of LWP::UserAgent to allow the user to type in username/password information if required for authentication."

An HTTP Authentication Example:
The Unicode Mailing Archive

Most password-protected sites (whether protected via HTTP Basic Authentication or otherwise) are that way because the sites' owners don't want just anyone to look at the content. And it would be a bit odd if I gave away such a username and password by mentioning it in this book! However, there is one well-known site whose content is password protected without being secret: the mailing list archive of the Unicode mailing lists.

In an effort to keep email-harvesting bots from finding the Unicode mailing list archive while spidering the Web for fresh email addresses, the Unicode.org sysadmins have put a password on that part of their site. But to allow people (actual not-bot humans) to access the site, the site administrators publicly state the password, on an unprotected page, at *http://www.unicode.org/mail-arch/*, which links to the protected part, but also states the username and password you should use.

The main Unicode mailing list (called *unicode*) once in a while has a thread that is really very interesting and you really must read, but it's buried in a thousand other messages that are not even worth downloading, even in digest form. Luckily, this problem meets a tidy solution with LWP: I've written a short program that, on the first of every month, downloads the index of all the previous month's messages and reports the number of messages that has each topic as its subject.

The trick is that the web pages that list this information are password protected. Moreover, the URL for the index of last month's posts is different every month, but in a fairly obvious way. The URL for March 2002, for example, is:

```
http://www.unicode.org/mail-arch/unicode-ml/y2002-m03/
```

Deducing the URL for the month that has just ended is simple enough:

```
# To be run on the first of every month...
use POSIX ('strftime');
my $last_month = strftime("y%Y-m%m", localtime(time - 24 * 60 * 60));
# Since today is the first, one day ago (24*60*60 seconds) is in
#  last month.
my $url = "http://www.unicode.org/mail-arch/unicode-ml/$last_month/";
```

But getting the contents of that URL involves first providing the username and password *and* realm name. The Unicode web site doesn't publicly declare the realm name, because it's an irrelevant detail for users with interactive browsers, but we need to know it for our call to the credential method. To find out the realm name, try accessing the URL in an interactive browser. The realm will be shown in the authentication dialog box, as shown in Figure 11-1.

In this case, it's "Unicode-MailList-Archives," which is all we needed to make our request:

```perl
my $browser = LWP::UserAgent->new;
$browser->credentials(
  'www.unicode.org:80',  # Don't forget the ":80"!
  # This is no secret...
  'Unicode-MailList-Archives',
  'unicode-ml' => 'unicode'
);
print "Getting topics for last month, $last_month\n",
      " from $url\n";
my $response = $browser->get($url);
die "Error getting $url: ", $response->status_line
  if $response->is_error;
```

If this fails (if the Unicode site's admins have changed the username or password or even the realm name), that will die with this error message:

```
Error getting http://www.unicode.org/mail-arch/unicode-ml/y2002-m03/:
401 Authorization Required at unicode_list001.pl line 21.
```

But assuming the authorization data is correct, the page is retrieved as if it were a normal, unprotected page. From there, counting the topics and noting the absolute URL of the first message of each thread is a matter of extracting data from the HTML source and reporting it concisely.

```perl
my(%posts, %first_url);
while( ${ $response->content_ref }
 =~ m{<li><a href="(\d+.html)"><strong>(.*?)</strong>}g
   # Like: <li><a href="0127.html"><strong>Klingon</strong>
) {
  my($url, $topic) = ($1,$2);

  # Strip any number of "Re:" prefixes.
  while( $topic =~ s/^Re:\s+//i ) {}

  ++$posts{$topic};
  use URI;   # For absolutizing URLs...
  $first_url{$topic} ||= URI->new_abs($url, $response->base);
}

print "Topics:\n", reverse sort map   # Most common first:
  sprintf("% 5s %s\n        %s\n",
          $posts{$_}, $_, $first_url{$_}
  ), keys %posts;
```

Typical output starts out like this:

```
Getting topics for last month, y2002-m02
 from http://www.unicode.org/mail-arch/unicode-ml/y2002-m02/
Topics:
    86 Unicode and Security
        http://www.unicode.org/mail-arch/unicode-ml/y2002-m02/0021.html
    47 ISO 3166 (country codes) Maintenance Agency Web pages move
        http://www.unicode.org/mail-arch/unicode-ml/y2002-m02/0390.html
    41 Unicode and end users
        http://www.unicode.org/mail-arch/unicode-ml/y2002-m02/0260.html
    27 Unicode Search Engines
        http://www.unicode.org/mail-arch/unicode-ml/y2002-m02/0360.html
    22 Smiles, faces, etc
        http://www.unicode.org/mail-arch/unicode-ml/y2002-m02/0275.html
    18 This spoofing and security thread
        http://www.unicode.org/mail-arch/unicode-ml/y2002-m02/0216.html
    16 Standard Conventions and euro
        http://www.unicode.org/mail-arch/unicode-ml/y2002-m02/0418.html
```

This continues for a few pages.

## CHAPTER 12

Spiders

So far we have focused on the mechanics of getting and parsing data off the Web, just a page here and a page there, without much attention to the ramifications. In this section, we consider issues that arise from writing programs that send more than a few requests to given web sites. Then we move on to how to writing recursive web user agents, or *spiders*. With these skills, you'll be able to write programs that automatically navigate web sites, from simple link checkers to powerful bulk-download tools.

Types of Web-Querying Programs

Let's say your boss comes to you and says "I need you to write a spider." What does he mean by "spider"? Is he talking about the simple one-page screen scrapers we wrote in earlier chapters? Or does he want to extract many pages from a single server? Or maybe he wants you to write a new Google, which attempts to find and download every page on the Web. Roughly speaking, there are four kinds of programs that make requests to web servers:

Type One Requester
> This program requests a couple items from a server, knowing ahead of time the URL of each. An example of this is our program in Chapter 7 that requested just the front page of the BBC News web site.

Type Two Requester
> This program requests a few items from a server, then requests the pages to which those link (or possibly just a subset of those). An example of this is the program we alluded to in Chapter 11 that would download the front page of the *New York Times* web site, then downloaded every story URL that appeared there.

Type Three Requester
> This single-site spider requests what's at a given URL, finds links on that page that are on the same host, and requests *those*. Then, for each of those, it finds links to things on the same host, and so on, until potentially it visits every URL on the host.

Type Four Requester

> This host-spanning spider requests what's at a given URL, finds links on that page that are anywhere on the Web, and requests those. Then, for each of those, it finds links to things anywhere on the Web (or at least things that are accessed via HTTP) and so on, until it visits every URL on the Web, in theory.

From each of the above types to the next, there is an added bit of logic that radically changes the scope and nature of the program.

A Type One Requester makes only a few requests. This is not normally a noticeable imposition on the remote server, unless one of these requests is for a document that's very large or that has to be dynamically generated with great difficulty.

A Type Two Requester places rather more burden on the remote server, simply because it generates many more requests. For example, our *New York Times* story downloader in Chapter 11 downloads not one or two pages, but several dozen. Because we don't want this to burden the *Times*'s servers, we considerately called sleep(2) after every request.

In fact, that probably makes our program much kinder to the remote server than a typical browser would be. Typically, browsers create several simultaneous connections when downloading all the various images, stylesheets, and applets they need to render a given web page. However, a typical session with a graphical browser doesn't involve downloading so many *different* pages.

Note that with this sort of program, the scope of the program is clearly finite; it processes only the presumably small number of links that appear on a few pages. So there is no real chance of the program surprising you by requesting vastly more pages than you'd expect. For example, if you run your program that downloads links off the *New York Times*'s front page, it downloads just those and that's it. If you run it, and the total count of downloaded pages is 45, you can assume that when you run it tomorrow, it will be about that many: maybe 30, 60, maybe even 70, but not 700 or 70,000. Moreover, when you see that the average length of each story downloaded is 30 KB, you can assume that it's unlikely for any future story to be 100 KB, and extremely unlikely for any to be 10 MB.

But a Type Three Requester is the first kind that could potentially go seriously awry. Previously, we could make safe assumptions about the nature of the pages whose links we were downloading. But when a program (or, specifically, a spider, as we can freely call these sorts of recursive programs) could request *anything and everything* on the server, it will be visiting pages we know nothing about, and about which we can't make any assumptions. For example, suppose we request the main page of our local paper's web site, and suppose that it links to a local events calendar for this month. If the events calendar is dynamically generated from a database, this month's page probably has a link to next month's page, and next month's to the month after, and so on forever, probably regardless of whether each "next month" has any events to it.

So if you wrote a spider that wouldn't stop until it had requested every object on the server, for this server, it would never stop, because the number of pages on the server is infinite. In webmaster jargon, these are referred to as "infinite URL spaces."

A Type Four Requester has all the problems of Type Threes, except that instead of running the risk of annoying just the webmaster of the local paper, it can annoy any number of webmasters all over the world. Just one of the many things that can go wrong with these kinds of host-spanning spiders is if it sees a link to Yahoo!. It will follow that link, and then start recursing through all of Yahoo!, and visiting every site to which Yahoo! links. Because these sorts of spiders demand typically immense resources and are not "general purpose" by any means, we will not be discussing them.

If you are interested in this type of spider, you should read this chapter to understand the basic ideas of single-site spiders, then read Totty et al's *HTTP: The Definitive Guide* (O'Reilly), which goes into great detail on the special problems that await large-scale spiders.

A User Agent for Robots

So far in this book, we've been using one type of user-agent object: objects of the class LWP::UserAgent. This is generally appropriate for a program that makes only a few undemanding requests of a remote server. But for cases in which we want to be quite sure that the robot behaves itself, the best way to start is by using LWP::RobotUA instead of LWP::UserAgent.

An LWP::RobotUA object is like an LWP::UserAgent object, with these exceptions:

- Instead of calling $browser = LWP::UserAgent->new( ), you call:

    $robot = LWP::RobotUA->new('botname/1.2', 'me@myhost.int')

    Specify a reasonably unique name for the bot (with an *X.Y* version number) and an email address where you can be contacted about the program, if anyone needs to do so.

- When you call $robot->get(...) or any other method that performs a request (head( ), post( ), request( ), simple_request( )), LWP calls sleep( ) to wait until enough time has passed since the last request was made to that server.

- When you request anything from a given HTTP server using an LWP::RobotUA $robot object, LWP will make sure it has consulted that server's *robots.txt* file, where the server's administrator can stipulate that certain parts of his server are off limits to some or all bots. If you request something that's off limits, LWP won't actually request it, and will return a response object with a 403 (Forbidden) error, with the explanation "Forbidden by robots.txt."

    For specifics on *robots.txt* files, see the documentation for the LWP module called WWW::RobotRules, and also be sure to read *http://www.robotstxt.org*.

Besides having all the attributes of an LWP::UserAgent object, an LWP::RobotUA object has one additional interesting attribute, $robot->delay($minutes), which controls how long this object should wait between requests to the same host. The current default value is one minute. Note that you can set it to a non-integer number of minutes. For example, to set the delay to seven seconds, use $robot->delay(7/60).

So we can take our *New York Times* program from Chapter 11 and make it into a scrupulously well-behaved robot by changing this one line:

```
my $browser = LWP::UserAgent->new( );
```

to this:

```
use LWP::RobotUA;
my $browser = LWP::RobotUA->new( 'JamiesNYTBot/1.0',
  'jamie@newsjunkie.int' # my address
);
$browser->delay(5/60); # 5 second delay between requests
```

We may not notice any particular effect on how the program behaves, but it makes quite sure that the $browser object won't perform its requests too quickly, nor request anything the *Times*'s webmaster thinks robots shouldn't request.

In new programs, I typically use $robot as the variable for holding LWP::RobotUA objects instead of $browser. But this is a merely cosmetic difference; nothing requires us to replace every $browser with $robot in the *Times* program when we change it from using an LWP::UserAgent object to an LWP::RobotUA object.

You *can* freely use LWP::RobotUA anywhere you could use LWP::UserAgent, in a Type One or Type Two spider. And you *really should* use LWP::RobotUA as the basis for any Type Three or Type Four spiders. You should use it not just so you can effortlessly abide by *robots.txt* rules, but also so that you don't have to remember to write in sleep statements all over your programs to keep it from using too much of the remote server's bandwidth—or yours!

Example: A Link-Checking Spider

So far in the book, we've produced little single-use programs that are for specific tasks. In this section, we will diverge from that approach by walking through the development of a Type Three Requester robot whose internals are modular enough that with only minor modification, it could be used as any sort of Type Three or Type Four Requester.

The Basic Spider Logic

The specific task for our program is checking all the links in a given web site. This means spidering the site, i.e., requesting every page in the site. To do that, we request a page in the site (or a few pages), then consider each link on that page. If it's a link to somewhere offsite, we should just check it. If it's a link to a URL that's in this site, we will not just check that the URL is retrievable, but in fact retrieve it and see what links *it* has, and so on, until we have gotten every page on the site and checked every link.

So, for example, if I start the spider out at *http://www.mybalalaika.com/oggs/*, it will request that page, get back HTML, and analyze that HTML for links. Suppose that page contains only three links:

```
http://bazouki-consortium.int/
http://www.mybalalaika.com/oggs/studio_credits.html
http://www.mybalalaika.com/oggs/plinky.ogg
```

We can tell that the first URL is not part of this site; in fact, we will define "site" in terms of URLs, so a URL is part of this site if starts with this site's URL. So because *http://bazouki-consortium.int* doesn't start with *http://www.mybalalaika.com/oggs/*, it's not part of this site. As such, we can check it (via an HTTP HEAD request), but we won't actually look at its contents for links. However, the second URL, which is *http://www.mybalalaika.com/oggs/studio_credits.html*, actually does start with *http://www.mybalalaika.com/oggs/*, so it's part of this site and can be retrieved and scanned for links. Similarly, the third link, *http://www.mybalalaika.com/oggs/plinky.ogg*, does start with *http://www.mybalalaika.com/oggs/*, so it's part of this site and can be retrieved, and its HTML checked for links.

But I happen to know that *http://www.mybalalaika.com/oggs/plinky.ogg* is a 90-megabyte Ogg Vorbis (compressed audio) file of a 50-minute long balalaika solo, and it would be a very bad idea for our user agent to go getting this file, much less to try scanning it as HTML! So the way we'll save our robot from this bother is by having it HEAD any URLs before it GETs them. If HEAD reports that the URL is gettable (i.e., doesn't have an error status, nor a redirect) *and* that its Content-Type header says it's HTML (text/html), only then will we actually get it and scan its HTML for links.

We could always hardcode a list of strings such as *.gif*, *.jpg*, etc., including *.ogg*, such that any URL ending in any such string will be assumed to not be HTML. However, we could never know that our list is complete, so we must carefully avoid the possibility of ever downloading a massive binary file that our suffix list just didn't happen to catch.

Now, what to do if we check (or try to get) a URL, and we get an error status? We will have to make note of this in some way. Now, at bare minimum we could do something like have a hash called %notable_url_error, and when we see an error, we could do:

```
$notable_url_error{$url} = $response->status_code;
```

In fact, we will be a bit more ambitious in our program, by also making note of what links to what, so that in the end, instead of saying "something links to *http://somebadurl.int*, but it's 404 Not Found," we can list the URLs that link to it, so that those links can be fixed.

Incidentally, when we get *http://www.mybalalaika.com/oggs/studio_credits.html* and scan its HTML, suppose it contains a link to *http://www.mybalalaika.com/oggs/*. We shouldn't go and request that URL, because we've already been there. So we'll need to keep track of what we've already seen. This is as simple as having a hash %seen_url_before, and when we see a URL, if we see $seen_url_before{$url} is true, we'll skip it. But if it's false, we know we haven't dealt with this URL before, so we can set $seen_url_before{$url} = 1 and go deal with it, for what we can be sure will be the only time this session.

Overall Design in the Spider

Now that we've settled on the basic logic behind the spider, we can start coding. For example, our idea of how to process a URL is expressed as this simple routine:

```
sub process_url {
  my $url = $_[0];
  if( near_url($url) )   { process_near_url($url) }
  else                   { process_far_url($url) }
  return;
}
```

This is the first of the two dozen routines (mostly small) that make up this spider framework, and clearly it requires us to write three more routines, near_url( ), process_near_url( ), and process_far_url( ). But before we go further, we must consider the question of how we would interact with the program. Ideally, we can just write it as a command-line utility that we start up and let run, and in the end it will email us. So, *in theory*, we could call it like so:

```
% thatdarnedbot http://mybazouki.com/ | mail $USER &
```

Then we don't have to think about it again until the program finishes and the report it generates comes to our mailbox. But that is like tightrope-walking without a net, because suppose we get email from someone saying "Hey, wassamatta you? A bot from your host just spent a solid hour hammering my server, checking the same links over and over again! Fix it!" But if all we have is a bad links report, we'll have no idea why the bot visited his site, whether it did indeed request "the same links" over and over, or even what URLs it visited (aside from the ones we see in our bad links report), so we'd have no idea how to fix the problem.

To avoid that situation, we must build logging into the spider right from the beginning. We'll implement this with two basic routines: say( ), used for important messages, and mutter( ), used for less important messages. When we have a part of the program call say( ), like so:

```
say("HEADing $url\n");
```

That is a message that we'll save in a log file, as well as write to STDOUT for the edification of the user who's watching the process. We can call mutter( ), like so:

```
mutter("  That was hit #$hit_count\n");
```

That message will be saved to the log file (in case we need it), but isn't considered important enough to send to STDOUT, unless of course the user is running this program with a switch that means "say everything to STDOUT, no matter how trivial."

And because it's helpful to know not just what happened but when, we'll make say( ) and mutter( ) emit a timestamp, unless it's the same time as the last thing we said or muttered. Here are the routines:

```perl
my $last_time_anything_said;
sub say {
  # Add timestamps as needed:
  unless(time( ) == ($last_time_anything_said || 0)) {
    $last_time_anything_said = time( );
    unshift @_, "[T$last_time_anything_said = " .
      localtime($last_time_anything_said) . "]\n";
  }
  print LOG @_ if $log;
  print @_;
}

my $last_time_anything_muttered;
sub mutter {
  # Add timestamps as needed:
  unless(time( ) == ($last_time_anything_muttered || 0)) {
    $last_time_anything_muttered = time( );
    unshift @_, "[T$last_time_anything_muttered = " .
      localtime($last_time_anything_muttered) . "]\n";
  }
  print LOG @_ if $log;
  print @_ if $verbose;
}
```

This relies on a flag $log (indicating whether we're logging), a filehandle LOG (open on our log file, if we are logging), and a flag $verbose that signals whether mutter messages should go to STDOUT too. These variables will be set by code that you'll see in the complete listing at the end of this chapter, which simply gets those values from @ARGV using the standard Perl module Getopt::Std.

With those two logging routines in place, we can return to our first substantial routine, here repeated:

```perl
sub process_url {
  my $url = $_[0];
  if (near_url($url))  { process_near_url($url) }
  else                 { process_far_url($url) }
  return;
}
```

Not only does this implicate near_url(), process_near_url(), and process_far_url(), but it also begs the question: what will actually call process_url()? We will implement the basic control of this program in terms of a schedule (or queue) of URLs that need to be processed. Three things need to be done with the schedule: we need a way to see how many entries there are in it (at least so we can know when it's empty); we need to be able to pull a URL from it, to be processed now; and we need a way to feed a URL into the schedule. Call those functions schedule_count( ), next_scheduled_url( ), and schedule($url) (with code that we'll define later on), and we're in business. We can now write the main loop of this spider:

```
my $QUIT_NOW;
 # a flag we can set to indicate that we stop now!

sub main_loop {
  while(
    schedule_count( )
    and $hit_count < $hit_limit
    and time( ) < $expiration
    and ! $QUIT_NOW
  ) {
    process_url( next_scheduled_url( ) );
  }
  return;
}
```

This assumes we've set $hit_limit (a maximum number of hits that this bot is allowed to perform on the network) and $expiration (a time after which this bot must stop running), and indeed our @ARGV processing will get those from the command line. But once we know that's the program's main loop, we know that the program's main code will just be the processing of switches in @ARGV, followed by this code:

```
initialize( );
process_starting_urls(@ARGV);
main_loop( );
report( ) if $hit_count;
say("Quitting.\n");
exit;
```

And from this point on, the design of the program is strictly top-down stepwise refinement, just fleshing out the details of the remaining routines that we have mentioned but not yet defined.

HEAD Response Processing

Consider our basic routine, repeated again:

```
sub process_url {
  my $url = $_[0];
  if( near_url($url) )  { process_near_url($url) }
  else                  { process_far_url($url) }
  return;
}
```

The first thing this needs in a function that, given a URL, can tell whether it's "near" or not, i.e., whether it's part of this site. Because we've decided that a URL is part of this site only if it starts with any of the URLs with which we started this program, just as *http://www.mybalalaika.com/oggs/studio_credits.html* starts with *http://www.mybalalaika.com/oggs/*, but *http://bazouki-consortium.int/* doesn't. This is a simple matter of using substr( ):

```perl
my @starting_urls;

sub near_url {   # Is the given URL "near"?
  my $url = $_[0];
  foreach my $starting_url (@starting_urls) {
    if( substr($url, 0, length($starting_url))
      eq $starting_url
      # We assume that all URLs are in canonical form!
    ) {
      mutter("  So $url is near\n");
      return 1;
    }
  }
  mutter("  So $url is far\n");
  return 0;
}
```

We will have to have fed things into @starting_urls first, and we can do that in the process_starting_urls( ) routine that gets called right before we start off the program's main loop. That routine needn't do anything more than this:

```perl
sub process_starting_urls {
  foreach my $url (@_) {
    my $u = URI->new($url)->canonical;
    schedule($u);
    push @starting_urls, $u;
  }
  return;
}
```

Note that we feed URLs through the canonical method, which converts a URL to its single most "proper" form; i.e., turning any capital letters in the hostname into lowercase, removing a redundant :80 port specification at the end of the hostname, and so on. We'll use the canonical method throughout this program when dealing with URLs. If we had failed to use the canonical method, we would, for example, not know that http://nato.int, http://NATO.int/ and http://nato.int:80/ all certainly denote the same thing, in that they all translate to exactly the same request to exactly the same server.

To get process_url( ) fleshed out fully, we need to define process_near_url($url) and process_far_url($url). We'll start with the first and simplest one. Processing a "far" URL (one that's not part of any site we're spidering, but is instead a URL we're merely checking the validity of), is a simple matter of HEADing the URL.

```perl
my $robot;

sub process_far_url {
  my $url = $_[0];
  say("HEADing $url\n");
```

```
++$hit_count;
my $response = $robot->head($url, refer($url));
mutter("  That was hit #$hit_count\n");
consider_response($response);  # that's all we do!
return;
}
```

The minor routine `refer($url)` should generate a Referer header for this request (or no header at all, if none can be generated). This is so if our request produces a 404 and this shows up in the remote server's hit logs, that server's webmaster won't be left wondering "What on Earth links to that broken URL?" This routine merely checks the hash-of-hashes `$points_to{$url}{$any_from_url}`, and either returns empty list (for no header) if there's no entry for `$url`, or `Referer => $some_url` if there is an entry.

```
my %points_to;

sub refer {
  # Generate a good Referer header for requesting this URL.
  my $url = $_[0];
  my $links_to_it = $points_to{$url};
   # the set (hash) of all things that link to $url
  return() unless $links_to_it and keys %$links_to_it;

  my @urls = keys %$links_to_it; # in no special order!
  mutter "  For $url, Referer => $urls[0]\n";
  return "Referer" => $urls[0];
}
```

The more important routine `consider_response( )` is where we will have to mull over the results of `process_far_url( )`'s having headed the given URL. This routine should decide what HTTP statuses are errors, and not all errors are created equal. Some are merely "405 Method Not Allowed" errors from servers or CGIs that don't understand HEAD requests; these apparent errors should presumably not be reported to the user as broken links. We could just define this routine like so:

```
sub consider_response {
  # Return 1 if it's successful, otherwise return 0
  my $response = $_[0];
  mutter("  ", $response->status_line, "\n");
  return 1 if $response->is_success;
  note_error_response($response);
  return 0;
}
```

We then further break down the task of deciding what errors are worthy of reporting and delegate that to a `note_error_response( )` routine:

```
my %notable_url_error;  # URL => error messageS

sub note_error_response {
  my $response = $_[0];
  return unless $response->is_error;
```

```
  my $code = $response->code;
  my $url = URI->new( $response->request->uri )->canonical;

  if( $code == 404 or $code == 410 or $code == 500  ) {
    mutter(sprintf "Noting {%s} error at %s\n",
           $response->status_line, $url );
    $notable_url_error{$url} = $response->status_line;
  } else {
    mutter(sprintf "Not really noting {%s} error at %s\n",
           $response->status_line, $url );
  }
  return;
}
```

This note_error_response( ) only really notes (in %notable_url_error) error messages
that are 404 "Not Found", 410 "Gone", or 500 (which could be any number of
things, from LWP having been unable to DNS the hostname, to the server actually
reporting a real 500 error on a CGI). Among the errors that this is meant to avoid
reporting is the 403 "Forbidden" error, which is what LWP::RobotUA generates if we
try accessing a URL that we are forbidden from accessing by that server's *robots.txt*
file. In practice, if you base a spider on this code, you should routinely consult the
logs (as generated by the above calls to mutter) to see what errors are being noted,
versus what kinds of errors are being "not really noted." This is an example of how
each will show up in the log:

```
[T1017138941 = Tue Mar 26 03:35:41 2002]
  For http://www.altculture.com/aentries/a/absolutely.html, Referer \
  => http://www.speech.cs.cmu.edu/~sburke/
[T1017139042 = Tue Mar 26 03:37:22 2002]
  That was hit #10
  500 Can't connect to www.altculture.com:80 (Timeout)
Noting {500 Can't connect to www.altculture.com:80 (Timeout)} error \
  at http://www.altculture.com/aentries/a/absolutely.html
[T1017139392 = Tue Mar 26 03:43:12 2002]
HEADing http://www.amazon.com/exec/obidos/ASIN/1565922840
  For http://www.amazon.com/exec/obidos/ASIN/1565922840, Referer \
  => http://www.speech.cs.cmu.edu/~sburke/pub/perl.html
[T1017139404 = Tue Mar 26 03:43:24 2002]
That was hit #51
405 Method Not Allowed
Not really noting {405 Method Not Allowed} error at \
  http://www.amazon.com/exec/obidos/ASIN/1565922840
```

Redirects

Implicit in our consider_request( ) function, above, is the idea that something either
succeeded or was an error. However, there is an important and frequent middle-
ground in HTTP status codes: redirection status codes.

Normally, these are handled internally by the LWP::UserAgent/LWP::RobotUA object, assuming that we have left that object with its default setting of following redirects wherever possible. But do we want it following redirects at all? There's a big problem with such automatic redirect processing: if we request a URL with options appropriate for a "far" URL, and it redirects to a URL that's part of our site, we've done the wrong thing. Or, going the other way, if we GET a URL that's part of our site, and it redirects to a "far" URL, we'll have broken our policy of never GETting "far" URLs.

The solution is to turn off automatic redirect following for the $robot that we use for HEADing and GETting (by calling $robot->requests_redirectable([]) when we initialize it), and to deal with redirects ourselves, in an expanded consider_response() routine, like so:

```
sub consider_response {
  # Return 1 if it's successful, otherwise return 0
  my $response = $_[0];
  mutter("  ", $response->status_line, "\n");
  return 1 if $response->is_success;

  if($response->is_redirect) {
    my $to_url = $response->header('Location');
    if(defined $to_url and length $to_url and
      $to_url !~ m/\s/
    ) {
      my $from_url = $response->request->uri;
      $to_url = URI->new_abs($to_url, $from_url);
      mutter("Noting redirection\n  from $from_url\n",
        "       to $to_url\n");
      note_link_to( $from_url => $to_url );
    }
  } else {
    note_error_response($response);
  }

  return 0;
}
```

By now we have completely fleshed out process_url() and everything it calls, except for process_near_url() and the less-important note_link_to() routine. Processing "near" (in-site) URLs is just an elaboration of what we do to "far" URLs. As discussed earlier, we will HEAD this URL, and if it's a successful URL (as shown by the return value of consider_response(), remember!), and if it will contain HTML, we GET it and scan its content for links. The fully defined function seems long, but only because of our many calls to say() and mutter(), and all our sanity checking, such as not bothering to GET the URL if the HEAD actually returned content, as happens now and then.

```
sub process_near_url {
  my $url = $_[0];
  mutter("HEADing $url\n");
  ++$hit_count;
  my $response = $robot->head($url, refer($url));
  mutter("  That was hit #$hit_count\n");
  return unless consider_response($response);

  if($response->content_type ne 'text/html') {
    mutter("  HEAD-response says it's not HTML!  Skipping ",
        $response->content_type, "\n");
    return;
  }
  if(length ${ $response->content_ref }) {
    mutter("  Hm, that had content!  Using it...\n" );
    say("Using head-gotten $url\n");
  } else {
    mutter("It's HTML!\n");
    say("Getting $url\n");
    ++$hit_count;
    $response = $robot->get($url, refer($url));
    mutter("  That was hit #$hit_count\n");
    return unless consider_response($response);
  }
  if($response->content_type eq 'text/html') {
    mutter("  Scanning the gotten HTML...\n");
    extract_links_from_response($response);
  } else {
    mutter("  Skipping the gotten non-HTML (",
      $response->content_type, ") content.\n");
  }
  return;
}
```

All the routines this uses are already familiar, except extract_links_from_response( ).

Link Extraction

Our extract_links_from_response( ) routine has to take a successful HTTP::Response object containing HTML and extract the URLs from the links in it. But in practice, "link" can be an imprecise term. Clearly, this constitutes a link:

```
<a href="pie.html">I like pie!</a>
```

But what about the area element here?

```
<map>
...
<area shape="rect" href="pie.html" coords="0,0,80,21">
...
</map>
```

Or what about the frame element here?

```
<frameset rows="*,76">
 ...
 <frame src="pie.html" name="eat_it">
 ...
</frameset>
```

And what about the background attribute value here?

```
<body bgcolor="#000066" background="images/bg.gif" ... >
```

You will have to decide for each kind of spider task what sort of links it should be interested in and implement a different extract_links_from_response( ) accordingly. For purposes of simplicity, we'll consider only <a href="..."> tags to be links. This is easy to implement using the HTML::TokeParser approach we covered in Chapter 7 and using the URI class we covered in Chapter 4.

```perl
use HTML::TokeParser;
use URI;

sub extract_links_from_response {
  my $response = $_[0];

  my $base = URI->new( $response->base )->canonical;
    # "canonical" returns it in the one "official" tidy form

  my $stream = HTML::TokeParser->new( $response->content_ref );
  my $page_url = URI->new( $response->request->uri );

  mutter( "Extracting links from $page_url\n" );

  my($tag, $link_url);
  while( $tag = $stream->get_tag('a') ) {
    next unless defined($link_url = $tag->[1]{'href'});
    next if $link_url =~ m/\s/; # If it's got whitespace, it's a bad URL.
    next unless length $link_url; # sanity check!

    $link_url = URI->new_abs($link_url, $base)->canonical;
    next unless $link_url->scheme eq 'http'; # sanity

    $link_url->fragment(undef); # chop off any "#foo" part
    note_link_to($page_url => $link_url)
      unless $link_url->eq($page_url); # Don't note links to itself!
  }
  return;
}
```

This does lots of sanity checking on the href attribute value but ends up feeding to note_link_to( ) new (absolute) URI objects for URLs such as *http://bazouki-consortium.int/* or *http://www.mybalalaika.com/oggs/studio_credits.html*, while skipping non-HTTP URLs such as *mailto:info@mybalalaika.com*, as well as invalid URLs that might arise from parsing bad HTML.

This is about as complex as our spider code gets, and it's easy from here on.

Fleshing Out the URL Scheduling

So far we've used a note_link_to( ) routine twice. That routine need only do a bit of accounting to update the %points_to hash we mentioned earlier and schedule this URL to be visited.

```
sub note_link_to {
  my($from_url => $to_url) = @_;
  $points_to{ $to_url }{ $from_url } = 1;
  mutter("Noting link\n  from $from_url\n    to $to_url\n");
  schedule($to_url);
  return;
}
```

That leaves routines such as schedule( ) left to write. As a reminder, three things need to be done with the schedule (as we're calling the big set of URLs that need to be visited). We need a way to see how many entries there are in it with schedule_count( ) (at least so main_loop( ) can know when it's empty). We'll need to pull a URL from the schedule with next_scheduled_url(), so main_loop() can feed it to process_url(). And we need a way to feed a URL into the schedule, with schedule($url), as called from note_link_to( ) and process_starting_urls( ).

A simple Perl array is a perfectly sufficient data structure for our schedule, so we can write schedule_count( ) like so:

```
my @schedule;
sub schedule_count    { return scalar @schedule }
```

The implementation of next_scheduled_url( ) depends on exactly what we mean by "next." If our @schedule is a proper stack, scheduling a URL means we push @schedule, $url, and next_scheduled_url( ) is just a matter of $url = pop @schedule. If our @schedule is a proper queue, then scheduling a URL means we push @schedule, $url, and next_scheduled_url( ) is just a matter of $url = shift @schedule.

Both of these approaches make our spider quite predictable, in the sense that when run on the same site, it will always do the same things in the same order. This could theoretically be an advantage for debugging, and would be a necessary feature if we were trying to debug without the benefit of the logging we've written into the spider.

However, that predictability is also a problem: if the spider happens on a page with dozens of slow-responding URLs, it could spend the rest of its life trying to check those links; i.e., until main_loop( ) quits because $hit_count reaches $hit_limit or because time( ) reaches $expiration. In practice, this problem is greatly alleviated (although not completely eliminated) by pulling URLs not from the beginning or end of @schedule, but instead from a random point in it:

```
sub next_scheduled_url {
  my $url = splice @schedule, rand(@schedule), 1;

  mutter("\nPulling from schedule: ", $url || "[nil]",
    "\n  with ", scalar(@schedule),
```

```
      " items left in schedule.\n");
    return $url;
  }
```

This leaves us with the schedule($url) routine to flesh out. It would be as simple as:

```
sub schedule {
  my $url = $_[0];
  push @schedule, URI->new($url);
  return;
}
```

However, we don't do much sanity checking on URLs everywhere else, so we need to do lots of it all here. First off, we need to make sure we don't schedule a URL that we've scheduled before. Not only does this keep there from being duplicates in @schedule at any one time, it means we never process the same URL twice in any given session.

Second off, we want to skip non-HTTP URLs, because other schemes (well, except HTTPS) aren't HEADable and don't have MIME types, two things our whole spider logic depends on. Moreover, we probably want to skip URLs that have queries (*http:// foo.bar/thing?baz*) because those are usually CGIs, which typically don't understand HEAD requests. Moreover, we probably want to skip HTTP URLs that inexplicably have userinfo components (*http://joeschmo@foo.bar/thing*), which are typically typos for FTP URLs, besides just being bizarre.

We also want to regularize the hostname, so we won't think *http://www.Perl.com/*, *http://www.perl.com/*, and *http://www.perl.com./* are all different hosts, to be visited separately. We also want to skip URLs that are too "deep," such as *http://www.foo.int/ docs/docs/docs/docs/docs/docs/about.html*, which are typically a sign of a wild symlink or some other similar problem. We also want to skip unqualified hostnames, such as *http://www/* or *http://mailhost/*, and URLs with path weirdness, such as *http://thing. com/.l.l.///foo.html*. Then we chop off any *#foo* fragment at the end of the URL, and finally add the URL to @schedule if it's new.

All that sort of sanity checking adds up to this:

```
my %seen_url_before;

sub schedule {
  # Add these URLs to the schedule
  foreach my $url (@_) {
    my $u = ref($url) ? $url : URI->new($url);
    $u = $u->canonical;  # force canonical form

    next unless 'http' eq ($u->scheme || '');
    next if defined $u->query;
    next if defined $u->userinfo;

    $u->host( regularize_hostname( $u->host() ) );
    return unless $u->host() =~ m/\./;
```

```
      next if url_path_count($u) > 6;
      next if $u->path =~ m<//> or $u->path =~ m</\.+(/|$)>;

      $u->fragment(undef);

      if( $seen_url_before{ $u->as_string }++ ) {
        mutter("  Skipping the already-seen $u\n");
      } else {
        mutter("  Scheduling $u\n");
        push @schedule, $u;
      }
    }
  }
  return;
}
```

All we need is the routine that regularizes a given hostname:

```
sub regularize_hostname {
  my $host = lc $_[0];
  $host =~ s/\.+/\./g; # foo..com => foo.com
  $host =~ s/^\.//;    # .foo.com => foo.com
  $host =~ s/\.$//;    # foo.com. => foo.com
  return 'localhost' if $host =~ m/^0*127\.0+\.0+\.0*1$/;
  return $host;
}
```

then a routine that counts the number of /-separated parts in the URL path:

```
sub url_path_count {
  # Return 4 for "http://foo.int/fee/fie/foe/fum"
  #                             1    2   3   4
  my $url = $_[0];
  my @parts = $url->path_segments;
  shift @parts if @parts and $parts[ 0] eq '';
  pop   @parts if @parts and $parts[-1] eq '';
  return scalar @parts;
}
```

The Rest of the Code

That's a fully functioning checker-spider—at least once you add in the boring switch
processing, initialize( ), and the report( ) that dumps the contents of %notable_
url_error, which are as follows:

```
use strict;
use warnings;
use URI;
use LWP;

# Switch processing:
my %option;
use Getopt::Std;
getopts('m:n:t:l:e:u:t:d:hv', \%option) || usage_quit(1);
usage_quit(0) if $option{'h'} or not @ARGV;
```

```perl
sub usage_quit {
  # Emit usage message, then exit with given error code.
  print <<"END_OF_MESSAGE"; exit($_[0] || 0);
Usage:
$0 [switches] [urls]
  This will spider for bad links, starting at the given URLs.

Switches:
 -h        display this help message
 -v        be verbose in messages to STDOUT  (default off)
 -m 123    run for at most 123 minutes.  (default 20)
 -n 456    cause at most 456 network hits.  (default 500)
 -d 7      delay for 7 seconds between hits.  (default 10)
 -l x.log  log to text file x.log. (default is to not log)
 -e y\@a.b  set bot admin address to y\@a.b  (no default!)
 -u Xyz    set bot name to Xyz.  (default: Verifactrola)
 -t 34     set request timeout to 34 seconds.  (default 15)

END_OF_MESSAGE
}

my $expiration = ($option{'m'} ||  20) * 60 + time( );
my $hit_limit  = $option{'h'} || 500;
my $log        = $option{'l'};
my $verbose    = $option{'v'};
my $bot_name   = $option{'u'} || 'Verifactrola/1.0';
my $bot_email  = $option{'e'} || '';
my $timeout    = $option{'t'} || 15;
my $delay      = $option{'d'} || 10;
die "Specify your email address with -e\n"
  unless $bot_email and $bot_email =~ m/\@/;

my $hit_count = 0;
my $robot;  # the user-agent itself

# Then the top-level code we've already seen:
initialize( );
process_starting_urls(@ARGV);
main_loop( );
report( ) if $hit_count;
say("Quitting.\n");
exit;

sub initialize {
  init_logging( );
  init_robot( );
  init_signals( );
  return;
}

sub init_logging {
  my $selected = select(STDERR);
  $| = 1; # Make STDERR unbuffered.
  if($log) {
```

```perl
      open LOG, ">>$log" or die "Can't append-open $log: $!";
      select(LOG);
      $| = 1; # Make LOG unbuffered
    }
    select($selected);
    print "Logging to $log\n" if $log;
    return;
  }

  sub init_robot {
    use LWP::RobotUA;
    $robot = LWP::RobotUA->new($bot_name, $bot_email);
    $robot->delay($delay/60); # "/60" to do seconds->minutes
    $robot->timeout($timeout);
    $robot->requests_redirectable([]);
       # don't follow any sort of redirects
    $robot->protocols_allowed(['http']);  # disabling all others
    say("$bot_name ($bot_email) starting at ", scalar(localtime), "\n");
    return;
  }

  sub init_signals {  # catch control-C's
    $SIG{'INT'} = sub { $QUIT_NOW = 1; return;};
     # That might not be emulated right under MSWin.
    return;
  }


  sub report {  # This that gets run at the end.
    say(
      "\n\nEnding at ", scalar(localtime),
      " after ", time() - $^T,
      "s of runtime and $hit_count hits.\n\n",
    );
    unless(keys %notable_url_error) {
      say( "\nNo bad links seen!\n" );
      return;
    }

    say( "BAD LINKS SEEN:\n" );
    foreach my $url (sort keys %notable_url_error) {
      say( "\n$url\n  Error: $notable_url_error{$url}\n" );
      foreach my $linker (sort keys %{ $points_to{$url} } ) {
        say( "  < $linker\n" );
      }
    }
    return;
  }
```

And that's all of it!

Ideas for Further Expansion

In its current form, this bot is a passable implementation framework for a Type Three Requester spider that checks links on typical HTML web sites. In actual use, you would want to fine tune its heuristics. For example, if you want to check the validity of lots of URLs to sites that don't implement HEAD, you'd want to improve on the logic that currently just considers those URLs a lost cause; or you might want to add code that will skip any attempt at HEADing a URL on a host that has previously responded to any HEAD request with a "Method Not Supported" error, or has otherwise proven uncooperative.

If you wanted the spider to check large numbers of URLs, or spider a large site, it might be prudent to have some of its state saved to disk (specifically @schedule, %seen_url_before, %points_to, and %notable_url_error); that way you could stop the spider, start it later, and have it resume where it left off, to avoid wastefully duplicating what it did the last time. It would also be wise to have the spider enforce some basic constraints on documents and requests, such as aborting any HTML transfer that exceeds 200K or that seems to not actually be HTML, or by having the spider put a maximum limit on the number of times it will hit any given host (see the no_visits( ) method mentioned in the LWP::RobotUA documentation, and specifically consider $bot->no_visits($url->host_port)).

Moreover, the spider's basic behavior could be altered easily by changing just a few of the routines. For example, to turn it into a robot that merely checks URLs that you give it on the command line, you need only redefine one routine like this:

```
sub near_url { 0; }   # no URLs are "near", i.e., spiderable
```

Conversely, to turn it into a pure Type Four Requester spider that recursively looks for links to which any web pages it finds link, all it takes is this:

```
sub near_url { 1; }   # all URLs are "near", i.e., spiderable
```

But as pointed out earlier in this chapter, that is a risky endeavor. It requires careful monitoring and log analysis, constant adjustments to its response-processing heuristics, intelligent caching, and other matters regrettably beyond what can be sufficiently covered in this book.

LWP Modules

While the text of this book has covered the LWP modules that you need to know about to get things done, there are many additional modules in LWP. Most of them are behind the scenes or have limited use that we couldn't spare the space to discuss. But if you want to further your knowledge of LWP's internals, here's a road-map to get you started.

These are the LWP modules, listed alphabetically, from the CPAN distributions most current at time of writing, libwww-perl v5.64, URI v1.18, HTML-Parser v3.26, HTML-Tree v3.11, and HTML-Format v1.23. Especially noteworthy modules have an "*" in front of their names.

Module	Description
File::Listing	Module for parsing directory listings. Used by Net::FTP.
HTML::Form	Class for objects representing HTML forms.
HTML::FormatPS	Class for objects that can render HTML::TreeBuilder tree contents as PostScript.
HTML::Formatter	Internal base class for HTML::FormatPS and HTML::FormatText.
*HTML::FormatText	Class for objects that can render HTML::TreeBuilder tree contents as plain text.
*HTML::Entities	Useful module providing functions that &-encode/decode strings (such as C. & E. Brontë to and from C. & E. Brontë).
HTML::Filter	Deprecated class for HTML parsers that reproduce their input by default.
HTML::HeadParser	Parse <HEAD> section of an HTML document.
HTML::LinkExtor	Class for HTML parsers that parse out links.
HTML::PullParser	Semi-internal base class used by HTML::TokeParser.
*HTML::TokeParser	Friendly token-at-a-time HTML pull-parser class.
HTML::Parser	Base class for HTML parsers; used by the friendlier HTML::TokeParser and HTML::TreeBuilder.
HTML::AsSubs	Semi-deprecated module providing functions that each construct an HTML::Element object.
*HTML::Element	Class for objects that each represent an HTML element.

Module	Description
HTML::Parse	Deprecated module that provides functions accessing HTML::TreeBuilder.
HTML::Tree	Module that exists just so you can run `perldoc HTML-Tree`.
*HTML::TreeBuilder	Class for objects representing an HTML tree into which you can parse source.
*HTTP::Cookies	Class for objects representing databases of cookies.
HTTP::Daemon	Base class for writing HTTP server daemons.
HTTP::Date	Module for date conversion routines. Used by various LWP protocol modules.
HTTP::Headers	Class for objects representing the group of headers in an HTTP::Response or HTTP::Request object.
HTTP::Headers::Auth	Experimental/internal for improving HTTP::Headers's authentication support.
HTTP::Headers::ETag	Experimental/internal module adding HTTP ETag support to HTTP::Headers.
HTTP::Headers::Util	Module providing string functions used internally by various other LWP modules.
*HTTP::Message	Base class for methods common to HTTP::Response and HTTP::Request.
HTTP::Negotiate	Module implementing an algorithm for content negotiation. Not widely used.
HTTP::Request	Class for objects representing a request that carried out with an LWP::UserAgent object.
HTTP::Request::Common	Module providing functions used for constructing common kinds of HTTP::Request objects.
*HTTP::Response	Class for objects representing the result of an HTTP::Request that was carried out.
*HTTP::Status	Module providing functions and constants involving HTTP status codes.
*LWP	Module that exists merely so you can say "use LWP" and have all the common LWP modules (notably LWP::UserAgent, HTTP::Request, and HTTP::Response). Saying `"use LWP 5.64"` also asserts that the current LWP distribution had better be Version 5.64 or later. The module also contains generous documentation.
LWP::Authen::Basic	Module used internally by LWP::UserAgent for doing common ("Basic") HTTP authentication responses.
LWP::Authen::Digest	Module used internally by LWP::UserAgent for doing less-common HTTP Digest authentication responses.
LWP::ConnCache	Class used internally by some LWP::Protocol::protocol modules to reuse socket connections.
*LWP::Debug	Module for routines useful in tracing how LWP performs requests.
LWP::MediaTypes	Module used mostly internally for guessing the MIME type of a file or URL.
LWP::MemberMixin	Base class used internally for accessing object attributes.
LWP::Protocol	Mostly internal base class for accessing and managing LWP protocols.
LWP::Protocol::data	Internal class that handles the new `data:` URL scheme (RFC 2397).
LWP::Protocol::file	Internal class that handles the `file:` URL scheme.
LWP::Protocol::ftp	Internal class that handles the `ftp:` URL scheme.
LWP::Protocol::GHTTP	Internal class for handling `http:` URL scheme using the HTTP::GHTTP library.
LWP::Protocol::gopher	Internal class that handles the `gopher:` URL scheme.
LWP::Protocol::http	Internal class that normally handles the `http:` URL scheme.
LWP::Protocol::http10	Internal class that handles the `http:` URL scheme via just HTTP v1.0 (without the 1.1 extensions and features).

Module	Description
LWP::Protocol::https	Internal class that normally handles the https: URL scheme, assuming you have an SSL library installed.
LWP::Protocol::https10	Internal class that handles the https: URL scheme, if you don't want HTTP v1.1 extensions.
LWP::Protocol::mailto	Internal class that handles the mailto: URL scheme; yes, it sends mail!
LWP::Protocol::nntp	Internal class that handles the nntp: and news: URL schemes.
LWP::Protocol::nogo	Internal class used in handling requests to unsupported protocols.
*LWP::RobotUA	Class based on LWP::UserAgent, for objects representing virtual browsers that obey robots.txt files and don't abuse remote servers.
*LWP::Simple	Module providing the get, head, getprint, getstore, and mirror shortcut functions.
*LWP::UserAgent	Class for objects representing "virtual browsers."
Net::HTTP	Internal class used for HTTP socket connections.
Net::HTTP::Methods	Internal class used for HTTP socket connections.
Net::HTTP::NB	Internal class used for HTTP socket connections with nonblocking sockets.
Net::HTTPS	Internal class used for HTTP Secure socket connections.
*URI	Main class for objects representing URIs/URLs, relative or absolute.
URI::_foreign	Internal class for objects representing URLs for schemes for which we don't have a specific class.
URI::_generic	Internal base class for just about all URLs.
URI::_login	Internal base class for connection URLs such as telnet:, rlogin:, and ssh:.
URI::_query	Internal base class providing methods for URL types that can have query strings (such as foo://...?bar).
URI::_segment	Internal class for representing some return values from $url->path_segments( ) calls.
URI::_server	Internal base class for URL types where the first bit represents a server name (most of them except mailto:).
URI::_userpass	Internal class providing methods for URL types with an optional user[:pass] part (such as ftp://itsme:foo@secret.int/).
URI::data	Class for objects representing the new data: URLs (RFC 2397).
*URI::Escape	Module for functions that URL-encode and URL-decode strings (such as pot pie to and from pot%20pie).
URI::file	Class for objects representing file: URLs.
URI::file::Base	Internal base class for file: URLs.
URI::file::FAT	Internal base class for file: URLs under legacy MSDOS (with 8.3 filenames).
URI::file::Mac	Internal base class for file: URLs under legacy (before v10) MacOS.
URI::file::OS2	Internal base class for file: URLs under OS/2.
URI::file::QNX	Internal base class for file: URLs under QNX.
URI::file::Unix	Internal base class for file: URLs under Unix.
URI::file::Win32	Internal base class for file: URLs under MS Windows.

Module	Description
URI::ftp	Class for objects representing `ftp:` URLs.
URI::gopher	Class for objects representing `gopher:` URLs.
URI::Heuristic	Module for functions that expand abbreviated URLs such as *ora.com*.
URI::http	Class for objects representing `http:` URLs.
URI::https	Class for objects representing `https:` URLs.
URI::ldap	Class for objects representing `ldap:` URLs.
URI::mailto	Class for objects representing `mailto:` URLs.
URI::news	Class for objects representing `news:` URLs.
URI::nntp	Class for objects representing `nntp:` URLs.
URI::pop	Class for objects representing `pop:` URLs.
URI::rlogin	Class for objects representing `rlogin:` login URLs.
URI::rsync	Class for objects representing `rsync:` URLs.
URI::snews	Class for objects representing `snews:` (Secure News) URLs.
URI::ssh	Class for objects representing `ssh:` login URLs.
URI::telnet	Class for objects representing `telnet:` login URLs.
URI::URL	Deprecated class that is like URI; use URI instead.
URI::WithBase	Like the class URI, but objects of this class can "remember" their base URLs.
WWW::RobotsRules	Class for objects representing restrictions parsed from various *robots.txt* files.
WWW::RobotRules::AnyDBM_File	Subclass of WWW::RobotRules that uses a DBM file to cache its contents.

HTTP Status Codes

You can find a detailed explanation of each status code in RFC 2616 *(Hypertext Transfer Protocol—HTTP/1.1)* at *http://www.rfc-editor.org.*

100s: Informational

If an LWP request gets either of these rarely used codes, $response->is_info will be true. For all other status codes, $response->is_info will be false.

```
100 Continue
101 Switching Protocols
```

200s: Successful

If an LWP request gets any of these codes, $response->is_success will be true. For all other status codes, $response->is_success will be false.

```
200 OK
201 Created
202 Accepted
203 Non-Authoritative Information
204 No Content
205 Reset Content
206 Partial Content
```

300s: Redirection

If an LWP request gets any of these codes, $response->is_redirect will be true. For all other status codes, $response->is_redirect will be false.

```
300 Multiple Choices
301 Moved Permanently
302 Found
```

```
303 See Other
304 Not Modified
305 Use Proxy
307 Temporary Redirect
```

400s: Client Errors

If an LWP request gets any of these 400-series codes, $response->is_error will be true, as it will be for any of the 500-series codes. For all other status codes, $response->is_error will be false.

```
400 Bad Request
401 Unauthorized
402 Payment Required
403 Forbidden
404 Not Found
405 Method Not Allowed
406 Not Acceptable
407 Proxy Authentication Required
408 Request Timeout
409 Conflict
410 Gone
411 Length Required
412 Precondition Failed
413 Request Entity Too Large
414 Request-URI Too Long
415 Unsupported Media Type
416 Requested Range Not Satisfiable
417 Expectation Failed
420-424: (Planned extensions involving WebDAV)
426 Upgrade Required (RFC 2817)
```

500s: Server Errors

If an LWP request gets any of these 500-series codes, $response->is_error will be true, as it will be for any of the 400-series codes. For all other status codes, $response->is_error will be false.

Note that at the time of this writing, the "500 Internal Server Error" code is also used by LWP to signal some error conditions where the remote server can't even be contacted, such as when there's a DNS failure or a TCP/IP connection error.

```
500 Internal Server Error
501 Not Implemented
502 Bad Gateway
503 Service Unavailable
504 Gateway Timeout
505 HTTP Version Not Supported
```

Common MIME Types

Every HTTP response that's more than just headers must specify a MIME type via the Content-Type header (accessible as $response->content_type( )). Here is a list of the usual MIME type for each of the most common file types on the Internet. The items are sorted alphabetically by the usual extensions.

Regrettably, this list is neither complete nor authoritative, as there are more file types in use than those given "official" MIME types. For more information, see *HTTP: The Definitive Guide* (O'Reilly). Also consider the *mime.types* file that comes with Apache and/or your browser's "Helper Applications" configuration menus. For the list of official MIME types, see *http://www.isi.edu/in-notes/iana/assignments/media-types/*.

Extension	MIME type
.au	audio/basic
.avi	video/msvideo, video/avi, video/x-msvideo
.bmp	image/bmp
.bz2	application/x-bzip2
.css	text/css
.dtd	application/xml-dtd
.doc	application/msword
.exe	application/octet-stream
.gif	image/gif
.gz	application/x-gzip
.hqx	application/mac-binhex40
.html	text/html
.jar	application/java-archive
.jpg	image/jpeg
.js	application/x-javascript
.midi	audio/x-midi
.mp3	audio/mpeg

Extension	MIME type
.mpeg	video/mpeg
.ogg	audio/vorbis, application/ogg
.pdf	application/pdf
.pl	application/x-perl
.png	image/png
.ppt	application/vnd.ms-powerpoint
.ps	application/postscript
.qt	video/quicktime
.ra	audio/x-pn-realaudio, audio/vnd.rn-realaudio
.ram	audio/x-pn-realaudio, audio/vnd.rn-realaudio
.rdf	application/rdf, application/rdf+xml
.rtf	application/rtf
.sgml	text/sgml
.sit	application/x-stuffit
.svg	image/svg+xml
.swf	application/x-shockwave-flash
.tar.gz	application/x-tar
.tgz	application/x-tar
.tiff	image/tiff
.tsv	text/tab-separated-values
.txt	text/plain
.wav	audio/wav, audio/x-wav
.xls	application/vnd.ms-excel
.xml	application/xml
.zip	application/zip, application/x-compressed-zip

Language Tags

Language tags are a system defined in RFC 3066, which is used in various Internet protocols and formats, including HTML, HTTP, and XML. For example, an HTTP request often has an `Accept-Language` header, an HTTP response can have a `Content-Language` header, and any HTML element can have a `lang="en-US"` or (in XML and XHTML) an `xml:lang="en-US"` attribute to indicate that its content is in that language.

There are *many* more language tags than are presented here; for the full list, see documentation for the Perl module I18N::LangTags::List. This appendix lists major languages, in alphabetical order by their English names.

Tag	Language	Tag	Language
sq	Albanian	en-us	American English
ar	Arabic	en-gb	British English
hy	Armenian	et	Estonian
as	Assamese	fa	Farsi
eu	Basque	fi	Finnish
be	Belarusian	fr	French
bn	Bengali/Bangla	fr-ca	Canadian French
bg	Bulgarian	fr-fr	French French
ca	Catalan	ga	Irish Gaelic
zh	Chinese	gd	Scots Gaelic
zh-cn	Mainland Chinese	de	German
zh-tw	Taiwan Chinese	el	Modern Greek
hr	Croatian	grc	Ancient Greek
cs	Czech	gu	Gujarati
da	Danish	haw	Hawaiian
nl	Dutch	he	Hebrew
en	English	hi	Hindi

Tag	Language	Tag	Language
hu	Hungarian	pt	Portuguese
is	Icelandic	pt-br	Brazilian Portuguese
id	Indonesian	pt-pt	European Portuguese
it	Italian	pa	Punjabi
ja	Japanese	ro	Romanian
kn	Kannada	ru	Russian
ks	Kashmiri	sa	Sanskrit
kok	Konkani	sr	Serbian
ko	Korean	sd	Sindhi
la	Latin	sk	Slovak
lv	Latvian	sl	Slovene
lt	Lithuanian	es	Spanish
mk	Macedonian	es-es	European Spanish
ms	Malay	es-mx	Mexican Spanish
ml	Malayalam	sv	Swedish
mt	Maltese	tl	Tagalog
mi	Maori	ta	Tamil
mr	Marathi	te	Telugu
mni	Meithei/Manipuri	th	Thai
ne	Nepali	tr	Turkish
no	Norwegian	uk	Ukrainian
nb	Norwegian Bokmål	ur	Urdu
nn	Norwegian Nynorsk	vi	Vietnamese
or	Oriya	cy	Welsh
pl	Polish		

Common Content Encodings

In an ideal world, the only character encoding (or, loosely, "character set") that you'd ever see would be UTF-8 (utf-8), and Latin-1 (iso-8859-1) for all those legacy documents. However, the encodings mentioned below exist and can be found on the Web. They are listed below in order of their English names, with the lefthand side being the value you'd get returned from $response->content_charset. The complete list of character sets can be found at *http://www.iana.org/assignments/character-sets*.

Value	Encoding
us-ascii	ASCII plain (just characters 0x00–0x7F)
asmo-708	Arabic ASMO-708
iso-8859-6	Arabic ISO
dos-720	Arabic MSDOS
windows-1256	Arabic MSWindows
iso-8859-4	Baltic ISO
windows-1257	Baltic MSWindows
iso-8859-2	Central European ISO
ibm852	Central European MSDOS
windows-1250	Central European MSWindows
hz-gb-2312	Chinese Simplified (HZ)
gb2312	Chinese Simplified (GB2312)
euc-cn	Chinese Simplified EUC
big5	Chinese Traditional (Big5)
cp866	Cyrillic DOS
iso-8859-5	Cyrillic ISO
koi8-r	Cyrillic KOI8-R
koi8-u	Cyrillic KOI8-U
windows-1251	Cyrillic MSWindows
iso-8859-7	Greek ISO

Value	Encoding
windows-1253	Greek MSWindows
iso-8859-8-i	Hebrew ISO Logical
iso-8859-8	Hebrew ISO Visual
dos-862	Hebrew MSDOS
windows-1255	Hebrew MSWindows
euc-jp	Japanese EUC-JP
iso-2022-jp	Japanese JIS
shift_jis	Japanese Shift-JIS
iso-2022-kr	Korean ISO
euc-kr	Korean Standard
windows-874	Thai MSWindows
iso-8859-9	Turkish ISO
windows-1254	Turkish MSWindows
utf-8	Unicode expressed as UTF-8
utf-16	Unicode expressed as UTF-16
windows-1258	Vietnamese MSWindows
viscii	Vietnamese VISCII
iso-8859-1	Western European (Latin-1)
windows-1252	Western European (Latin-1) with extra characters in 0x80-0x9F

ASCII Table

Gone are the days when ASCII meant just US-ASCII characters 0–127. For over a decade now, Latin-1 support (US-ASCII plus characters 160–255) has been the bare minimum for any Internet application, and support for Unicode (Latin-1 plus characters 256 and up) is becoming the rule more than the exception. Although a full Unicode character chart is a book on its own, this appendix lists all US-ASCII characters, plus all the Unicode characters that are common enough that the current HTML specification (4.01) defines a named entity for them.

Note that at time of this writing, not all browsers support all these characters, and not all users have installed the fonts needed to display some characters.

Also note that in HTML, XHTML, and XML, you can refer to any Unicode character regardless of whether it has a named entity (such as €) by using a decimal character reference such as € or a hexadecimal character reference such as € (note the leading x). See *http://www.unicode.org/charts/* for a complete reference for Unicode characters.

Dec	Hex	Char	Octal	Raw encoding	UTF8 encoding	HTML entity	Description
0	0000		000	0x00	0x00		NUL
1	0001		001	0x01	0x01		SOH
2	0002		002	0x02	0x02		STX
3	0003		003	0x03	0x03		ETX
4	0004		004	0x04	0x04		EOT
5	0005		005	0x05	0x05		ENQ
6	0006		006	0x06	0x06		ACK
7	0007		007	0x07	0x07		BEL, bell, alarm, \a
8	0008		010	0x08	0x08		BS, backspace, \b
9	0009		011	0x09	0x09		HT, tab, \t
10	000a		012	0x0A	0x0A		LF, line feed, \cj

Dec	Hex	Char	Octal	Raw encoding	UTF8 encoding	HTML entity	Description
11	000b		013	0x0B	0x0B		VT
12	000c		014	0x0C	0x0C		FF, NP, form feed, \f
13	000d		015	0x0D	0x0D		CR, carriage return, \cm
14	000e		016	0x0E	0x0E		SO
15	000f		017	0x0F	0x0F		SI
16	0010		020	0x10	0x10		DLE
17	0011		021	0x11	0x11		DC1
18	0012		022	0x12	0x12		DC2
19	0013		023	0x13	0x13		DC3
20	0014		024	0x14	0x14		DC4
21	0015		025	0x15	0x15		NAK
22	0016		026	0x16	0x16		SYN
23	0017		027	0x17	0x17		ETB
24	0018		030	0x18	0x18		CAN
25	0019		031	0x19	0x19		EM
26	001a		032	0x1A	0x1A		SUB
27	001b		033	0x1B	0x1B		ESC, escape, \e
28	001c		034	0x1C	0x1C		FS
29	001d		035	0x1D	0x1D		GS
30	001e		036	0x1E	0x1E		RS
31	001f		037	0x1F	0x1F		US
32	0020		040	0x20	0x20		SPC, space
33	0021	!	041	0x21	0x21		Exclamation point, bang
34	0022	"	042	0x22	0x22	"	Quote, double quote
35	0023	#	043	0x23	0x23		Number, pound, hash
36	0024	$	044	0x24	0x24		Dollar
37	0025	%	045	0x25	0x25		Percent
38	0026	&	046	0x26	0x26	&	Ampersand, and
39	0027	'	047	0x27	0x27	'	Apostrophe, single quote
40	0028	(	050	0x28	0x28		Open parenthesis, open parens
41	0029	)	051	0x29	0x29		Close parenthesis, close parens
42	002a	*	052	0x2A	0x2A		Asterisk, star, glob
43	002b	+	053	0x2B	0x2B		Plus
44	002c	,	054	0x2C	0x2C		Comma
45	002d	-	055	0x2D	0x2D		Hyphen, dash, minus

Dec	Hex	Char	Octal	Raw encoding	UTF8 encoding	HTML entity	Description
46	002e	.	056	0x2E	0x2E		Period, dot, decimal, full stop
47	002f	/	057	0x2F	0x2F		Slash, forward slash, stroke, virgule, solidus
48	0030	0	060	0x30	0x30		
49	0031	1	061	0x31	0x31		
50	0032	2	062	0x32	0x32		
51	0033	3	063	0x33	0x33		
52	0034	4	064	0x34	0x34		
53	0035	5	065	0x35	0x35		
54	0036	6	066	0x36	0x36		
55	0037	7	067	0x37	0x37		
56	0038	8	070	0x38	0x38		
57	0039	9	071	0x39	0x39		
58	003a	:	072	0x3A	0x3A		Colon
59	003b	;	073	0x3B	0x3B		Semicolon
60	003c	<	074	0x3C	0x3C	<	Less-than sign
61	003d	=	075	0x3D	0x3D		Equals sign
62	003e	>	076	0x3E	0x3E	>	Greater-than sign
63	003f	?	077	0x3F	0x3F		Question mark
64	0040	@	100	0x40	0x40		At sign
65	0041	A	101	0x41	0x41		
66	0042	B	102	0x42	0x42		
67	0043	C	103	0x43	0x43		
68	0044	D	104	0x44	0x44		
69	0045	E	105	0x45	0x45		
70	0046	F	106	0x46	0x46		
71	0047	G	107	0x47	0x47		
72	0048	H	110	0x48	0x48		
73	0049	I	111	0x49	0x49		
74	004a	J	112	0x4A	0x4A		
75	004b	K	113	0x4B	0x4B		
76	004c	L	114	0x4C	0x4C		
77	004d	M	115	0x4D	0x4D		
78	004e	N	116	0x4E	0x4E		
79	004f	O	117	0x4F	0x4F		
80	0050	P	120	0x50	0x50		
81	0051	Q	121	0x51	0x51		

Dec	Hex	Char	Octal	Raw encoding	UTF8 encoding	HTML entity	Description
82	0052	R	122	0x52	0x52		
83	0053	S	123	0x53	0x53		
84	0054	T	124	0x54	0x54		
85	0055	U	125	0x55	0x55		
86	0056	V	126	0x56	0x56		
87	0057	W	127	0x57	0x57		
88	0058	X	130	0x58	0x58		
89	0059	Y	131	0x59	0x59		
90	005a	Z	132	0x5A	0x5A		
91	005b	[	133	0x5B	0x5B		Left (square) bracket, open (square) bracket
92	005c	\	134	0x5C	0x5C		Backslash
93	005d	]	135	0x5D	0x5D		Right (square) bracket, close (square) bracket
94	005e	^	136	0x5E	0x5E		Caret, up-arrow, circumflex
95	005f	_	137	0x5F	0x5F		Underscore
96	0060	`	140	0x60	0x60		Backtick, backquote
97	0061	a	141	0x61	0x61		
98	0062	b	142	0x62	0x62		
99	0063	c	143	0x63	0x63		
100	0064	d	144	0x64	0x64		
101	0065	e	145	0x65	0x65		
102	0066	f	146	0x66	0x66		
103	0067	g	147	0x67	0x67		
104	0068	h	150	0x68	0x68		
105	0069	i	151	0x69	0x69		
106	006a	j	152	0x6A	0x6A		
107	006b	k	153	0x6B	0x6B		
108	006c	l	154	0x6C	0x6C		
109	006d	m	155	0x6D	0x6D		
110	006e	n	156	0x6E	0x6E		
111	006f	o	157	0x6F	0x6F		
112	0070	p	160	0x70	0x70		
113	0071	q	161	0x71	0x71		
114	0072	r	162	0x72	0x72		
115	0073	s	163	0x73	0x73		
116	0074	t	164	0x74	0x74		

Dec	Hex	Char	Octal	Raw encoding	UTF8 encoding	HTML entity	Description
117	0075	u	165	0x75	0x75		
118	0076	v	166	0x76	0x76		
119	0077	w	167	0x77	0x77		
120	0078	x	170	0x78	0x78		
121	0079	y	171	0x79	0x79		
122	007a	z	172	0x7A	0x7A		
123	007b	{	173	0x7B	0x7B		Open brace
124	007c	|	174	0x7C	0x7C		Pipe, vertical bar
125	007d	}	175	0x7D	0x7D		Close brace
126	007e	~	176	0x7E	0x7E		Tilde, twiddle, squiggle
127	007f		177	0x7F	0x7F		DEL, delete
128	0080		200	0x80	0xC2,0x80		(Undefined)
129	0081		201	0x81	0xC2,0x81		(Undefined)
130	0082		202	0x82	0xC2,0x82		(Undefined)
131	0083		203	0x83	0xC2,0x83		(Undefined)
132	0084		204	0x84	0xC2,0x84		(Undefined)
133	0085		205	0x85	0xC2,0x85		(Undefined)
134	0086		206	0x86	0xC2,0x86		(Undefined)
135	0087		207	0x87	0xC2,0x87		(Undefined)
136	0088		210	0x88	0xC2,0x88		(Undefined)
137	0089		211	0x89	0xC2,0x89		(Undefined)
138	008a		212	0x8A	0xC2,0x8A		(Undefined)
139	008b		213	0x8B	0xC2,0x8B		(Undefined)
140	008c		214	0x8C	0xC2,0x8C		(Undefined)
141	008d		215	0x8D	0xC2,0x8D		(Undefined)
142	008e		216	0x8E	0xC2,0x8E		(Undefined)
143	008f		217	0x8F	0xC2,0x8F		(Undefined)
144	0090		220	0x90	0xC2,0x90		(Undefined)
145	0091		221	0x91	0xC2,0x91		(Undefined)
146	0092		222	0x92	0xC2,0x92		(Undefined)
147	0093		223	0x93	0xC2,0x93		(Undefined)
148	0094		224	0x94	0xC2,0x94		(Undefined)
149	0095		225	0x95	0xC2,0x95		(Undefined)
150	0096		226	0x96	0xC2,0x96		(Undefined)
151	0097		227	0x97	0xC2,0x97		(Undefined)
152	0098		230	0x98	0xC2,0x98		(Undefined)

Dec	Hex	Char	Octal	Raw encoding	UTF8 encoding	HTML entity	Description
153	0099		231	0x99	0xC2,0x99		(Undefined)
154	009a		232	0x9A	0xC2,0x9A		(Undefined)
155	009b		233	0x9B	0xC2,0x9B		(Undefined)
156	009c		234	0x9C	0xC2,0x9C		(Undefined)
157	009d		235	0x9D	0xC2,0x9D		(Undefined)
158	009e		236	0x9E	0xC2,0x9E		(Undefined)
159	009f		237	0x9F	0xC2,0x9F		(Undefined)
160	00a0		240	0xA0	0xC2,0xA0		No-break space, nonbreaking space
161	00a1	¡	241	0xA1	0xC2,0xA1	¡	Inverted exclamation mark
162	00a2	¢	242	0xA2	0xC2,0xA2	¢	Cent sign
163	00a3	£	243	0xA3	0xC2,0xA3	£	Pound sign
164	00a4	¤	244	0xA4	0xC2,0xA4	¤	Currency sign
165	00a5	¥	245	0xA5	0xC2,0xA5	¥	Yen sign, yuan sign
166	00a6	¦	246	0xA6	0xC2,0xA6	¦	Broken bar, broken vertical bar
167	00a7	§	247	0xA7	0xC2,0xA7	§	Section sign
168	00a8	¨	250	0xA8	0xC2,0xA8	¨	Diaeresis, spacing diaeresis
169	00a9	©	251	0xA9	0xC2,0xA9	©	Copyright sign
170	00aa	ª	252	0xAA	0xC2,0xAA	ª	Feminine ordinal indicator
171	00ab	«	253	0xAB	0xC2,0xAB	«	Left-pointing double angle quotation mark, left pointing guillemet
172	00ac	¬	254	0xAC	0xC2,0xAC	¬	Not sign, angled dash
173	00ad	(-)	255	0xAD	0xC2,0xAD	­	Soft hyphen, discretionary hyphen
174	00ae	®	256	0xAE	0xC2,0xAE	®	Registered sign, registered trademark sign
175	00af	¯	257	0xAF	0xC2,0xAF	¯	Macron, spacing macron, overline, APL overbar
176	00b0	°	260	0xB0	0xC2,0xB0	°	Degree sign
177	00b1	±	261	0xB1	0xC2,0xB1	±	Plus-minus sign, plus-or-minus sign
178	00b2	²	262	0xB2	0xC2,0xB2	²	Superscript two, superscript digit two, squared
179	00b3	³	263	0xB3	0xC2,0xB3	³	Superscript three, superscript digit three, cubed
180	00b4	´	264	0xB4	0xC2,0xB4	´	Acute accent, spacing acute
181	00b5	μ	265	0xB5	0xC2,0xB5	µ	Micro sign

Dec	Hex	Char	Octal	Raw encoding	UTF8 encoding	HTML entity	Description
182	00b6	¶	266	0xB6	0xC2,0xB6	¶	Pilcrow sign, paragraph sign
183	00b7	•	267	0xB7	0xC2,0xB7	·	Middle dot, Georgian comma, Greek middle dot
184	00b8	¸	270	0xB8	0xC2,0xB8	¸	Cedilla, spacing cedilla
185	00b9	¹	271	0xB9	0xC2,0xB9	¹	Superscript one, superscript digit one
186	00ba	º	272	0xBA	0xC2,0xBA	º	Masculine ordinal indicator
187	00bb	»	273	0xBB	0xC2,0xBB	»	Right-pointing double angle quotation mark, right pointing guillemet
188	00bc	¼	274	0xBC	0xC2,0xBC	¼	Vulgar fraction one quarter, fraction one quarter
189	00bd	½	275	0xBD	0xC2,0xBD	½	Vulgar fraction one half, fraction one half
190	00be	¾	276	0xBE	0xC2,0xBE	¾	Vulgar fraction three quarters, fraction three quarters
191	00bf	¿	277	0xBF	0xC2,0xBF	¿	Inverted question mark, turned question mark
192	00c0	À	300	0xC0	0xC3,0x80	À	Capital A grave, capital A grave
193	00c1	Á	301	0xC1	0xC3,0x81	Á	Capital A acute
194	00c2	Â	302	0xC2	0xC3,0x82	Â	Capital A circumflex
195	00c3	Ã	303	0xC3	0xC3,0x83	Ã	Capital A tilde
196	00c4	Ä	304	0xC4	0xC3,0x84	Ä	Capital A diaeresis
197	00c5	Å	305	0xC5	0xC3,0x85	Å	Capital A ring above, capital A ring
198	00c6	Æ	306	0xC6	0xC3,0x86	Æ	Capital AE, capital ligature AE
199	00c7	Ç	307	0xC7	0xC3,0x87	Ç	Capital C cedilla
200	00c8	È	310	0xC8	0xC3,0x88	È	Capital E grave
201	00c9	É	311	0xC9	0xC3,0x89	É	Capital E acute
202	00ca	Ê	312	0xCA	0xC3,0x8A	Ê	Capital E circumflex
203	00cb	Ë	313	0xCB	0xC3,0x8B	Ë	Capital E diaeresis
204	00cc	Ì	314	0xCC	0xC3,0x8C	Ì	Capital I grave
205	00cd	Í	315	0xCD	0xC3,0x8D	Í	Capital I acute
206	00ce	Î	316	0xCE	0xC3,0x8E	Î	Capital I circumflex
207	00cf	Ï	317	0xCF	0xC3,0x8F	Ï	Capital I diaeresis
208	00d0	Ð	320	0xD0	0xC3,0x90	Ð	Capital Eth, Edh, crossed D
209	00d1	Ñ	321	0xD1	0xC3,0x91	Ñ	Capital N tilde
210	00d2	Ò	322	0xD2	0xC3,0x92	Ò	Capital O grave

Dec	Hex	Char	Octal	Raw encoding	UTF8 encoding	HTML entity	Description
211	00d3	Ó	323	0xD3	0xC3,0x93	Ó	Capital O acute
212	00d4	Ô	324	0xD4	0xC3,0x94	Ô	Capital O circumflex
213	00d5	Õ	325	0xD5	0xC3,0x95	Õ	Capital O tilde
214	00d6	Ö	326	0xD6	0xC3,0x96	Ö	Capital O diaeresis
215	00d7	×	327	0xD7	0xC3,0x97	×	Multiplication sign
216	00d8	Ø	330	0xD8	0xC3,0x98	Ø	Capital O stroke, capital O slash
217	00d9	Ù	331	0xD9	0xC3,0x99	Ù	Capital U grave
218	00da	Ú	332	0xDA	0xC3,0x9A	Ú	Capital U acute
219	00db	Û	333	0xDB	0xC3,0x9B	Û	Capital U circumflex
220	00dc	Ü	334	0xDC	0xC3,0x9C	Ü	Capital U diaeresis
221	00dd	Ý	335	0xDD	0xC3,0x9D	Ý	Capital Y acute
222	00de	Þ	336	0xDE	0xC3,0x9E	Þ	Capital Thorn
223	00df	ß	337	0xDF	0xC3,0x9F	ß	Sharp s, ess-zed
224	00e0	à	340	0xE0	0xC3,0xA0	à	a grave
225	00e1	á	341	0xE1	0xC3,0xA1	á	a acute
226	00e2	â	342	0xE2	0xC3,0xA2	â	a circumflex
227	00e3	ã	343	0xE3	0xC3,0xA3	ã	a tilde
228	00e4	ä	344	0xE4	0xC3,0xA4	ä	a diaeresis
229	00e5	å	345	0xE5	0xC3,0xA5	å	a ring above, a ring
230	00e6	æ	346	0xE6	0xC3,0xA6	æ	ae, ligature ae
231	00e7	ç	347	0xE7	0xC3,0xA7	ç	c cedilla
232	00e8	è	350	0xE8	0xC3,0xA8	è	e grave
233	00e9	é	351	0xE9	0xC3,0xA9	é	e acute
234	00ea	ê	352	0xEA	0xC3,0xAA	ê	e circumflex
235	00eb	ë	353	0xEB	0xC3,0xAB	ë	e diaeresis
236	00ec	ì	354	0xEC	0xC3,0xAC	ì	i grave
237	00ed	í	355	0xED	0xC3,0xAD	í	i acute
238	00ee	î	356	0xEE	0xC3,0xAE	î	i circumflex
239	00ef	ï	357	0xEF	0xC3,0xAF	ï	i diaeresis
240	00f0	ð	360	0xF0	0xC3,0xB0	ð	eth, edh, crossed d
241	00f1	ñ	361	0xF1	0xC3,0xB1	ñ	n tilde
242	00f2	ò	362	0xF2	0xC3,0xB2	ò	o grave
243	00f3	ó	363	0xF3	0xC3,0xB3	ó	o acute
244	00f4	ô	364	0xF4	0xC3,0xB4	ô	o circumflex
245	00f5	õ	365	0xF5	0xC3,0xB5	õ	o tilde
246	00f6	ö	366	0xF6	0xC3,0xB6	ö	o diaeresis

Dec	Hex	Char	Octal	Raw encoding	UTF8 encoding	HTML entity	Description
247	00f7	÷	367	0xF7	0xC3,0xB7	÷	Division sign
248	00f8	ø	370	0xF8	0xC3,0xB8	ø	o stroke, o slash
249	00f9	ù	371	0xF9	0xC3,0xB9	ù	u grave
250	00fa	ú	372	0xFA	0xC3,0xBA	ú	u acute
251	00fb	û	373	0xFB	0xC3,0xBB	û	u circumflex
252	00fc	ü	374	0xFC	0xC3,0xBC	ü	u diaeresis
253	00fd	ý	375	0xFD	0xC3,0xBD	ý	y acute
254	00fe	þ	376	0xFE	0xC3,0xBE	þ	Thorn
255	00ff	ÿ	377	0xFF	0xC3,0xBF	ÿ	y diaeresis
338	0152	Œ			0xC5,0x92	Œ	Capital ligature OE
339	0153	œ			0xC5,0x93	œ	Ligature oe
352	0160	Š			0xC5,0xA0	Š	Capital S caron
353	0161	š			0xC5,0xA1	š	s caron
376	0178	Ÿ			0xC5,0xB8	Ÿ	Capital Y diaeresis
402	0192	ƒ			0xC6,0x92	ƒ	F hook, function, florin
710	02c6	ˆ			0xCB,0x86	ˆ	Modifier letter circumflex accent
732	02dc	˜			0xCB,0x9C	˜	Small tilde
913	0391	A			0xCE,0x91	Α	Capital alpha
914	0392	B			0xCE,0x92	Β	Capital beta
915	0393	Γ			0xCE,0x93	Γ	Capital gamma
916	0394	Δ			0xCE,0x94	Δ	Capital delta
917	0395	E			0xCE,0x95	Ε	Capital epsilon
918	0396	Z			0xCE,0x96	Ζ	Capital zeta
919	0397	H			0xCE,0x97	Η	Capital eta
920	0398	Θ			0xCE,0x98	Θ	Capital theta
921	0399	I			0xCE,0x99	Ι	Capital iota
922	039a	K			0xCE,0x9A	Κ	Capital kappa
923	039b	Λ			0xCE,0x9B	Λ	Capital lambda
924	039c	M			0xCE,0x9C	Μ	Capital mu
925	039d	N			0xCE,0x9D	Ν	Capital nu
926	039e	Ξ			0xCE,0x9E	Ξ	Capital xi
927	039f	O			0xCE,0x9F	Ο	Capital omicron
928	03a0	Π			0xCE,0xA0	Π	Capital pi
929	03a1	P			0xCE,0xA1	Ρ	Capital rho
931	03a3	Σ			0xCE,0xA3	Σ	Capital sigma
932	03a4	T			0xCE,0xA4	Τ	Capital tau

Dec	Hex	Char	Octal	Raw encoding	UTF8 encoding	HTML entity	Description
933	03a5	Υ			0xCE,0xA5	Υ	Capital upsilon
934	03a6	Φ			0xCE,0xA6	Φ	Capital phi
935	03a7	Χ			0xCE,0xA7	Χ	Capital chi
936	03a8	Ψ			0xCE,0xA8	Ψ	Capital psi
937	03a9	Ω			0xCE,0xA9	Ω	Capital omega
945	03b1	α			0xCE,0xB1	α	Alpha
946	03b2	β			0xCE,0xB2	β	Beta
947	03b3	γ			0xCE,0xB3	γ	Gamma
948	03b4	δ			0xCE,0xB4	δ	Delta
949	03b5	ε			0xCE,0xB5	ε	Epsilon
950	03b6	ζ			0xCE,0xB6	ζ	Zeta
951	03b7	η			0xCE,0xB7	η	Eta
952	03b8	θ			0xCE,0xB8	θ	Theta
953	03b9	ι			0xCE,0xB9	ι	Iota
954	03ba	κ			0xCE,0xBA	κ	Kappa
955	03bb	λ			0xCE,0xBB	λ	Lambda
956	03bc	μ			0xCE,0xBC	μ	Mu
957	03bd	ν			0xCE,0xBD	ν	Nu
958	03be	ξ			0xCE,0xBE	ξ	Xi
959	03bf	ο			0xCE,0xBF	ο	Omicron
960	03c0	π			0xCF,0x80	π	Pi
961	03c1	ρ			0xCF,0x81	ρ	Rho
962	03c2	ς			0xCF,0x82	ς	Final sigma
963	03c3	σ			0xCF,0x83	σ	Sigma
964	03c4	τ			0xCF,0x84	τ	Tau
965	03c5	υ			0xCF,0x85	υ	Upsilon
966	03c6	φ			0xCF,0x86	φ	Phi
967	03c7	χ			0xCF,0x87	χ	Chi
968	03c8	ψ			0xCF,0x88	ψ	Psi
969	03c9	ω			0xCF,0x89	ω	Omega
977	03d1	ϑ			0xCF,0x91	ϑ	Theta symbol
978	03d2	ϒ			0xCF,0x92	ϒ	Greek upsilon with hook symbol
982	03d6	ϖ			0xCF,0x96	ϖ	Greek pi symbol
8194	2002				0xE2,0x80,0x82		En space
8195	2003				0xE2,0x80,0x83		Em space
8201	2009				0xE2,0x80,0x89		Thin space

Dec	Hex	Char	Octal	Raw encoding	UTF8 encoding	HTML entity	Description
8204	200c	ZWNJ			0xE2,0x80,0x8C	‌	Zero width non-joiner
8205	200d	ZWJ			0xE2,0x80,0x8D	‍	Zero width joiner
8206	200e	LRM			0xE2,0x80,0x8E	‎	Left-to-right mark
8207	200f	RLM			0xE2,0x80,0x8F	‏	Right-to-left mark
8211	2013	–			0xE2,0x80,0x93	–	En dash
8212	2014	—			0xE2,0x80,0x94	—	Em dash
8216	2018	'			0xE2,0x80,0x98	‘	Left single quotation mark
8217	2019	'			0xE2,0x80,0x99	’	Right single quotation mark
8218	201a	‚			0xE2,0x80,0x9A	‚	Single low-9 quotation mark
8220	201c	"			0xE2,0x80,0x9C	“	Left double quotation mark
8221	201d	"			0xE2,0x80,0x9D	”	Right double quotation mark
8222	201e	„			0xE2,0x80,0x9E	„	Double low-9 quotation mark
8224	2020	†			0xE2,0x80,0xA0	†	Dagger
8225	2021	‡			0xE2,0x80,0xA1	‡	Double dagger
8226	2022	•			0xE2,0x80,0xA2	•	Bullet, black small circle
8230	2026	…			0xE2,0x80,0xA6	…	Horizontal ellipsis, three dot leader
8240	2030	‰			0xE2,0x80,0xB0	‰	Per mille sign
8242	2032	′			0xE2,0x80,0xB2	′	Prime, minutes, feet
8243	2033	″			0xE2,0x80,0xB3	″	Double prime, seconds, inches
8249	2039	‹			0xE2,0x80,0xB9	‹	Single left-pointing angle quotation mark
8250	203a	›			0xE2,0x80,0xBA	›	Single right-pointing angle quotation mark
8254	203e	‾			0xE2,0x80,0xBE	‾	Overline, spacing overscore
8260	2044	⁄			0xE2,0x81,0x84	⁄	Fraction slash
8364	20ac	€			0xE2,0x82,0xAC	€	Euro sign
8465	2111	ℑ			0xE2,0x84,0x91	ℑ	Blackletter capital I, imaginary part
8472	2118	℘			0xE2,0x84,0x98	℘	Script capital P, power set, Weierstrass p
8476	211c	ℜ			0xE2,0x84,0x9C	ℜ	Blackletter capital R, real part symbol
8482	2122	™			0xE2,0x84,0xA2	™	Trademark sign
8501	2135	ℵ			0xE2,0x84,0xB5	ℵ	Alef symbol, first transfinite cardinal
8592	2190	←			0xE2,0x86,0x90	←	Leftward arrow
8593	2191	↑			0xE2,0x86,0x91	↑	Upward arrow

Dec	Hex	Char	Octal	Raw encoding	UTF8 encoding	HTML entity	Description
8594	2192	→			0xE2,0x86,0x92	→	Rightward arrow
8595	2193	↓			0xE2,0x86,0x93	↓	Downward arrow
8596	2194	↔			0xE2,0x86,0x94	↔	Left-right arrow
8629	21b5	↵			0xE2,0x86,0xB5	↵	Downward arrow with corner leftward, carriage return
8656	21d0	⇐			0xE2,0x87,0x90	⇐	Leftward double arrow
8657	21d1	⇑			0xE2,0x87,0x91	⇑	Upward double arrow
8658	21d2	⇒			0xE2,0x87,0x92	⇒	Rightward double arrow
8659	21d3	⇓			0xE2,0x87,0x93	⇓	Downward double arrow
8660	21d4	⇔			0xE2,0x87,0x94	⇔	Left-right double arrow
8704	2200	∀			0xE2,0x88,0x80	∀	For all
8706	2202	∂			0xE2,0x88,0x82	∂	Partial differential
8707	2203	∃			0xE2,0x88,0x83	∃	There exists
8709	2205	∅			0xE2,0x88,0x85	∅	Empty set, null set, diameter
8711	2207	∇			0xE2,0x88,0x87	∇	Nabla, backward difference
8712	2208	∈			0xE2,0x88,0x88	∈	Element of
8713	2209	∉			0xE2,0x88,0x89	∉	Not an element of
8715	220b	∋			0xE2,0x88,0x8B	∋	Contains as member
8719	220f	∏			0xE2,0x88,0x8F	∏	n-ary product, product sign
8721	2211	∑			0xE2,0x88,0x91	∑	n-ary sumation
8722	2212	-			0xE2,0x88,0x92	−	Minus sign
8727	2217	∗			0xE2,0x88,0x97	∗	Asterisk operator
8730	221a	√			0xE2,0x88,0x9A	√	Square root, radical sign
8733	221d	∝			0xE2,0x88,0x9D	∝	Proportional to
8734	221e	∞			0xE2,0x88,0x9E	∞	Infinity
8736	2220	∠			0xE2,0x88,0xA0	∠	Angle
8743	2227	∧			0xE2,0x88,0xA7	∧	Logical and, wedge
8744	2228	∨			0xE2,0x88,0xA8	∨	Logical or, vee
8745	2229	∩			0xE2,0x88,0xA9	∩	Intersection, cap
8746	222a	∪			0xE2,0x88,0xAA	∪	Union, cup
8747	222b	∫			0xE2,0x88,0xAB	∫	Integral
8756	2234	∴			0xE2,0x88,0xB4	∴	Therefore
8764	223c	~			0xE2,0x88,0xBC	∼	Tilde operator, varies with, similar to
8773	2245	≅			0xE2,0x89,0x85	≅	Approximately equal to
8776	2248	≈			0xE2,0x89,0x88	≈	Almost equal to, asymptotic to
8800	2260	≠			0xE2,0x89,0xA0	≠	Not equal to

Dec	Hex	Char	Octal	Raw encoding	UTF8 encoding	HTML entity	Description
8801	2261	≡			0xE2,0x89,0xA1	≡	Identical to
8804	2264	≤			0xE2,0x89,0xA4	≤	Less-than or equal to
8805	2265	≥			0xE2,0x89,0xA5	≥	Greater-than or equal to
8834	2282	⊂			0xE2,0x8A,0x82	⊂	Subset of
8835	2283	⊃			0xE2,0x8A,0x83	⊃	Superset of
8836	2284	⊄			0xE2,0x8A,0x84	⊄	Not a subset of
8838	2286	⊆			0xE2,0x8A,0x86	⊆	Subset of or equal to
8839	2287	⊇			0xE2,0x8A,0x87	⊇	Superset of or equal to
8853	2295	⊕			0xE2,0x8A,0x95	⊕	Circled plus, direct sum
8855	2297	⊗			0xE2,0x8A,0x97	⊗	Circled times, vector product
8869	22a5	⊥			0xE2,0x8A,0xA5	⊥	Up tack, orthogonal to, perpendicular
8901	22c5	·			0xE2,0x8B,0x85	⋅	Dot operator
8968	2308	⌈			0xE2,0x8C,0x88	⌈	Left ceiling, APL upstile
8969	2309	⌉			0xE2,0x8C,0x89	⌉	Right ceiling
8970	230a	⌊			0xE2,0x8C,0x8A	⌊	Left floor, APL downstile
8971	230b	⌋			0xE2,0x8C,0x8B	⌋	Right floor
9001	2329	⟨			0xE2,0x8C,0xA9	⟨	Left-pointing angle bracket, bra
9002	232a	⟩			0xE2,0x8C,0xAA	⟩	Right-pointing angle bracket, ket
9674	25ca	◊			0xE2,0x97,0x8A	◊	Lozenge
9824	2660	♠			0xE2,0x99,0xA0	♠	Black spade suit
9827	2663	♣			0xE2,0x99,0xA3	♣	Black club suit, shamrock
9829	2665	♥			0xE2,0x99,0xA5	♥	Black heart suit, valentine
9830	2666	♦			0xE2,0x99,0xA6	♦	Black diamond suit

User's View of Object-Oriented Modules

The following article by Sean M. Burke first appeared in *The Perl Journal* #17 and is copyright 2000, *The Perl Journal*. It appears courtesy of Jon Orwant and *The Perl Journal*. This document may be distributed under the same terms as Perl itself.

A User's View of Object-Oriented Modules

The first time that most Perl programmers run into object-oriented programming is when they need to use a module whose interface is object-oriented. This is often a mystifying experience, since talk of "methods" and "constructors" is unintelligible to programmers who thought that functions and variables was all there was to worry about.

Articles and books that explain object-oriented programming (OOP), do so in terms of how to program that way. That's understandable, and if you learn to write object-oriented code of your own, you'd find it easy to use object-oriented code that others write. But this approach is the *long* way around for people whose immediate goal is just to use existing object-oriented modules, but who don't yet want to know all the gory details of having to write such modules for themselves.

This article is for those programmers—programmers who want to know about objects from the perspective of using object-oriented modules.

Modules and Their Functional Interfaces

Modules are the main way that Perl provides for bundling up code for later use by yourself or others. As I'm sure you can't help noticing from reading *The Perl Journal*, CPAN (the Comprehensive Perl Archive Network) is the repository for modules (or groups of modules) that others have written, to do anything from composing music to accessing web pages. A good deal of those modules even come with every installation of Perl.

One module that you may have used before, and which is fairly typical in its interface, is Text::Wrap. It comes with Perl, so you don't even need to install it from CPAN. You use it in a program of yours, by having your program code say early on:

```
use Text::Wrap;
```

and after that, you can access a function called wrap, which inserts line-breaks in text that you feed it, so that the text will be wrapped to 72 (or however many) columns.

The way this use Text::Wrap business works is that the module Text::Wrap exists as a file *Text/Wrap.pm* somewhere in one of your library directories. That file contains Perl code* which, among other things, defines a function called Text::Wrap::wrap, and then exports that function, which means that when you say wrap after having said use Text::Wrap, you'll be actually calling the Text::Wrap::wrap function. Some modules don't export their functions, so you have to call them by their full name, like Text::Wrap::wrap(*parameters*).

Regardless of whether the typical module exports the functions it provides, a module is basically just a container for chunks of code that do useful things. The way the module allows for you to interact with it, is its interface. And when, like with Text::Wrap, its interface consists of functions, the module is said to have a *functional interface*.†

Using modules with functional interfaces is straightforward—instead of defining your own "wrap" function with sub wrap { ... }, you entrust use Text::Wrap to do that for you, along with whatever other functions its defines and exports, according to the module's documentation. Without too much bother, you can even write your own modules to contain your frequently used functions; I suggest having a look at the *perlmod* manpage for more leads on doing this.

Modules with Object-Oriented Interfaces

So suppose that one day you want to write a program that will automate the process of ftping a bunch of files from one server down to your local machine, and then off to another server.

A quick browse through *search.cpan.org* turns up the module Net::FTP, which you can download and install using normal installation instructions (unless your sysadmin has already installed it, as many have).

---

* And mixed in with the Perl code, there's documentation, which is what you read with perldoc Text::Wrap. The *perldoc* program simply ignores the code and formats the documentation text, whereas use Text::Wrap loads and runs the code while ignoring the documentation.

† The term "function" (and therefore "function*al*") has various senses. I'm using the term here in its broadest sense, to refer to routines—bits of code that are called by some name and take parameters and return some value.

Like Text::Wrap or any other module with a familiarly functional interface, you start off using Net::FTP in your program by saying:

```
use Net::FTP;
```

However, that's where the similarity ends. The first hint of difference is that the documentation for Net::FTP refers to it as a *class*. A class is a kind of module, but one that has an object-oriented interface.

Whereas modules like Text::Wrap provide bits of useful code as *functions*, to be called like function(*parameters*) or like PackageName::function(*parameters*), Net::FTP and other modules with object-oriented interfaces provide *methods*. Methods are sort of like functions in that they have a name and parameters; but methods look different, and are different, because you have to call them with a syntax that has a class name or an object as a special argument. I'll explain the syntax for method calls, and then later explain what they all mean.

Some methods are meant to be called as *class methods*, with the class name (same as the module name) as a special argument. Class methods look like this:

```
ClassName->methodname(parameter1, parameter2, ...)
ClassName->methodname()   # if no parameters
ClassName->methodname     # same as above
```

which you will sometimes see written:

```
methodname ClassName (parameter1, parameter2, ...)
methodname ClassName     # if no parameters
```

Basically, all class methods are for making new objects, and methods that make objects are called *constructors* (and the process of making them is called "constructing" or "instantiating"). Constructor methods typically have the name "new," or something including "new" (new_from_file, etc.); but they can conceivably be named anything—DBI's constructor method is named "connect," for example.

The object that a constructor method returns is typically captured in a scalar variable:

```
$object = ClassName->new(param1, param2...);
```

Once you have an object (more later on exactly what that is), you can use the other kind of method call syntax, the syntax for *object method* calls. Calling object methods is just like class methods, except that instead of the ClassName as the special argument, you use an expression that yields an object. Usually this is just a scalar variable that you earlier captured the output of the constructor in. Object method calls look like this:

```
$object->methodname(parameter1, parameter2, ...);
$object->methodname()   # if no parameters
$object->methodname     # same as above
```

which is occasionally written as:

```
methodname $object (parameter1, parameter2, ...)
methodname $object     # if no parameters
```

Examples of method calls are:

```
my $session1 = Net::FTP->new("ftp.myhost.com");
  # Calls a class method "new", from class Net::FTP,
  #  with the single parameter "ftp.myhost.com",
  #  and saves the return value (which is, as usual,
  #  an object), in $session1.
  # Could also be written:
  #  new Net::FTP('ftp.myhost.com')
$session1->login("sburke","aoeuaoeu")
  || die "failed to login!\n";
  # calling the object method "login"
print "Dir:\n", $session1->dir(), "\n";
$session1->quit;
  # same as $session1->quit()
print "Done\n";
exit;
```

Incidentally, I suggest always using the syntaxes with parentheses and -> in them,[*] and avoiding the syntaxes that start out methodname $object or methodname ModuleName. When everything's going right, they all mean the same thing as the -> variants, but the syntax with -> is more visually distinct from function calls, as well as being immune to some kinds of rare but puzzling ambiguities that can arise when you're trying to call methods that have the same name as subroutines you've defined.

But, syntactic alternatives aside, all this talk of constructing objects and object methods begs the question—what *is* an object? There are several angles to this question that the rest of this article will answer in turn: what can you do with objects? what's in an object? what's an object value? and why do some modules use objects at all?

What Can You Do with Objects?

You've seen that you can make objects and call object methods with them. But what are object methods for? The answer depends on the class:

A Net::FTP object represents a session between your computer and an FTP server. So the methods you call on a Net::FTP object are for doing whatever you'd need to do across an FTP connection. You make the session and log in:

```
my $session = Net::FTP->new('ftp.aol.com');
die "Couldn't connect!" unless defined $session;
  # The class method call to "new" will return
  # the new object if it goes OK, otherwise it
  # will return undef.

$session->login('sburke', 'p@ssw3rD')
  || die "Did I change my password again?";
  # The object method "login" will give a true
```

---

[*] The character-pair -> is supposed to look like an arrow, not "negative greater-than"!

```
# return value if actually logs in, otherwise
# it'll return false.
```

You can use the session object to change directory on that session:

```
$session->cwd("/home/sburke/public_html")
    || die "Hey, that was REALLY supposed to work!";
# if the cwd fails, it'll return false
```

...get files from the machine at the other end of the session:

```
foreach my $f ('log_report_ua.txt', 'log_report_dom.txt',
               'log_report_browsers.txt')
{
   $session->get($f) || warn "Getting $f failed!"
};
```

...and plenty else, ending finally with closing the connection:

```
$session->quit( );
```

In short, object methods are for doing things related to (or with) whatever the object represents. For FTP sessions, it's about sending commands to the server at the other end of the connection, and that's about it—there, methods are for doing something to the world outside the object, and the objects is just something that specifies what bit of the world (well, what FTP session) to act upon.

With most other classes, however, the object itself stores some kind of information, and it typically makes no sense to do things with such an object without considering the data that's in the object.

What's in an Object?

An object is (with rare exceptions) a data structure containing a bunch of attributes, each of which has a value, as well as a name that you use when you read or set the attribute's value. Some of the object's attributes are private, meaning you'll never see them documented because they're not for you to read or write; but most of the object's documented attributes are at least readable, and usually writeable, by you. Net::FTP objects are a bit thin on attributes, so we'll use objects from the class Business::US_Amort for this example. Business::US_Amort is a very simple class (available from CPAN) that I wrote for making calculations to do with loans (specifically, amortization, using U.S.-style algorithms).

An object of the class Business::US_Amort represents a loan with particular parameters, i.e., attributes. The most basic attributes of a "loan object" are its interest rate, its principal (how much money it's for), and it's term (how long it'll take to repay). You need to set these attributes before anything else can be done with the object. The way to get at those attributes for loan objects is just like the way to get at attributes for any class's objects: through accessors. An *accessor* is simply any method that accesses (whether reading or writing, a.k.a. getting or putting) some attribute in the given object. Moreover, accessors are the *only* way that you can change an object's attributes. (If a module's documentation wants you to know about any other way, it'll tell you.)

Usually, for simplicity's sake, an accessor is named after the attribute it reads or writes. With Business::US_Amort objects, the accessors you need to use first are principal, interest_rate, and term. Then, with at least those attributes set, you can call the run method to figure out several things about the loan. Then you can call various accessors, like total_paid_toward_interest, to read the results:

```
use Business::US_Amort;
my $loan = Business::US_Amort->new;
# Set the necessary attributes:
$loan->principal(123654);
$loan->interest_rate(9.25);
$loan->term(20); # twenty years

# NOW we know enough to calculate:
$loan->run;

# And see what came of that:
print
  "Total paid toward interest: A WHOPPING ",
  $loan->total_paid_interest, "!!\n";
```

This illustrates a convention that's common with accessors: calling the accessor with no arguments (as with $loan->total_paid_interest) usually means to read the value of that attribute, but providing a value (as with $loan->term(20)) means you want that attribute to be set to that value. This stands to reason: why would you be providing a value, if not to set the attribute to that value?

Although a loan's term, principal, and interest rates are all single numeric values, an object's values can be any kind of scalar, or an array, or even a hash. Moreover, an attribute's value(s) can be objects themselves. For example, consider MIDI files (as I wrote about in TPJ#13): a MIDI file usually consists of several tracks. A MIDI file is complex enough to merit being an object with attributes like its overall tempo, the file-format variant it's in, and the list of instrument tracks in the file. But tracks themselves are complex enough to be objects too, with attributes like their track-type, a list of MIDI commands if they're a MIDI track, or raw data if they're not. So I ended up writing the MIDI modules so that the "tracks" attribute of a MIDI::Opus object is an array of objects from the class MIDI::Track. This may seem like a runaround—you ask what's in one object, and get *another* object, or several! But in this case, it exactly reflects what the module is for—MIDI files contain MIDI tracks, which contain data.

What Is an Object Value?

When you call a constructor like Net::FTP->new(*hostname*), you get back an object value, which is a value you can later use, in combination with a method name, to call object methods.

Now, so far we've been pretending, in the above examples, that the variables $session or $loan *are* the objects you're dealing with. This idea is innocuous up to a point, but it's really a misconception that will, at best, limit you in what you know how to do. The reality is not that the variables $session or $query are objects; it's a little more indirect—they hold values that symbolize objects. The kind of value that $session or $query hold is what I'm calling an object value.

To understand what kind of value this is, first think about the other kinds of scalar values you know about: The first two types of scalar values you probably ever ran into in Perl are *numbers* and *strings*, which you learned (or just assumed) will usually turn into each other on demand; that is, the three-character string "2.5" can become the quantity two and a half, and vice versa. Then, especially if you started using perl -w early on, you learned about the *undefined value*, which can turn into 0 if you treat it as a number, or the empty-string if you treat it as a string.*

And now you're learning about *object values*. An object value is a value that points to a data structure somewhere in memory, which is where all the attributes for this object are stored. That data structure as a whole belongs to a class (probably the one you named in the constructor method, like ClassName->new), so that the object value can be used as part of object method calls.

If you want to actually *see* what an object value is, you might try just saying print $object. That'll get you something like this:

    Net::FTP=GLOB(0x20154240)

or:

    Business::US_Amort=HASH(0x15424020)

That's not very helpful if you wanted to really get at the object's insides, but that's because the object value is only a symbol for the object. This may all sound very abstruse and metaphysical, so a real-world allegory might be very helpful.

You get an advertisement in the mail saying that you have been (im)personally selected to have the rare privilege of applying for a credit card. For whatever reason, *this* offer sounds good to you, so you fill out the form and mail it back to the credit card company. They gleefully approve the application and create your account, and send you a card with a number on it.

Now, you can do things with the number on that card—clerks at stores can ring up things you want to buy, and charge your account by keying in the number on the card. You can pay for things you order online by punching in the card number as part of your online order. You can pay off part of the account by sending the credit

---

* You may *also* have been learning about references, in which case you're ready to hear that object values are just a kind of reference, except that they reflect the class that created thing they point to, instead of merely being a plain old array reference, hash reference, etc. If this makes sense to you, and you want to know more about how objects are implemented in Perl, have a look at the *perltoot* manpage.

card people some of your money (well, a check) with some note (usually the pre-printed slip) that has the card number for the account you want to pay toward. And you should be able to call the credit card company's computer and ask it things about the card, like its balance, its credit limit, its APR, and maybe an itemization of recent purchases and payments.

Now, what you're *really* doing is manipulating a credit card *account*, a completely abstract entity with some data attached to it (balance, APR, etc.). But for ease of access, you have a credit card *number* that is a symbol for that account. Now, that symbol is just a bunch of digits, and the number is effectively meaningless and use-less in and of itself—but in the appropriate context, it's understood to *mean* the credit card account you're accessing.

This is exactly the relationship between objects and object values, and from this analogy, several facts about object values are a bit more explicable:

- An object value does nothing in and of itself, but it's useful when you use it in the context of an $object->method call, the same way that a card number is use-ful in the context of some operation dealing with a card account.

  Moreover, several copies of the same object value all refer to the same object, the same way that making several copies of your card number won't change the fact that they all still refer to the same single account (this is true whether you're "copying" the number by just writing it down on different slips of paper, or whether you go to the trouble of forging exact replicas of your own plastic credit card). That's why this:

  ```
  $x = Net::FTP->new("ftp.aol.com");
  $x->login("sburke", "aoeuaoeu");
  ```

  does the same thing as this:

  ```
  $x = Net::FTP->new("ftp.aol.com");
  $y = $x;
  $z = $y;
  $z->login("sburke", "aoeuaoeu");
  ```

  That is, $z and $y and $x are three different *slots* for values, but what's in those slots are all object values pointing to the same object—you don't have three different FTP connections, just three variables with values pointing to the some single FTP connection.

- You can't tell much of anything about the object just by looking at the object value, any more than you can see your credit account balance by holding the plas-tic card up to the light, or by adding up the digits in your credit card number.*

---

* URI.pm objects are an exception to this general rule: when you use them as a string, instead of getting a use-less value like URI=HASH(0x15404220), you instead get the string representation of that URL: *http://www.perl.com/thingamabob/* or whatever.

- You can't just make up your own object values and have them work—they can come only from constructor methods of the appropriate class. Similarly, you get a credit card number *only* by having a bank approve your application for a credit card account—at which point *they* let *you* know what the number of your new card is.

  Now, there's even more to the fact that you can't just make up your own object value: even though you can print an object value and get a string like Net::FTP=GLOB(0x20154240), that's just a *representation* of an object value.

Internally, an object value has a basically different type from a string, or a number, or the undefined value—if $x holds a real string, then that value's slot in memory says "this is a value of type *string*, and its characters are...," whereas if it's an object value, the value's slot in memory says, "this is a value of type *reference*, and the location in memory that it points to is..." (and by looking at what's at that location, Perl can tell the class of what's there).

Perl programmers typically don't have to think about all these details of Perl's internals. Many other languages force you to be more conscious of the differences between all of these (and also between types of numbers, which are stored differently depending on their size and whether they have fractional parts). But Perl does its best to hide the different types of scalars from you—it turns numbers into strings and back as needed, and takes the string or number representation of undef or of object values as needed. However, you can't go from a string representation of an object value, back to an object value. And that's why this doesn't work:

```
$x = Net::FTP->new('ftp.aol.com');
$y = Net::FTP->new('ftp.netcom.com');
$z = Net::FTP->new('ftp.qualcomm.com');
$all = join(' ', $x,$y,$z);          # !!!
...later...
($aol, $netcom, $qualcomm) = split(' ', $all);  # !!!
$aol->login("sburke", "aoeuaoeu");
$netcom->login("sburke", "qjkxqjkx");
$qualcomm->login("smb", "dhtndhtn");
```

This fails because $aol ends up holding merely the *string representation* of the object value from $x, not the object value itself—when join tried to join the characters of the "strings" $x, $y, and $z, Perl saw that they weren't strings at all, so it gave join their string representations.

Unfortunately, this distinction between object values and their string representations doesn't really fit into the analogy of credit card numbers, because credit card numbers really *are* numbers—even thought they don't express any meaningful quantity, if you stored them in a database as a quantity (as opposed to just an ASCII string), that wouldn't stop them from being valid as credit card numbers.

This may seem rather academic, but there's two common mistakes programmers new to objects often make, which make sense only in terms of the distinction between object values and their string representations.

The first common error involves forgetting (or never having known in the first place) that when you go to use a value as a hash key, Perl uses the string representation of that value. When you want to use the numeric value two and a half as a key, Perl turns it into the three-character string "2.5." But if you then want to use that string as a number, Perl will treat it as meaning two and a half, so you're usually none the wiser that Perl converted the number to a string and back. But recall that Perl can't turn strings back into objects—so if you tried to use a Net::FTP object value as a hash key, Perl actually used its string representation, like Net::FTP=GLOB(0x20154240), but that string is unusable as an object value. (Incidentally, there's a module Tie::RefHash that implements hashes that *do* let you use real object-values as keys.)

The second common error with object values is in trying to save an object value to disk (whether printing it to a file, or storing it in a conventional database file). All you'll get is the string, which will be useless.

When you want to save an object and restore it later, you may find that the object's class already provides a method specifically for this. For example, MIDI::Opus provides methods for writing an object to disk as a standard MIDI file. The file can later be read back into memory by a MIDI::Opus constructor method, which will return a new MIDI::Opus object representing whatever file you tell it to read into memory. Similar methods are available with, for example, classes that manipulate graphic images and can save them to files, which can be read back later.

But some classes, like Business::US_Amort, provide no such methods for storing an object in a file. When this is the case, you can try using any of the Data::Dumper, Storable, or FreezeThaw modules. Using these is unproblematic for objects of most classes, but may run into limitations with others. For example, a Business::US_Amort object can be turned into a string with Data::Dumper, and that string written to a file. When it's restored later, its attributes will be accessible as normal. But in the unlikely case that the loan object was saved in mid-calculation, the calculation may not be resumable. This is because of the way that that *particular* class does its calculations, but similar limitations may occur with objects from other classes.

But often, even *wanting* to save an object is basically wrong—what would saving an ftp *session* even mean? Saving the hostname, username, and password? current directory on both machines? the local TCP/IP port number? In the case of "saving" a Net::FTP object, you're better off just saving whatever details you actually need for your own purposes, so that you can make a new object later and just set those values for it.

So Why Do Some Modules Use Objects?

All these details of using objects are definitely enough to make you wonder—is it worth the bother? If you're a module author, writing your module with an object-oriented interface restricts the audience of potential users to those who understand the basic concepts of objects and object values, as well as Perl's syntax for calling methods. Why complicate things by having an object-oriented interface?

A somewhat esoteric answer is that a module has an object-oriented interface because the module's insides are written in an object-oriented style. This article is about the basics of object-oriented *interfaces*, and it'd be going far afield to explain what object-oriented *design* is. But the short story is that object-oriented design is just one way of attacking messy problems. It's a way that many programmers find very helpful (and which others happen to find to be far more of a hassle than it's worth, incidentally), and it just happens to show up for you, the module user, as merely the style of interface.

The Gory Details

For sake of clarity of explanation, I had to oversimplify some of the facts about objects. Here's a few of the gorier details:

- Every example I gave of a constructor was a class method. But object methods can be constructors, too, if the class was written to work that way: $new = $old->copy, $node_y = $node_x->new_subnode, or the like.

- I've given the impression that there's two kinds of methods: object methods and class methods. In fact, the same method can be both, because it's not the kind of method it is, but the kind of calls it's written to accept—calls that pass an object, or calls that pass a class name.

- The term "object value" isn't something you'll find used much anywhere else. It's just my shorthand for what would properly be called an "object reference" or "reference to a blessed item." In fact, people usually say "object" when they properly mean a reference to that object.

- I mentioned creating objects with *con*structors, but I didn't mention destroying them with *de*structor—a destructor is a kind of method that you call to tidy up the object once you're done with it, and want it to neatly go away (close connections, delete temporary files, free up memory, etc.). But because of the way Perl handles memory, most modules won't require the user to know about destructors.

- I said that class method syntax has to have the class name, as in $session = Net::FTP->new($host). Actually, you can instead use any expression that returns a class name: $ftp_class = 'Net::FTP'; $session = $ftp_class->new($host). Moreover, instead of the method name for object- or class-method calls, you can use a scalar holding the method name: $foo->$method($host). But, in practice, these syntaxes are rarely useful.

And finally, to learn about objects from the perspective of writing your own classes, see the *perltoot* documentation, or Damian Conway's exhaustive and clear book *Object Oriented Perl* (Manning Publications, 1999).

Index

We'd like to hear your suggestions for improving our indexes. Send email to *index@oreilly.com*.

uri_escape( ) function, 16, 60
URI::Escape module, 16
URI->new_abs method, 49
URL encoded characters, 16
URLs (Uniform Resource Locators), 15
  absolute
    converting from relative, 57
    converting to relative, 55
  brackets, stripping, 49
  characters allowed, 16
  comparing, 51
  components, 51
  extracting all in document, 52
  fixed, GET forms and, 59
  normalizing, 50
  parsing, 48
  quotes, stripping, 49
  relative, 46, 54
    constructors and, 49
    converting from absolute URLs, 55
    converting to absolute URLs, 57
    fragments, 55
    implicit information, 54
  scheduling, 192
  schemes, 54
  story URLs, 108
  whitespace, stripping, 49
url_scan( ) function, 111
user agents, 34
  authentication, 38
  imitating others, 170

LWP::RobotUA, 180
  protocols, 36
  proxies, 38
  redirection, 37
  request methods, 39
User-Agent header, 35
userinfo( ) method, 51

V

values, queries in named values, 53
value=string attribute, option element, 69

W

Weather Underground web site, link
    extraction, 98
Web as data source, 1
web automation, 1
web services, 3
while loop, link extraction and, 97
whitespace
    HTML::TreeBuider, 150
    regular expressions and, 87
WWW-Authentication header, 172

X

XML-RPC, 3

About the Author

Sean M. Burke is an active member of the Perl community and one of CPAN's most prolific module authors. He has been a columnist for *The Perl Journal* since 1998 and is an authority on markup languages. Trained as a linguist, he also develops tools for software internationalization and native language preservation.

Colophon

Our look is the result of reader comments, our own experimentation, and feedback from distribution channels. Distinctive covers complement our distinctive approach to technical topics, breathing personality and life into potentially dry subjects.

The animals on the cover of *Perl and LWP* are blesbok. Blesbok are African antelopes related to the hartebeest. These grazing animals, native to Africa's grasslands are extinct in the wild but preserved in farms and parks.

Blesbok have slender, horselike bodies that are shorter than four feet at the shoulder. They are deep red, with white patches on their faces and rumps. A white blaze extends from between a blesbok's horns to the end of its nose, broken only by a brown band above the eyes. The blesbok's horns sweep back, up, and inward. Both male and female blesbok have horns, though the males' are thicker.

Blesbok are diurnal, most active in the morning and evening. They sleep in the shade during the hottest part of the day, as they are very susceptible to the heat. They travel from place to place in long single-file lines, leaving distinct paths. Their life span is about 13 years.

Linley Dolby was the production editor and copyeditor for *Perl and LWP*, and Sarah Sherman was the proofreader. Rachel Wheeler and Claire Cloutier provided quality control. Johnna VanHoose Dinse wrote the index. Emily Quill provided production support.

Emma Colby designed the cover of this book, based on a series design by Edie Freedman. The cover image is a 19th-century engraving from the Dover Pictorial Archive. Emma Colby produced the cover layout with QuarkXPress 4.1 using Adobe's ITC Garamond font.

Melanie Wang designed the interior layout, based on a series design by David Futato. This book was converted to FrameMaker 5.5.6 with a format conversion tool created by Erik Ray, Jason McIntosh, Neil Walls, and Mike Sierra that uses Perl and XML technologies. The text font is Linotype Birka; the heading font is Adobe Myriad Condensed; and the code font is LucasFont's TheSans Mono Condensed. The illustrations that appear in the book were produced by Robert Romano and Jessamyn Read using Macromedia FreeHand 9 and Adobe Photoshop 6. This colophon was written by Linley Dolby.

Other Titles Available from O'Reilly

Perl

Learning Perl, 3rd Edition

By Randal Schwartz & Tom Phoenix
3rd Edition July 2001
330 pages, ISBN 0-596-00132-0

Learning Perl is the quintessential tutorial for the Perl programming language. The third edition has not only been updated to Perl Version 5.6, but has also been rewritten from the ground up to reflect the needs of programmers learning Perl today. Other books may teach you to program in Perl, but this book will turn you into a Perl programmer.

Mastering Regular Expressions, 2nd Edition

By Jeffrey E. F. Friedl
2nd Edition July 2002 (est.)
456 pages (est.), ISBN 0-596-00289-0

Written by an expert in the topic, this book shows programmers not only how to use regular expressions, but how to think in regular expressions. Updated with a wealth of new material, the second edition explains how to use regular expressions to code complex and subtle text processing that you never imagined could be automated. Included are such key topics as avoiding common errors and optimizing expressions. The book covers many new features added to Perl—a language well endowed with regular expressions—as well as other languages such as Java, Python, and Visual Basic that include support for this powerful tool.

Embedded Perl in HTML with Mason

By Dave Rolsky & Ken Williams
1st Edition October 2002
304 pages, ISBN 0-596-00225-4

Mason, a Perl-based templating system, is becoming more and more popular as a tool for building websites and managing other dynamic collections. While using Mason is not difficult, creating Mason-based sites can be tricky, and this concise book helps you navigate around the obstacles. The book covers the most recent release of Mason, 1.10, which has many new features including line number reporting based on source files, sub-requests, and simplified use as a CGI. It also explores using Mason for dynamic generation of XML documents.

Perl & XML

By Erik T. Ray & Jason McIntosh
1st Edition April 2002
224 pages, ISBN 0-596-00205-X

Perl & XML is aimed at Perl programmers who need to work with XML documents and data. This book gives a complete, comprehensive tour of the landscape of Perl and XML, making sense of the myriad of modules, terminology, and techniques. The last two chapters of Perl and XML give complete examples of XML applications, pulling together all the tools at your disposal.

Mastering Perl/Tk

By Steve Lidie & Nancy Walsh
1st Edition January 2002
768 pages, ISBN 1-56592-716-8

Beginners and seasoned Perl/Tk programmers alike will find *Mastering Perl/Tk* to be the definitive book on creating graphical user interfaces with Perl/Tk. After a fast-moving tutorial, the book goes into detail on creating custom widgets, working with bindings and callbacks, IPC techniques, and examples using many of the non-standard add-on widgets for Perl/Tk (including Tix widgets). Every Perl/Tk programmer will need this book.

Perl Cookbook

By Tom Christiansen &
Nathan Torkington
1st Edition August 1998
794 pages, ISBN 1-56592-243-3

The *Perl Cookbook* is a comprehensive collection of problems, solutions, and practical examples for anyone programming in Perl. You'll find hundreds of rigorously reviewed Perl "recipes" for manipulating strings, numbers, dates, arrays, and hashes; pattern matching and text substitutions; references, data structures, objects, and classes; signals and exceptions; and much more.

O'REILLY®

To order: 800-998-9938 • *order@oreilly.com* • *www.oreilly.com*
Online editions of most O'Reilly titles are available by subscription at *safari.oreilly.com*
Also available at most retail and online bookstores.

Perl

Computer Science & Perl Programming: Best of The Perl Journal

Edited by Jon Orwant
1st Edition, November 2002 (est.)
600 pages (est.), ISBN 0-596-00310-2

The first of three volumes from the archives of *The Perl Journal* that O'Reilly has exclusive rights to distribute, this book is a compilation of the best from TPJ: 71 articles providing a comprehensive tour of how experts implement computer science concepts in the real world, with code walkthroughs, case studies, and explanations of difficult techniques that can't be found in any other book.

Perl Graphics Programming

By Shawn Wallace
1st Edition, December 2002 (est.)
504 pages (est.), 0-596-00219-X

This insightful volume focuses on scripting programs that enable programmers to manipulate graphics for the Web. The book also helps demystify the manipulation of graphics formats for web newcomers with a practical, resource-like approach. While most of the examples use Perl as a scripting language, the concepts are applicable to any programming language. The book documents ways to use several powerful Perl modules for generating graphics, including GD, PerlMagick, and GIMP.

Programming Web Services with Perl

By Randy J. Ray & Scott Guelich
1st Edition December 2002 (est.)
280 pages (est.), ISBN 0-596-00206-8

O'Reilly presents another Perl first: *Programming Web Services with Perl.* Like most O'Reilly books, it cuts through the hype on web services and concentrates on the useful and practical. It shows how to use Perl to create web services, introducing the major web service standards (XML-RPC, SOAP, WSDL, UDDI) and how to implement Perl servers and clients using these standards. Moving beyond the basics, the book offers solutions to the problems of security, authentication, and scalability.

How to stay in touch with O'Reilly

1. Visit our award-winning web site

http://www.oreilly.com/

★ "Top 100 Sites on the Web"—PC Magazine
★ CIO Magazine's Web Business 50 Awards

Our web site contains a library of comprehensive product information (including book excerpts and tables of contents), downloadable software, background articles, interviews with technology leaders, links to relevant sites, book cover art, and more. File us in your bookmarks or favorites!

2. Join our email mailing lists

Sign up to get email announcements of new books and conferences, special offers, and O'Reilly Network technology newsletters at:

http://www.elists.oreilly.com

It's easy to customize your free elists subscription so you'll get exactly the O'Reilly news you want.

3. Get examples from our books

To find example files for a book, go to:

http://www.oreilly.com/catalog

select the book, and follow the "Examples" link.

4. Work with us

Check out our web site for current employment opportunities:

http://jobs.oreilly.com/

5. Register your book

Register your book at:

http://register.oreilly.com

6. Contact us

O'Reilly & Associates, Inc.
1005 Gravenstein Hwy North
Sebastopol, CA 95472 USA
TEL: 707-827-7000 or 800-998-9938
(6am to 5pm PST)
FAX: 707-829-0104

order@oreilly.com
For answers to problems regarding your order or our products. To place a book order online visit:

http://www.oreilly.com/order_new/

catalog@oreilly.com
To request a copy of our latest catalog.

booktech@oreilly.com
For book content technical questions or corrections.

corporate@oreilly.com
For educational, library, and corporate sales.

proposals@oreilly.com
To submit new book proposals to our editors and product managers.

international@oreilly.com
For information about our international distributors or translation queries. For a list of our distributors outside of North America check out:

http://international.oreilly.com/distributors.html

O'REILLY®